Collins   W9-CQI-220

easy
Italian

HarperCollins Publishers
Westerhill Rd, Bishopbriggs, Glasgow, G64 2QT

www.harpercollins.co.uk

First published 2001
This edition published 2006

© HarperCollins Publishers 2006

Reprint 10 9 8 7 6 5 4 3 2 1 0

ISBN 0 00 720836 7

A catalogue reference for this book is available from
The British Library

Photography: Angelo Gai and Diana Grandi
With additional photography/material from:
Ian Brooke, Sheila Ferguson, Ian and James Smart,
The Printer's Devil, Artville (pp 95, 96, 98, 99, 100, 101, 102,
103, 106, 107, 110, 111, 112)
The Anthony Blake Photo Library (pp 79, 83, 87, 93[tl & br],
97[tr,bl], 98[bl], 99(bl), 100[br], 101[br], 102[tl], 103[tl],
104[tl,br], 105, 106[br], 108, 109, 110[t])
Wine material: Andrea Gillies
Map: Heather Moore
Layout & Origination: The Printer's Devil and
Davidson Pre-Press Graphics Ltd, Glasgow

Other titles in the Collins Easy Photo Phrase Book series:
French (0 00 720840 5)
German (0 00 720839 1)
Greek (0 00 720837 5)
Portuguese (0 00 720835 9)
Spanish (0 00 720833 2)
These titles are also published in a CD pack containing
a 60-minute CD and Easy Photo Phrase Book.

Printed in China by Imago

Contents

Useful Websites

Currency converters
www.xe.com
www.oanda.com

UK Passport Office
www.passport.gov.uk

Foreign Office travel advice
www.fco.gov.uk

Health advice
www.traveldoctor.co.uk
www.dh.gov.uk/PolicyAndGuidance/
  HealthAdviceForTravellers/fs/en

Pet advice
www.defra.gov.uk/animalh/
  quarantine/index.htm

Facts and figures
www.cia.gov/cia/publications/
  factbook

Weather
www.bbc.co.uk/weather
www.italy-weather-and-maps.com

Internet cafes
www.cybercafes.com

Hostels
www.hostels.com
europeanhostels.com

Hotel bookings
www.hrs.com

Rail fares and tickets
www.raileurope.co.uk

Skiing
www.goski.com

Transport
www.trenitalia.com/en/index.html

Italian airport websites
www.aeroporti.com/aeroporti.html

Driving abroad
www.drivingabroad.co.uk

Italian motorways
www.autostrade.it/en/index.html

Planning your trip
www.willgoto.com

Maps
www.big-italy-map.co.uk

Italian tourist board
www.enit.it

Holidays and festivals
www.hostetler.net/italy/italy.cfm

Sightseeing
www.initaly.com
www.romeguide.it (Rome)
www.doge.it (Venice)
www.italianvisits.com/sardegna/
  index.htm (pictorial tour of
  regions)

Introduction

In the age of the euro, the internet and cash machines that offer a choice of languages, foreign travel might seem less of an adventure than it once was. But English is not the universal language yet, and there is much more to communication than knowing the right words for things. Once out of the airport you will not get far without some idea of the language, and also the way things are done in an unfamiliar culture. Things you might assume are the same everywhere, such as road signs and colour-coding, can turn out not to be. Red for trunk roads and skimmed milk, blue for motorways and full cream? Not everywhere! You may know the word for 'coffee' but what sort of coffee will you get? Will they understand what you mean when you say you're a vegetarian? What times do the shops open, and which ticket gives you the best deal? *Collins Easy Photo Phrase Books* keep you up to speed with handy tips for each topic, and a wealth of pictures of signs and everyday objects to help you understand what you see around you. Even if your knowledge of the language is excellent, you may still find yourself on the back foot when trying to understand what's on offer in a restaurant, so the food and drink section features a comprehensive menu reader to make sure eating out is a pleasure.

The unique combination of practical information, photos and phrases found in this book provides the key to hassle-free travel. The colour-coding below shows how information is presented and how to access it as quickly as possible.

General, practical information which will provide useful tips on getting the best out of your trip.

keywords

destra
***des**-tra*
right
sinistra
*see-**nees**-tra*
left

< keywords

these are words that are useful to know both when you see them written down or when you hear them spoken

key talk >

short, simple phrases that you can change and adapt to suit your own situation

excuse me!
scusi!
***skoo**-zee*

we're looking for...
cerchiamo...
*cherk-**ya**-mo...*

do you know where ... is?
sa dov'è...?
*sa do-**ve**...*

talking

The **food and drink section** allows you to choose more easily from what is on offer, both for snacks and at restaurants.

The practical **Dictionary** means that you will never be stuck for words.

Speaking Italian

We've tried to make the pronunciation under the phrases as clear as possible. We've split up the words to make them easy to read, but don't pause too long between syllables. Italian isn't really hard to pronounce and once you learn a few basic rules, it shouldn't be too long before you can read straight from the Italian.

Longer words are usually stressed on the next to last syllable, but we show all stressed syllables in **heavy type**, so you won't be caught out by any exceptions.

The spellings **c** and **ch** might confuse you, because **c** is sometimes pronounced like English **ch** as in church, while the Italian **ch** is pronounced like the English **k**. (Look at the English for kilogram and the Italian **chilogrammo**.) So **c'è** (there is) is pronounced like English check without the final **k** sound, while **che?** (what?) is pronounced **kay**. The rule to remember is that **c** followed by **e** or **i** makes it a soft **ch** sound. But **c** followed by **a**, **o** or **u** has a hard **k** sound. Try practising saying and reading the following words:

chiave *kee-a-vay* (key)   **cibo** *chee-bo* (food)

chiesa *kee-ay-za* (church)   **cena** *chay-na* (dinner)

The letter **g** behaves in a similar way. When followed by **a**, **o** or **u**, **g** will be hard. When followed by **e** or **i**, **g** will be soft. The word for lake is **lago**, for lakes the word is **laghi**. The **h** has been added to keep the **g** hard. So when you see a **ch** or **gh** combination in Italian, remember to make the **c** and **g** hard.

Finally, pronounce all **r**'s when you see them in Italian words.

Basic rules to remember are:

italian	sounds like	example	pronunciation
a	cat	**pasta**	*pas-ta*
e	bet/day	**letto/per**	*let-to/payr*
i	meet	**vino**	*vee-no*
o	got	**botta**	*bot-ta*
u	boot	**luna**	*loo-na*
gli	million	**figlio**	*feel-yo*
sc (*before* e/i)	shop	**sci**	*shee*
sc (*before* a/o/u)	scan	**scarpa**	*skar-pa*

There are two forms of address in Italian, formal and informal. You should always stick with the formal until you are on a first-name basis. For the purposes of this book we will use the formal.

yes
sì
see

no
no
no

ok/that's fine
va bene
va **be**-*nay*

please
per favore
*payr fa-**vo**-ray*

thank you
grazie
grats-*yay*

thanks very much
grazie mille
grats-*yay* **meel**-*lay*

don't mention it
prego
pray-*go*

that's very kind
molto gentile
mol-*to jen-**tee**-lay*

hello
buon giorno
bwon **jor**-*no*

goodbye
arrivederci
*ar-ree-ve-**der**-chee*

hi/bye
ciao
chow

good evening
buona sera
bwo-*na* **say**-*ra*

good night
buona notte
bwo-*na* **not**-*tay*

see you later
a più tardi
a pyoo **tar**-*dee*

excuse me!
scusi!
skoo-*zee*

excuse me! (*to get past*)
permesso!
*per-**mes**-so*

I am sorry
mi scusi
mee **skoo**-*zee*

I don't understand
non capisco
*non ka-**pees**-ko*

I don't know
non lo so
non lo so

Addressing people

Italians are quite formal when addressing each other. When greeting someone in the street or shop you can simply say *buon giorno, signora* (for a woman) and *buon giorno, signore* (for a man). If you are not sure how formal to be, a good alternative for hello is *salve* which you can use with anyone. Among young people and friends, you will hear *ciao*.

how are you?
come sta?
ko-*may sta*

fine thanks
bene grazie
be-*nay* **grats**-*yay*

and you?
e lei?
e lay

hi, Michele
ciao Michele
*chow mee-**ke**-lay*

bye, Luisa
ciao Luisa
*chow loo-**ee**-za*

piacere
nice to meet you
*pya-**cher**-ay*

*The simplest way to ask for something in a shop or bar is by naming what you want and adding **per favore**.*

keywords keywords keywords

1	**uno**	*oo-no*
2	**due**	*doo-ay*
3	**tre**	*tray*
4	**quattro**	*kwat-tro*
5	**cinque**	*cheen-kway*
6	**sei**	*say*
7	**sette**	*set-tay*
8	**otto**	*ot-to*
9	**nove**	*no-vay*
10	**dieci**	*dee-ay-chee*

a ... please
un/una ... per favore
oon/oo-na ... payr fa-vo-ray

a coffee please
un caffè per favore
oon kaf-fe payr fa-vo-ray

a beer please
una birra per favore
oo-na beer-ra payr fa-vo-ray

an ice cream
un gelato
oon jay-la-to

a phonecard
una scheda telefonica
oo-na sked-a te-le-fo-nee-ka

the (singular)
il/la
eel/la

the (plural)
i/le
ee/lay

the menu please
il menù per favore
eel me-noo payr fa-vo-ray

the bill please
il conto per favore
eel kon-to payr fa-vo-ray

my key
la mia chiave
la-mee-a kee-a-vay

my passport
il mio passaporto
eel mee-o pas-sa-por-to

another...
un altro/un'altra...
oon al-tro/oon al-tra...

more...
ancora...
an-ko-ra...

another beer
un'altra birra
oon al-tra beer-ra

another tea
un altro tè
oon al-tro te

2 more beers
ancora due birre
an-ko-ra doo-ay beer-ray

2 more coffees
ancora due caffè
an-ko-ra doo-ay kaf-fe

To catch someone's attention

The easiest way to catch someone's attention is by using *scusi*. If it is an older man or woman, it is polite to add *signore* (for the man) and *signora* (for the woman). If you are trying to get through a crowd, use *permesso*.

excuse me!
scusi, signore/signora!
skoo-zee seen-yo-ray/seen-yo-ra

can you help me?
può aiutarmi?
pwo a-yoo-tar-mee

do you know where ... is?
sa dov'è ...?
sa do-ve ...

do you know how I get to...?
sa come si va a...?
sa ko-may see va a...

By combining key words and phrases you can build up your language and adapt the phrases to suit your own situation.

avete...? **do you have...?**	**do you have a map?** avete una cartina? *a-vay-tay oo-na kar-tee-na*	**do you have a room?** avete una camera? *a-vay-tay oo-na ka-may-ra*
quanto costa? **how much is it?**	**how much is the wine?** quanto costa il vino? *kwan-ta kos-ta eel vee-no*	**how much is the trip?** quanto costa il viaggio? *kwan-ta kos-ta eel vee-ad-jo*
vorrei... **I'd like...**	**I'd like a red wine** vorrei un vino rosso *vor-ray oon vee-no ros-so*	**I'd like an ice cream** vorrei un gelato *vor-ray oon jay-la-to*
ho bisogno di... **I need...**	**I need a taxi** ho bisogno di un taxi *o bee-zon-yo dee oon tak-see*	**I need to go** ho bisogno di andare *o bee-zon-yo dee an-da-ray*
quando? **when?**	**when does it open?** quando apre? *kwan-do a-pray*	**when does it close?** quando chiude? *kwan-do kee-oo-day*
	when does it leave? quando parte? *kwan-do par-tay*	**when does it arrive?** quando arriva? *kwan-do ar-ree-va*
dove? **where?**	**where is the bank?** dov'è la banca? *do-ve la ban-ka*	**where is the hotel?** dov'è l'albergo? *do-ve lal-ber-go*
c'è...? **is there...?**	**is there a market?** c'è un mercato? *che oon mer-ka-to*	**where is there a market?** dove c'è un mercato? *do-vay che oon mer-ka-to*
non c'è... **there is no...**	**there is no bread** non c'è pane *non che pa-nay*	**is there no train?** non c'è un treno? *non che oon tray-no*
posso...? **can I...?**	**can I smoke?** posso fumare? *pos-so foo-ma-ray*	**can I go by train?** posso andare in treno? *pos-so an-da-ray een tray-no*
	where can I buy milk? dove posso comprare del latte? *do-vay pos-so kom-pra-ray del lat-tay*	
è...? **is it...?**	**is it near?** è vicino? *e vee-chee-no*	**is it far?** è lontano? *e lon-ta-no*
mi piace... **I like...**	**I like wine** mi piace il vino *mee pya-chay eel vee-no*	**I don't like dancing** non mi piace ballare *non mee pya-chay bal-la-ray*

These are a selection of small but very useful words to know.

grande
gran-day
large

piccolo(a)
pee-ko-lo(a)
small

un poco
oon po-ko
a little

basta
bas-ta
enough

più vicino(a)
pyoo vee-chee-no(a)
nearest

lontano(a)
lon-ta-no(a)
far

troppo caro(a)
trop-po ka-ro(a)
too expensive

pieno(a)
pee-ay-no(a)
full

libero(a)
lee-bay-ro(a)
free

e
ay
and

con/senza
kon/sent-sa
with/without

questo/quello
kwes-to/kwel-lo
this one/that one

subito
soo-bee-to
straightaway

più tardi
pyoo tar-dee
later

a large car
una macchina grande
oo-na mak-kee-na gran-day

a small house
una casa piccola
oo-na ka-za peek-ko-la

a little please
un poco per favore
oon po-ko payr fa-vo-ray

that's enough thanks
basta così grazie
bas-ta ko-zee grats-yay

where is the nearest chemist?
dov'è la farmacia più vicina?
do-ve la far-ma-chee-a pyoo vee-chee-na

is it far?
è lontano?
e lon-ta-no

it is too expensive
è troppo caro
e trop-po ka-ro

it is too small
è troppo piccolo
e trop-po peek-ko-lo

is it full?
e pieno?
e pee-ay-no

is it free? (unoccupied)
è libero?
e lee-bay-ro

a tea and 2 beers
un tè e due birre
oon te e doo-ay beer-ray

with sugar
con zucchero
kon tsook-kay-ro

with milk
col latte
kol lat-tay

without sugar
senza zucchero
sent-sa tsook-kay-ro

without milk
senza latte
sent-sa lat-tay

for me
per me
payr me

for her/for him
per lei/per lui
payr lay/per loo-ee

my passport
il mio passaporto
eel mee-o pas-sa-por-to

my keys
le mie chiavi
lay mee-ay kee-a-vee

I'd like this one
vorrei questo
vor-ray kwes-to

I'd like that one
vorrei quello
vor-ray kwel-lo

I need a taxi straightaway
ho bisogno di un taxi subito
o bee-zon-yo dee oon tak-see soo-bee-to

I'll call again later
richiamo più tardi
reek-ya-mo pyoo tar-dee

keywords keywords keywords keywords keywords

It is always good to be able to say a few words about yourself to break the ice, even if you won't be able tell your life story.

my name is...
mi chiamo...
*mee kee-**a**-mo...*

I am from...
sono di...
so-no dee...

I'm here on holiday
sono qui in vacanza
*so-no kwee een va-**kan**-za*

I'm here on business
sono qui per lavoro
*so-no kwee payr la-**vo**-ro*

I'm not married
non sono sposato(a)
*non so-no spo-**za**-to(a)*

I am married
sono sposato(a)
*so-no spo-**za**-to(a)*

I have a boyfriend
ho un ragazzo
*o oon rag-**at**-so*

I have a girlfriend
ho una ragazza
*o **oo**-na rag-**at**-sa*

I am a widow
sono vedova
*so-no **vay**-do-va*

I am a widower
sono vedovo
*so-no **vay**-do-vo*

I am divorced
sono divorziato(a)
*so-no dee-vorts-**ya**-to(a)*

I am separated
sono separato(a)
*so-no sep-a-**ra**-to(a)*

I have a son/daughter
ho un figlio/una figlia
*o oon **feel**-yo/**oo**-na **feel**-ya*

I have ... children
ho ... figli
*o ... **feel**-yee*

I work
lavoro
*la-**vo**-ro*

I am retired
sono in pensione
*so-no een pens-**yo**-nay*

I am a student
sono studente
*so-no stoo-**den**-tay*

Italy is very beautiful
l'Italia è molto bella
*lee-**tal**-ya e **mol**-to **bel**-la*

I love Italian food
mi piace molto la cucina italiana
*mee **pya**-chay **mol**-to la koo-**chee**-na ee-tal-**ya**-na*

Italian people are very kind
gli Italiani sono molto gentili
*lee ee-tal-**ya**-nee **so**-no **mol**-to jen-**tee**-lee*

I'd like to come back
vorrei ritornare
*vor-**ray** ree-**tor**-na-ray*

thank you very much for your kindness
grazie mille per la sua gentilezza
***grats**-yay **meel**-lay payr la **soo**-a jen-tee-**let**-sa*

you are very kind
lei è molto gentile
*lay e **mol**-to jen-**tee**-lay*

I have enjoyed myself very much
mi sono divertito(a) moltissimo
*mee so-no dee-ver-**tee**-to(a) mol-**tees**-see-mo*

we will be back next year
ritorniamo l'anno prossimo
*ree-torn-**ya**-mo **lan**-no **pros**-see-mo*

can I have your address?
potrei avere il suo indirizzo?
*po-**tray** a-**vay**-ray eel **soo**-o een-dee-**reet**-so*

see you next year!
all'anno prossimo!
*al-**lan**-no **pros**-see-mo*

Although problems are not something anyone wants, you might come across the odd difficulty, and it is best to be armed with a few phrases to cope with the situation.

excuse me!
scusi!
skoo-zee

can you help me?
può aiutarmi?
pwo a-yoo-tar-mee

I don't speak...
non parlo...
non par-lo...

I am sorry, I did not know
mi scusi, non lo sapevo
mee skoo-zee non lo sa-pay-vo

I am lost
mi sono smarrito(a)
mee so-no smar-ree-to(a)

we are lost
ci siamo persi
chee see-a-mo per-see

I have lost...	**my money**	**my tickets**	**my passport**
ho perso...	i soldi	i biglietti	il mio passaporto
ho payr-so...	*ee sol-dee*	*ee beel-yet-tee*	*eel mee-o pas-sa-por-to*

I have left...	**in the restaurant**		**on the train**
ho lasciato...	nel ristorante		sul treno
o la-sha-to...	*nel rees-to-ran-tay*		*sool tray-no*

I have missed...	**my flight**	**the train**	**the coach**
ho perso...	il volo	il treno	il pullman
ho per-so...	*eel vo-lo*	*eel tray-no*	*eel pool-man*

I need to get to...
devo andare a...
day-vo an-da-ray a...

how can I get there today?
come ci posso arrivare oggi?
ko-may chee pos-so ar-ree-va-ray od-jee

my luggage hasn't arrived
il mio bagaglio non è arrivato
eel mee-o ba-gal-yo non e ar-ree-va-to

my case has been damaged
la mia valigia è stata danneggiata
la mee-a va-lee-ja e sta-ta dan-nay-ja-ta

my bag	**my purse**	**my camera**
la mia borsa	il mio portafoglio	la mia macchina fotografica
la mee-a bor-sa	*eel mee-o por-ta-fol-yo*	*la mee-a mak-kee-na fo-to-gra-fee-ka*

... has been stolen
... è stato rubato(a)
... e sta-to roo-ba-to(a)

you can get me at this address
mi trova a questo indirizzo
mee tro-va a kwes-to een-dee-reet-so

I have to go to hospital
devo andare in ospedale
day-vo an-da-ray een os-pay-da-lay

I have no money
non ho soldi
non o sol-dee

I can't find my son
non trovo mio figlio
non tro-vo mee-yo feel-yo

I can't find my daughter
non trovo mia figlia
non tro-vo mee-a feel-ya

go away!
se ne vada!
say nay va-da

that man is following me
quell'uomo mi sta seguendo
kwel wo-mo mee sta seg-wen-do

Italians expect to receive good service and quality. They will complain when things are not to their liking.

there is no...
non c'è...
non che...

there is no soap
non c'è sapone
*non che sa-**po**-nay*

it is dirty
è sporco(a)
*e **spor**-ko(a)*

they are dirty
sono sporchi
*so-no **spor**-kee*

it is broken
è rotto(a)
*e **rot**-to(a)*

they are broken
sono rotti
*so-no **rot**-tee*

the ... does not work
il/la ... non funziona
*eel/la ... non foonts-**yo**-na*

the ... do not work
i/le ... non funzionano
*ee/lay ... non foonts-**yo**-na-no*

the window doesn't open
la finestra non si apre
*la fee-**nes**-tra non see **ap**-ray*

the window doesn't close
la finestra non si chiude
*la fee-**nes**-tra non see kee-**oo**-day*

there is too much noise
c'è troppo rumore
*che **trop**-po roo-**mor**-ay*

the room is too small
la camera è troppo piccola
*la **ka**-may-ra e **trop**-po peek-**ko**-la*

the room is too hot
la camera e troppo calda
*la **ka**-may-ra e **trop**-po **kal**-da*

the room is too cold
la camera è troppo fredda
*la **ka**-may-ra e **trop**-po **fred**-da*

it is too expensive
è troppo caro
*e **trop**-po **ka**-ro*

you are charging too much
lei mi chiede troppo
*lay mee **kyay**-day **trop**-po*

I want to complain
voglio fare un reclamo
***vol**-yo **fa**-ray oon rek-**la**-mo*

I want to speak to the manager
voglio parlare con il responsabile
***vol**-yo par-**la**-ray kon eel res-pon-**sa**-bee-lay*

we'd like to order
vorremmo ordinare
*vor-**rem**-mo or-dee-**na**-ray*

the service is bad
il servizio è pessimo
*eel ser-**veets**-yo e **pes**-see-mo*

this food is cold
il cibo è freddo
*eel **chee**-bo e **fred**-do*

this cappuccino is cold
questo cappuccino è freddo
***kwes**-to kap-poo-**chee**-no e **fred**-do*

there is a mistake
c'è un errore
*che oon er-**ro**-ray*

can we check the bill?
possiamo controllare il conto?
*poss-**ya**-mo kon-trol-**la**-ray eel **kon**-to*

I didn't order this
non ho ordinato questo
*non o or-dee-**na**-to **kwes**-to*

please take it off the bill
può toglierlo dal conto
*pwo **tol**-yer-lo dal **kon**-to*

Everyday Italy

The following four pages should give you an idea of the type of things you will come across in Italy.

open

opening hours

closed   closed Tuesdays

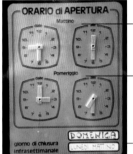

mattino
morning

pomeriggio
afternoon

giorno di chiusura
day closed
Sunday and Monday afternoon

Small shops are generally open from 9am to 12.30pm and from 3.30 until 7pm (closing on Saturday evening and reopening on Monday afternoon). In the summer (particularly in tourist areas) they stay open on Sunday. Big shopping centres are open all day 7 days a week until 10 or 11pm. In the south of Italy small shops tend to stay open much later.

pay here

pedestrian entrance

Spingere
push

Tirare
pull

do you have...?	**stamps**	**phonecards**
avete...?	francobolli	schede telefoniche
a-vay-tay...	*fran-ko-**bol**-lee*	***skay**-day te-le-**fo**-nee-kay*
where can I get...?	**a newspaper**	**postcards**
dove posso comprare...?	un giornale	cartoline
*do-vay **pos**-so komp-**ra**-ray...*	*oon jor-**na**-lay*	*kar-to-**lee**-nay*

tobacconist
These are often attached to a bar and sell cigarettes, stamps, bus tickets, lottery tickets etc.

out of service

in servizio

in service

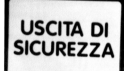

entrance

emergency exit

There are increasing numbers of automated machines with instructions given in different languages.

Postboxes are red. The blue postbox is for priority mail abroad.

USCITA DI SICUREZZA

You will also see the word **uscita** used for exit on the motorway.

excuse me...
scusi...
skoo-zee...

what do I have to do?
cosa devo fare?
ko-za day-vo fa-ray

how does this work?
come funziona?
ko-may foonts-yo-na

what does this mean?
cosa vuol dire?
ko-za vwol dee-ray

talking

Service is usually included in a restaurant bill so tipping is discretionary. However, it is usual to leave a small tip. In busy bars, there will often be a saucer to leave coins.

no fishing
divieto means
forbidden

from 1 April to
30 September

divieto
di
pesca

dal 1 Aprile
al 30 Settembre

VIETATO FUMARE

no smoking

*no entry for
unauthorised
persons*

**VIETATO
L'INGRESSO
AI NON ADDETTI
AI LAVORI**

Smoking is prohibited in all public buildings, including cinemas, bars and restaurants. It is also prohibited in stations, airports and shopping centres.

Vietato is another word that means *forbidden*.

---

talking

can I smoke?
posso fumare?
pos-so foo-ma-ray

I don't smoke
non fumo
non foo-mo

an ashtray
un portacenere
oon por-ta-chen-nay-ray

do you mind if I smoke?
le dà fastidio se fumo?
lay da fas-teed-yo say foo-mo

please don't smoke
le dispiace non fumare
lay deesp-ya-chay non foo-ma-ray

a smoking seat
un posto fumatore
oon pos-to foo-ma-tor-ay

There are toilets at railway stations, often with an attendant. Although you do not have to pay, you may see a plate for coins. The attendant may even hand out toilet paper. If you do come across a public toilet, it is unlikely to have toilet paper, so remember always to carry tissues. Bars and restaurants have toilets, but they will not look at you kindly if you use their facilities without buying something. Remember it is cheapest to buy a drink standing at the bar. Toilets are sometimes locked and you will have to ask for the key.

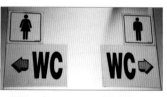

Toilets are usually indicated with a pictogram.

men   **women**

UOMINI   **DONNE**

non-drinking water

Don't be fooled:
caldo means hot,
freddo means cold.

Caldo   **Freddo**

excuse me! where is the toilet?
scusi! dov'è la toilette?
skoo-zee do-ve la twa-let

excuse me! may I use the bathroom?
scusi! posso usare il bagno?
skoo-zee pos-so oo-za-ray eel ban-yo

do you have the key for the toilet?
avete la chiave per la toilette?
a-vay-tay la kee-a-vay payr la twa-let

is there a disabled toilet?
ci sono le toilette per i disabili?
chee so-no lay twa-let payr ee dee-za-bee-lee

is there somewhere to change the baby?
c'è un posto per cambiare il bambino?
che oon pos-to payr kamb-ya-ray eel bam-bee-no

talking talking talking

Asking the Way

Tourist offices provide free maps, usually with an English version. They are usually well-stocked with brochures and leaflets about attractions in the area. They can also help finding somewhere to stay.

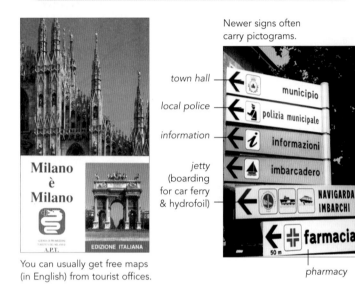

Newer signs often carry pictograms.

town hall — **municipio**

local police — **polizia municipale**

information — **informazioni**

jetty (boarding for car ferry & hydrofoil) — **imbarcadero** / **NAVIGARDA IMBARCHI**

pharmacy — **farmacia**

Milano è Milano
EDIZIONE ITALIANA

You can usually get free maps (in English) from tourist offices.

---

excuse me!
scusi!
skoo-zee

do you know where ... is?
sa dov'è...?
sa do-ve...

how do I get to...?
per andare a...?
payr an-da-ray a...

is this the right way to...?
è la strada giusta per...?
e la stra-da joos-ta payr...

do you have a map of the town?
avete una piantina della città?
a-vay-tay oo-na pyan-tee-na del-la cheet-ta

can you show me on the map?
mi può indicare sulla piantina?
mee pwo een-dee-ka-ray sool-la pyan-tee-na

we're looking for...
cerchiamo...
cherk-ya-mo...

where is the tourist office?
dov'è l'ufficio turistico?
do-ve loof-fee-cho too-rees-tee-ko

is it far?
è lontano?
e lon-ta-no

a street directory
uno stradario
oo-no stra-dar-ee-o

white signs indicate local destinations (green is for the **autostrada**, the motorway)

blue signs indicate main routes **tutte le direzioni** = *all routes*

brown signs indicate places of interest; **monumento ai caduti** is a war memorial.

other routes

duomo means *cathedral*

piazza means *square*

name of the road

indicates one-way street

centre (note pictogram)

parking

Church of the Crucifix

pedestrian area
bicycles allowed

keywords keywords keywords keywords keywords keywords

a destra
a des-tra
to the right

a sinistra
a see-nees-tra
to the left

vada
va-da
go

giri
jee-ree
turn

via
vee-a
road

piazza
pee-at-sa
square

semaforo
se-ma-fo-ro
traffic lights

chiesa
kee-ay-za
church

primo(a)
pree-mo(a)
first

secondo(a)
se-kon-do(a)
second

lontano(a)
lon-ta-no(a)
far

vicino a
vee-chee-no a
near to

accanto a
ak-kan-to a
next to

in faccia a
een fat-cha a
opposite

fino a
fee-no a
until

Banks & Money

i   *Banks offer the best rate of exchange, though changing
traveller's cheques can sometimes be quite lengthy. Remember to
take your passport with you and don't expect cashiers to speak English.
In smaller places banks tend to be shut in the afternoon, so it is best to
go in the mornings, when you can be sure that they are open. Banking
hours are generally 8.30am to 1.30pm Monday to Friday and in the
afternoon for an hour from 2.45 to 3.45. But check when you are there,
as times vary from place to place. Cash machines (**Bancomat**) are now
widespread. Credit cards and switch payments are widely accepted.*

Italy has many regional banks such
as *Banca Popolare di Sondrio*;
nationwide banks include
UniCredit and *San Paolini*.

Some cash
machines are
located inside
the bank.
Look out for
the *Bancomat*
sign.

Italian banks operate a double-
door or revolving-door system
with metal detectors to check you
aren't armed. To enter you press
a button and wait for a green
light to show and let you through.

Bureaux de
Change are
usually open
longer, but
tend not to
offer as good
rates as banks.

Symbol for the
euro. It is also
abbreviated to
EUR. A comma
is used between
euro and cent
and a full stop for thousands,
i.e. €6,50 or EUR 6.500,05.

Press the yellow button (**cancella**) to delete last part of the transaction and return to previous menu.

Press the red button (**annulla**) to delete the whole transaction and get your card back.

Press the green button (**esegui**) to go ahead.

Most cash machines let you select the language for your transaction.

The euro is the currency of Italy.
It breaks down into 100 euro cents.
Notes: 5, 10, 20, 50, 100, 200 and 500 euro.
Coins: 2 euro, 1 euro, 50 cent, 20 cent, 10 cent, 5 cent, 2 cent, 1 cent.
You find that Italians refer to them as **centesimi** (chen-**tes**-ee-mee). Euro notes are the same throughout Europe. The backs of coins carry different designs from each of the member European countries.

carta di credito
kar-ta dee kray-dee-to
credit card

bancomat
ban-ko-mat
cash machine

numero pin
noo-may-ro peen
pin number

spiccioli
speech-cho-lee
change

inserire
een-ser-ee-ray
insert

cambio
kamb-yo
exchange rate

contanti
kon-tan-tee
cash

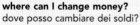

where can I change money?
dove posso cambiare dei soldi?
do-vay pos-so kamb-ya-ray day sol-dee

where is the nearest cash machine?
dov'è il bancomat più vicino?
do-ve eel ban-ko-mat pyoo vee-chee-no

where is there a bureau de change?
dove c'è un cambio?
do-vay che oon kamb-yo

where is the bank?
dov'è la banca?
do-ve la ban-ka

I want to change these traveller's cheques
vorrei cambiare questi travellers cheque
vor-ray kamb-ya-ray kwes-tee travellers cheques

small notes
biglietti piccoli
beel-yet-tee pee-ko-lee

the cash machine has swallowed my card
il bancomat ha mangiato la mia carta
eel ban-ko-mat a man-ja-to la mee-a kar-ta

When is...?

 Italy is one hour ahead of Great Britain.

at...

mattina
mat-tee-na
morning

pomeriggio
po-may-reed-jo
afternoon

stasera
sta-say-ra
this evening

oggi
od-jee
today

domani
do-ma-nee
tomorrow

ieri
yer-ee
yesterday

più tardi
pyoo tar-dee
later

subito
soo-bee-to
straightaway

adesso
a-des-so
now

13:00
14:00
15:00
16:00
17:00
18:00
19:00
20:00
21:00
22:00
23:00
24:00

alle ore tredici
al-lay o-ray tray-dee-chee

alle ore quattordici
al-lay o-ray kwat-tor-dee-chee

alle ore quindici
al-lay o-ray kween-dee-chay

alle ore sedici
al-lay o-ray say-dee-chee

alle ore diciassette
al-lay o-ray dee-chas-set-tay

alle ore diciotto
al-lay o-ray dee-chot-to

alle ore diciannove
al-lay o-ray dee-chan-no-vay

alle ore venti
al-lay o-ray ven-tee

alle ore ventuno
al-lay o-ray ven-too-no

alle ore ventidue
al-lay o-ray ven-tee-doo-ay

alle ore ventitre
al-lay o-ray ven-tee-tray

alle ore ventiquattro
al-lay o-ray ven-tee-kwat-tro

when is the next...?
quando c'è il prossimo...?
kwan-do che eel pros-see-mo...

what time is...?
a che ora è...?
a kay o-ra e...

when does it leave?
quando parte?
kwan-do par-tay

train
treno
tray-no

breakfast
la prima colazione
la pree-ma ko-lats-yo-nay

when does it arrive?
quando arriva?
kwan-do ar-ree-va

boat
battello
bat-tel-lo

dinner
la cena
la chay-na

at...

alle dodici
al-lay do-dee-chee

alle undici
al-lay oon-dee-chee

all'una
al-loo-na

alle dieci
al-lay dee-ay-chee

alle due
al-lay doo-ay

alle nove
al-lay no-vay

alle tre
al-lay tray

alle otto
al-lay ot-to

alle quattro
al-lay kwat-tro

alle sette
al-lay set-tay

alle cinque
al-lay cheen-kway

alle sei
al-lay say

alle ore diciotto e quarantacinque
al-lay o-ray dee-chot-to ay kwa-ran-ta-cheen-kway
at 18.45

alle ... meno un quarto
al-lay ... may-no oon kwar-to
at a quarter to...

a mezzanotte/mezzogiorno
a med-za-not-tay/med-zo-jor-no
at midnight/midday

alle ... e un quarto
al-lay ... e oon kwar-to
at a quarter past ...

alle ... meno venti
al-lay ... may-no ven-tee
at twenty to ...

alle ... e mezza
al-lay ... e med-za
at half past ...

what time is it?
che ore sono?
kay o-ray so-no

it's...
sono le...
so-no lay...

what is the date?
che giorno è oggi?
kay jor-no e od-jee

it is the 8th May
è l'otto maggio
e lot-to mad-jo

16 September 2006
il sedici settembre duemilaesei
eel say-dee-chee set-tem-bray doo-ay-mee-la-ay-say

talking

Timetables

Timetables use the 24 hour clock. The Italian for timetable is **orario**. *There are winter (**invernale**) and summer (**estivo**) timetables.*

CORSE BATTELLO - SCHIFF - BATEAU - SCHIP										BELLAGIO - LECCO
Annotazioni		❸ feriale 181	sabato e festivi 283	85	festiva 287	Rapido festiva SR253	87	❸ feriale 189	sabato e festivi 289
N° CORSE									
BELLAGIO	*part.*	6.40	8.20	11.45	12.45	14.34	16.50	18.05	18.05
Lierna	"	I	8.38	I					18.23
Limonta	"	6.57	8.46	12.02				18.22	18.31
Vassena	"	7.09	8.58	12.14	↓		↓	18.34	18.43

boat timetable *feriale* = weekdays (Monday-Friday)
sabato e festivi = Saturday and Sunday holidays

part. ore 19.28   arr. ore 23.45

part. ore = partenza alle ... ore
= departure at ... hours
arr. ore = arrivo alle ... ore
= arrival at ... hours

afternoon
pomeriggio

morning
mattino

orario
o-*rar*-yo
timetable

estivo(a)
es-*tee*-vo(a)
summer

invernale
een-ver-*na*-lay
winter

si effetua
see ef-*fet*-oo-a
operates

dalle/alle
dal-lay/*al*-lay
from/to

giorni
jor-nee
days

escluso(a)
es-*kloo*-zo(a)
except for

feriale
fer-*ya*-lay
Mon-Sat

festivo(a)
fes-*tee*-vo(a)
Sun and hols

bank opening hours
Monday-Friday

ORARIO SPORTELLO
da LUNEDÍ a VENERDÍ
8.20 - 13.20
14.35 - 15.35

MINISTERO DEI TRASPORTI E DELLA NAVIGAZIONE

Lago di COMO

ORARIO DAL 26 GIUGNO AL 1° OTTOBRE

timetable *from 26 June to 1 October*

lunedì
loo-nay-*dee*
Monday

martedì
mar-tay-*dee*
Tuesday

mercoledì
mer-ko-lay-*dee*
Wednesday

giovedì
jo-vay-*dee*
thursday

venerdì
ven-er-*dee*
Friday

sabato
sa-ba-to
Saturday

domenica
do-*me*-nee-ka
Sunday

bus timetable

services operating from there

number of bus service

SPT (bus company)

Scol = scolastici school term

Fest = festivo Sun & hols

Fer = feriale weekdays Mon-Sat

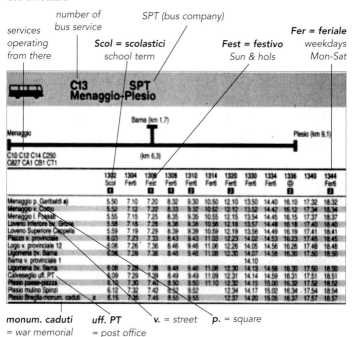

	1302 Scol ■	1304 Fer6	1306 Fest ■	1308 Fer6 ■	1310 Fer6 ■	1314 Fer6 ■	1320 Fer6 ■	1330 Fer6 ■	1334 Fer6 ■	1336 ⑪ ■	1340	1344 Fer6 ■
Menaggio p. Garibaldi a)	5.50	7.10	7.20	8.32	9.30	10.50	12.10	13.50	14.40	16.10	17.32	18.32
Menaggio v. Como	5.52	7.12	7.22	8.33	9.32	10.52	12.12	13.52	14.42	16.12	17.34	18.34
Menaggio l. Fossati	5.55	7.15	7.25	8.35	9.35	10.55	12.15	13.54	14.45	16.15	17.37	18.37
Loveno Inferiore bv. Grosa	5.58	7.18	7.28	8.38	9.38	10.58	12.18	13.57	14.48	16.18	17.40	18.40
Loveno Superiore Cappella	5.59	7.19	7.29	8.39	9.39	10.59	12.19	13.58	14.49	16.19	17.41	18.41
Plazzo v. provinciale	6.03	7.23	7.33	8.43	9.43	11.03	12.23	14.02	14.53	16.23	17.45	18.45
Logo v. provinciale 12	6.05	7.26	7.36	8.46	9.46	11.06	12.26	14.05	14.56	16.26	17.48	18.48
Ugomena bv. Barna	6.04	7.28	7.38	8.48	9.48	11.08	12.30	14.07	14.58	16.30	17.50	18.50
Barna v. provinciale 1								14.10				
Ugomena bv. Barna	6.06	7.28	7.38	8.48	9.48	11.08	12.30	14.13	14.58	16.30	17.50	18.50
Calvesegio uff. PT	6.09	7.29	7.39	8.49	9.49	11.09	12.31	14.14	14.59	16.31	17.51	18.51
Plesio paese-piazza	6.10	7.30	7.40	8.50	9.50	11.10	12.32	14.15	15.00	16.32	17.52	18.52
Plesio mulino Spinzi	6.12	7.32	7.42	8.52	9.52		12.34	14.17	15.02	16.34	17.54	18.54
Plesio Breglia-monum. caduti a	6.15	7.35	7.45	8.55	9.55		12.37	14.20	15.05	16.37	17.57	18.57

monum. caduti = war memorial

uff. PT = post office

v. = street

p. = square

winter timetable

Como
Orario Invernale

Partenze
departures

Arrivi
arrivals

summer timetable

ORARIO ESTIVO 2006

Como città del Lago di Volta della Seta ...e della S.P.T. ④

TRASPORTI REGIONE LOMBARDIA

gennaio Jan
febbraio Feb
marzo Mar
aprile Apr
maggio May
giugno Jun
luglio Jul
agosto Aug
settembre Sep
ottobre Oct
novembre Nov
dicembre Dec

do you have a timetable?	**can you explain the timetable?**
avete un orario?	mi può spiegare l'orario?
a-**vay**-tay oon o-**rar**-yo	mee pwo spyay-**ga**-ray lo-**rar**-yo

talk

Tickets

Tickets for bus, metro and trains need to be validated, otherwise you can be fined. Bus tickets are validated on board the bus. Train and metro tickets are validated at the special yellow/orange machines in the stations.

FERROVIE DELLO STATO
BIGLIETTERIA SIPAX
SELF-SERVICE

There is an increasing number of self-service ticket machines. You can choose the language for your transaction.

Tickets can be validated here instead of at machines on platforms.

Cod. 811003

Data di emissione
15-10-2006
Autolinea COMO-COLICO

COLICO	TREMEZZO
DUBINO	BOLVEDRO
SORICO	AZZANO
GERA	PORTEZZA
VERCANA	LENNO
DOMASO	ISOLA
GRAVEDONA	SPURANO
CONSIGLIO	SALA
DONGO	COLONNO
MUSSO	ARGEGNO
PIANELLO	BRIENNO
CREMIA	LAGLIO
REZZONICO	CARATE
MOLVEDO	URIO
ACQUASERIA	MOLTRASIO
NOBIALLO	CERNOBBIO
MENAGGIO	COMO
CADENABBIA	

N° 433528
TARIFFA **2**

Bus ticket listing all the stops en route. The destination is punched.

train ticket

valid for 6 hours from validating   *ticket valid for 2 months from date of issue*   2nd class   **adulti** *adults*   **ragazzi** *children*

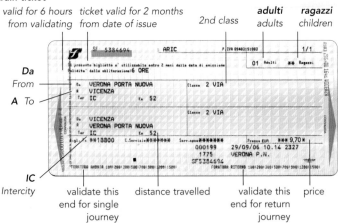

Da *From*
A *To*

IC *Intercity*   validate this end for single journey   distance travelled   validate this end for return journey   price

boat ticket

valid on all motorboats

retain ticket until end of journey

valid for one day

return

standard fare i.e. no reductions

single

journey

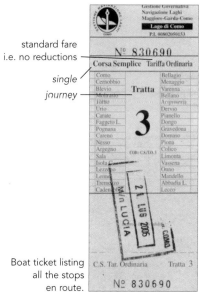

Boat ticket listing all the stops en route.

carnet di biglietti
kar-nay dee beel-yet-tee
book of tickets

biglietto
beel-yet-to
ticket

riduzione
ree-doots-yo-nay
reduction

andata
an-da-ta
single

andata e ritorno
an-da-ta ay ree-tor-no
return

adulto(a)
a-dool-to(a)
adult

ragazzo(a)
ra-gat-so(a)
child

studente(a)
stoo-den-tay(a)
student

terza età
tert-za ay-ta
over 60s

disabile
dee-za-bee-lay
disabled

famiglia
fa-meel-ya
family

City transport ticket which has been stamped. It is valid for 75 minutes from stamping and can be used for one metro ride and unlimited bus/tram rides.

Public Transport

Most Italian cities operate an integrated transport system, which means that all the different kinds of transport are part of one network, and you can use any of them with your ticket. Bus tickets must be bought in advance and you can buy them at newsagents/kiosks and at tobacconists. In smaller places they will be sold at the shop or bar near to the bus stop. Look out for a sign stating that bus tickets are on sale. You validate the ticket in the machine at the back of the bus, or on long-distance buses there will be a conductor to check your ticket, not to sell you one.

Tickets for Milan's integrated transport system.

City buses are generally orange. You enter from the back and validate your ticket at the machine as you enter.

Tram

Sign showing bus tickets for sale – here, at the local butcher's. Shops like this shut from 12.30 to 3.30pm, so you should buy tickets in advance.

Rural buses usually have a conductor. This does not mean you can buy a ticket on board – you still must buy it in advance.

Bus station are generally located near train stations. It is the most likely place to find a public toilet.

City bus stop showing the different lines, services and which buses stop at metro stations (indicated by an M).

Long-distance bus stop showing the different services and routes.

Italian airports are well served by buses. Tourist offices will have information.

is there a bus to...?
c'è un autobus per...?
*che oon **ow**-to-boos payr...*

where does the bus leave from?
da dove parte l'autobus?
*da **do**-vay **par**-tay **low**-to-boos*

which bus goes to the centre?
quale autobus va in centro?
*kwa-lay **ow**-to-boos va een **chen**-tro*

which number goes to...?
quale linea va a...?
*kwa-lay **lee**-nay-a va a...*

does this bus go to...?
questo autobus va a...?
*kwes-to **ow**-to-boos va a...*

when is the next bus to...?
quando c'è il prossimo autobus per...?
*kwan-do che eel **pros**-see-mo **ow**-to-boos payr...*

can you tell me when it is my stop
mi può dire quando è la mia fermata
*mee pwo **deer**-mee **kwan**-do e la **mee**-a fer-**ma**-ta*

I want to get off!
voglio scendere!
*vol-yo **shen**-day-ray*

talking talking

i Milan and Rome are the only two Italian cities to have metro systems. You can buy a book (**carnet**) of tickets which is cheaper than buying tickets individually. Tickets must be validated before you get on the train. You can also buy weekly tickets valid for 2 journeys per day 6 days a week. These are geared to commuters. There are also 24 and 48 hour tickets, which are ideal for tourists.

Metro station

ticket machine
A single ticket is valid for 75 minutes from validating and can be used for one metro ride and any number of bus and tram journeys within that time limit.

tickets on sale at kiosk or from ticket machines

Metro sign

Kiosk selling metro tickets and parking tickets.

The Milan underground has three colour-coded lines: MI is red, M2 is green and M3 yellow. There is also a fourth, blue line called the **passante ferroviario** linking with the main train stations.

a single ticket
un biglietto singolo
oon beel-yet-to seen-go-lo

a 24-hour ticket
un biglietto da ventiquattro ore
oon beel-yet-to da ven-tee-kwat-tro o-ray

a carnet of tickets
un carnet di biglietti
oon kar-nay dee beel-yet-tee

a 48-hour ticket
un biglietto da quarantotto ore
oon beel-yet-to da kwa-rant-ot-to o-ray

have you a map of the metro?
avete una piantina della metro?
a-vay-tay oo-na pyan-tee-na del-la met-ro

where is the nearest metro station?
dov'è la stazione della metropolitana più vicina?
do-ve la stats-yo-nay del-la met-ro-po-lee-ta-na pyoo vee-chee-na

I want to go to...
voglio andare a...
vol-yo an-da-ray a...

do I have to change?
devo cambiare?
day-vo kamb-ya-ray

where?
dove?
do-vay

which line do I take?
quale linea prendo?
kwa-lay lee-nay-a pren-do

in which direction?
in quale direzione?
een kwa-lay dee-rets-yo-nay

which station is it for...?
qual è la stazione per...?
kwa-le la stats-yo-nay payr...

what is the next stop?
qual è la prossima fermata?
kwa-le la pros-see-ma fer-ma-ta

excuse me! I want to get off
permesso! voglio scendere
payr-mes-so vol-yo shen-day-ray

talking talking talking talking talking

Italian trains are good value. Fares are charged according to the distance travelled, so buying a return does not make it any cheaper. Return tickets are valid only within 48 hours of outward journey, so it is not worth buying one if you are staying for a longer period. On Intercity trains you must pay a supplement when you purchase your ticket. If you do not, the train conductor can ask you to pay a surcharge that is more expensive than the supplement. On both Eurocity and Intercity trains, reservations are obligatory. Remember to validate your ticket before boarding the train.

departures   *Tues 29 Aug*

destination   *extra info.*   *class*

timetable   *delay*
(orario)   *(ritardo)*

platform
(binario)

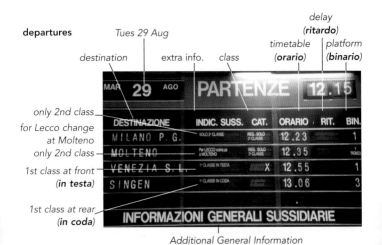

only 2nd class
for Lecco change at Molteno
only 2nd class
1st class at front *(in testa)*
1st class at rear *(in coda)*

Additional General Information

a single	2 returns	to...
un'andata	due andate e ritorno	per...
oon an-da-ta	*doo-ay an-da-tay ay ree-tor-no*	*payr...*

I want to book...	2 seats	a couchette
voglio prenotare...	due posti	una cuccetta
vol-yo pray-no-ta-ray...	*doo-ay pos-tee*	*oo-na koo-chet-ta*

what time is the next train to...?
a che ora c'è il prossimo treno per...?
a kay o-ra che eel pros-see-mo tray-no payr...

which platform?
quale binario?
kwa-lay bee-nar-yo

is there a supplement to pay?
c'e un supplemento da pagare?
che oon soop-lay-men-to da pa-ga-ray

do I have to change?
devo cambiare?
day-vo kam-bee-a-ray

talking

stazione →

station with rail logo

Milan Central Station information board

telephone booking collection
platforms
information desk

ticket office

automated ticket machine

Validating machines are usually situated at platform entrances and can easily be missed.

andata
an-da-ta
one-way

andata e ritorno
an-da-ta ay ree-tor-no
return

prima classe
pree-ma klas-say
first class

seconda classe
se-kon-da klas-say
second class

prezzo ridotto
pret-so ree-dot-to
reduced fare

prenotazione
pray-no-tats-yo-nay
reservation

carta d'argento
kar-ta dar-jen-to
over 60s pass

sportello
spor-tel-lo
ticket counter

tessera
tes-say-ra
pass

corridoio
ko-ree-doy-o
aisle

finestra
fee-nes-tra
window

does this train stop at...?
questo treno si ferma a...?
kwes-to tray-no see fer-ma a...

is this the train for...?
è questo il treno per...?
e kwes-to eel tray-no payr...

how long does the train stop for?
quanto tempo si ferma il treno?
kwan-to tem-po see fer-ma eel tray-no

this is my seat
questo è il mio posto
kwes-to e eel mee-o pos-to

Taxi

The easiest place to find a taxi is at a railway station. Be sure to take an official white taxi. In smaller places you can ask at the tourist office for the phone number of the local taxi. You may be charged extra to go to or from the airport. Watch out for pirate cab operators as they are more likely to overcharge. Try and establish in advance how much the fare will be.

taxi sign
Two phone numbers are given, one for the town centre and one for the station.

You can phone for a taxi. **Numero Verde** means free phone so you don't need any money to call.

Taxis are white. This is a taxi stand at a railway station.

where is the nearest taxi stand?
dov'è il posteggio dei taxi più vicino?
do-**ve** eel pos-**ted**-jo day **tak**-see pyoo vee-**chee**-no

to ... please
a ... per favore
a ... payr fa-**vo**-ray

how much is it to...?
quanto costa andare a...?
kwan-to **kos**-ta an-**da**-ray a...

please order me a taxi
per favore, mi chiami un taxi
payr fa-**vo**-ray mee kee-**a**-mee oon **tak**-see

now
subito
soo-bee-to

for ... o'clock
per le ...
payr lay ...

I need a receipt
ho bisogno di una ricevuta
o bee-**zon**-yo dee **oo**-na ree-chay-**voo**-ta

keep the change
tenga il resto
ten-ga eel **res**-to

is there a special rate for the airport?
c'è una tariffa speciale per l'aeroporto?
che **oo**-na ta-**reef**-fa spay-**cha**-lay payr lay-ro-**por**-to

talking talking talking

Car Hire

> You will find all the big car hire firms in Italy, but hiring a car on the spot can prove more expensive than arranging it before your trip. Depending on the company, it may be that you have to be at least 21 and to have held a driving licence for over a year to hire a car.

Most of the big hire firms operate in Italy.

— *car hire*

— *van hire*

I want to hire a car
vorrei noleggiare una macchina
vor-ray nol-ed-ja-ray oo-na mak-kee-na

for one day
per un giorno
payr oon jor-no

for ... days
per ... giorni
payr ... jor-nee

I want...
vorrei...
vor-ray...

a small car
una macchina piccola
oo-na mak-kee-na peek-ko-la

a large car
una macchina grande
oo-na mak-kee-na gran-day

a people carrier
una monovolume
oo-na mo-no-vo-loo-may

an automatic car
un macchina con cambio automatico
oo-na mak-kee-na kon kam-byo ow-to-ma-teek-ko

how much is it?
quanto costa?
kwan-to kos-ta

is there a kilometre charge?
si paga per chilometro?
see pa-ga payr kee-lo-may-tro

I am ... old
ho ... anni
o ... an-nee

here is my driving licence
ecco la mia patente
ek-ko la mee-a pa-ten-tay

what is included in the insurance?
cos'è compreso nell'assicurazione?
ko-ze kom-pray-zo nel-las-see-koo-rats-yo-nay

how do the controls work?
come funzionano i comandi?
ko-may foonts-yo-na-no ee ko-man-dee

where are the documents?
dove sono i documenti?
do-vay so-no ee do-koo-men-tee

what do we do if...?
cosa si deve fare se...?
ko-za see day-vay fa-ray say...

when there is a breakdown
quando c'è un guasto
kwan-do che oon gwas-to

can we have a babyseat?
si può avere un seggiolino per il bambino?
see pwo a-vay-ray oon sed-jo-lee-no payr eel bam-bee-no

how is it fitted?
come si monta?
ko-may see mon-ta

talking talking talking talking talking

Driving

*The minimum age for driving in Italy is 18. Italian drivers can sometimes be impatient and will often overtake dangerously. Zebra crossings show where you can cross the road but don't expect cars to stop for you. The **Polizia Stradale** look after the roads and their cars are equipped with speed-monitoring machines. You must carry your passport and car documents with you at all times and it is likely that the police will ask to look at these. Non EU-members need to have an international driving licence. If you are caught speeding they will fine you on the spot. If you break down, call 803116 (ACI, the Italian equivalent to the AA). They operate 24 hours a day and have multi-lingual staff. They will need to know where you are, the type of car and the registration number.*

Remember, speeds are in kilometres per hour.

Speed restrictions

built up area	50 km/h
main roads	90-110 km/h
motorway	130-140 km/h

North **Nord**

Ovest — **Est**

West *East*

Sud *South*

I is for *Italy*   *CO* is for region (*Como*)

BM·967DL co

Italian number plate.

One way street.

Late at night the amber light may be flashing. This means you can go through if nothing is coming.

green indicates motorway, prefixed A- (*autostrada*)

blue indicates main routes

centro centre local signs are white

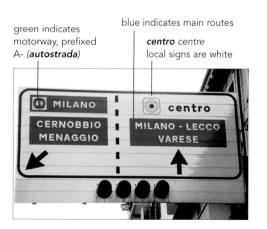

A9 MILANO
CERNOBBIO MENAGGIO

centro
MILANO - LECCO VARESE

pictograms on road signs indicate services available: hospital, post office and police

Beware! New roundabouts follow the same rules as the UK, ie you stop and give way to vehicles already on it. Old roundabouts are the opposite – you can drive straight onto them and cars on it have to give way to you. The problem is telling which system operates! Watch out carefully for signs and don't trust other drivers. Italians aren't yet used to the new system.

caution

electronic speed control

You must have your headlights on at all times on the motorways and outside built-up areas.

ACCENDERE I FARI

switch on lights

caution lorry exit

Pictograms are increasingly used. If you don't see your destination, follow **tutte le direzioni** (all routes) or **altre direzioni** (other routes). To get to the town centre, follow **centro**.

no sounding horn

we are going to...
andiamo a...
and-ya-mo a...

is it a good road?
è una buona strada?
e oo-na bwo-na stra-da

is the pass open?
il passo è aperto?
eel pas-so e a-payr-to

which is the best route?
qual è la strada migliore?
kwa-le la stra-da meel-yo-ray

can you show me on the map?
mi può indicare sulla cartina?
mee pwo een-dee-ka-ray sool-la kar-tee-na

do we need snow chains?
c'è bisogno delle catene da neve?
che bee-zon-yo del-lay ka-tay-nay da nev-ay

*Italian motorways (**autostrada**) are often two-laned and cars can come up very fast in the outside lane. Italian drivers are apt to come up very close behind you and to flash their lights if they want you to get out of the way. The speed limit on Italian motorways (in good weather) is 130km/h. In bad weather (when windscreen wipers in use), you must reduce speed to 110km/h. You must also keep your headlights on all the time on motorways and outside built-up areas.*

On most motorways you pay a toll.

entrance to motorway
Italian motorway signs are green.

no hitchhiking

toll to pay

pay station coming up

You must stop and pay unless you have a **Telepass**. This device, installed in the car, allows you to go through the automatic barrier.

motorway exit sign
Prossima Uscita on a motorway sign means *next exit*.

exit for Malpensa Airport

brown signs are for places of interest

SS 33 indicates a **Strada Statale**, a main road.

CH indicates border crossing to Switzerland.

Pay station in 2.5km. Do not use the yellow telepass lane unless you have an in-car device. The righthand lane is for cash. If you plan to pay by debit or credit card, choose the blue *carte* lane.

Service station 500m with facilities for the disabled and a cash machine.

SOS phones are every 2km on the motorway.

Italian service stations offer hot and cold food.

If you break down on the motorway

If you break down on the motorway, first put on your warning lights, then put on a fluorescent vest (compulsory for all vehicles) and place the warning triangle about 100m behind the car. There are SOS points every 2km. They are simple to use and instructions are in four languages. Simply press either the red cross button for ambulance assistance or the spanner button if you need breakdown recovery. The confirmation light (*lampada di conferma*) should light when your call has been acknowledged. You should then return to the car and wait for help to arrive.

my car has broken down
la mia macchina è in panne
la **mee**-a **mak**-kee-na e een **pan**-nay

what should I do?
cosa devo fare?
ko-za **day**-vo **fa**-ray

I'm a female on my own
sono da sola
so-no da **so**-la

my children are in the car
i miei figli sono nella macchina
ee mee-**ay feel**-yee so-no **nel**-la **mak**-kee-na

the car is...
la macchina è...
la **mak**-kee-na e...

after exit...
dopo l'uscita...
do-po loo-**shee**-ta...

before exit...
prima dell'uscita...
pree-ma del-loo-**shee**-ta...

it's a red Nissan
è una Nissan rossa
e **oo**-na **nees**-san **ros**-sa

registration number...
il numero di targa...
eel **noo**-may-ro dee **tar**-ga...

*There are a number of different systems used for parking. More and more automated machines are being used and you will need coins. Some machines will take credit cards and banknotes (but they must be in good condition). Some parking is with a parking disk (**disco orario**) and you can get these from petrol stations. Don't park in a **zona di rimozione** or you will be towed away.*

parking sign
More and more pictograms are being used on signs. It often makes them more baffling.

parking disk required

1 hour

cross = Sundays

crossed mallets = work day Mon–Sat

No parking outside authorised spaces.

Parking disk required. You must display it on the dashboard where it is visible.

maximum 60 minutes from 8am–8pm, holidays included

You will be towed away if you park here.

pay at the meter

giorni feriali means Mon–Sat from 9am–8pm

Inizio means begins (i.e. parking restriction begins here).

No parking at any time of the day (you will be towed away).

parking ticket machine
Instructions on the right are also in English.

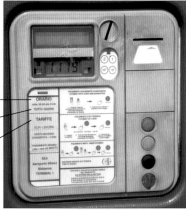

orario (when payment applies)
00.00 to 24.00 (i.e. all the time)

tutti i giorni means *every day*

tariffe *tariff*
maximum stay allowed 3 hours
minimum payment for 30 minutes

municipal parking

pedestrian entrance

Careful! *libero* means *spaces*, not that it's free and *completo* means *full*.

private property

free parking

multi-storey car park

where is there a car park?
dove c'è un parcheggio?
do-vay che oon par-ked-jo

where's the best place to park?
dov'è il posto migliore per parcheggiare?
do-ve eel pos-to meel-yo-ray payr par-ked-ja-ray

I don't have a parking disk
non ho un disco orario
non o oon deesk o-rar-yo

can I park here?
posso parcheggiare qui?
pos-so par-ked-ja-ray kwee

how long for?
per quanto tempo?
payr kwan-to tem-po

the ticket machine doesn't work
il parchimetro non funziona
eel par-kee-may-tro non foonts-yo-na

Petrol stations generally follow shop hours and are closed between 12.30 and 3.30pm. They stay open until 7.30pm and are shut on Sundays. However, they usually have automatic pumps which accept banknotes. Make sure you have 5, 10 and 20 euro notes. No change is given so be careful how much money you put in.

Senza Pb unleaded

Gasolio diesel

Many petrol stations have machines where you can select and pay for the petrol you want. Select the petrol, pay in advance and then the pump will release the petrol.

Pumps in large petrol stations are generally numbered and you just need to tell the attendant the pump number.

where is the nearest petrol station?
dov'è la stazione di servizio più vicina?
do-ve la stats-yo-nay dee ser-veets-yo pyoo vee-chee-na

... worth of unleaded petrol
... di benzina senza piombo
... dee bent-see-na sent-sa pee-om-bo

can I get the car washed?
si può lavare la macchina?
see pwo la-va-ray la mak-kee-na

fill it up
il pieno
eel pee-ay-no

pump number
pompa numero
pom-pa noo-may-ro

talking

*If you break down, phone 803116 for assistance. Garages that do repairs are known as **Autofficina**.*

car wash

car vacuum

I have broken down
sono in panne
*so-no een **pan**-nay*

the battery is flat
la batteria è scarica
*la bat-tay-**ree**-a e **ska**-ree-ka*

I need new tyres
ho bisogno di gomme nuove
*o bee-**zon**-yo di **gom**-may **nwov**-ay*

I have run out of petrol
ho finito la benzina
*o fee-**nee**-to la bent-**see**-na*

the ... is not working
il/la ... non funziona
*eel/la ... non foonts-**yo**-na*

can you repair it?
può ripararlo?
*pwo ree-par-**ar**-lo*

when will it be ready?
quando sarà pronta?
*kwan-do sa-**ra pron**-ta*

the car won't start
la macchina non parte
*la **mak**-kee-na non **par**-tay*

I have a flat tyre
ho forato una gomma
*o fo-**ra**-to **oo**-na **gom**-ma*

where is the nearest garage?
dov'è l'autofficina più vicina?
*do-**ve** low-tof-fee-**chee**-na pyoo vee-**chee**-na*

there is something wrong with...
c'è qualcosa che non va con...
*che kwal-**ko**-za kay non va kon...*

have you the parts?
avete i pezzi di ricambio?
*a-**vay**-tay ee **pet**-see dee ree-**kamb**-yo*

how long will it take?
quanto ci vuole?
*kwan-to chee **vwo**-lay*

how much will it cost?
quanto costerà?
*kwan-to kos-tay-**ra***

can you replace the windscreen?
può cambiare il parabrezza?
*pwo kamb-**ya**-ray eel pa-ra-**bret**-sa*

can you change...	**the oil**	**the water**	**the tyres**
mi può cambiare...	l'olio	l'acqua	le gomme
*mee pwo kamb-**ya**-ray...*	***lol**-yo*	***lak**-wa*	*lay **gom**-may*

Milan District

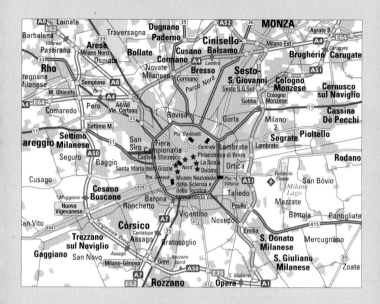

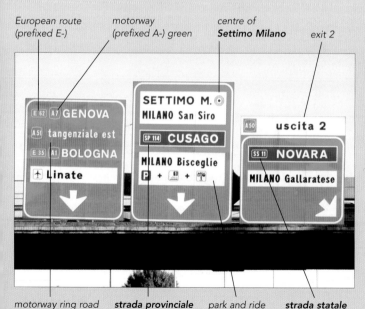

European route (prefixed E-)

motorway (prefixed A-) green

centre of **Settimo Milano**

exit 2

motorway ring road eastbound (est)

strada provinciale *(B road)*

park and ride

strada statale *(A road)*

Milan City

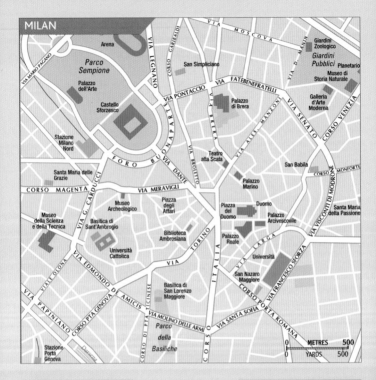

MILAN

CHIESA S. CECILIA
Church of St. Cecilia

PINACOTECA
art gallery

MUSEI CIVICI
local museum

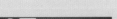
cathedral

150 m a destra
150m on right
a sinistra = on left

motorway ring road —  tangenziale

old part of town
(*centro storico*)

pedestrian area

private parking
no parking

municipio
town hall

1º piano
1st floor

piazza
Nuova
square (*piazza*)

Rome City

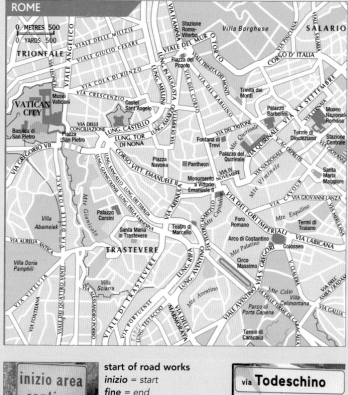

start of road works
inizio = start
fine = end

rallentare

slow down

P AUTOSILO

multi-storey parking

centro ⊚→

centre

DEVIAZIONE centro storico

Detour to the old part of town
(*centro storico*).

via **Todeschino**

town hall — ← 🏛 **municipio**

local police — ← 🔔 **polizia municipale**

schools — ← 🚸 **scuole**

medical centre — ← **guardia medica**

thermal spring — ← **terme di Virgilio**

Pictograms are increasingly
used on signs (hospital,
post office and police).

Rome District

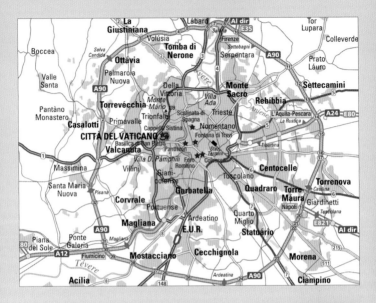

Matrix boards warn of any hold-ups. Here roadworks (*lavori*) are flagged up.

recommended speed 70kph

motorway service station

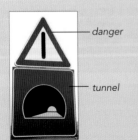

danger

tunnel

cash payment lane

priority road

Shopping

Smaller shops are generally shut on Monday mornings. Other days they are open in the mornings from 9am to 12.30pm and in the afternoons from 3.30pm to 7pm., shops are shut on Sundays except cake shops and shops in tourist areas.

Alimentari is the grocer's, selling fresh bread, milk and other foods. It tends to open early, about 8am.

Butcher & Pork products (e.g. ham, salami, sausage)

newspapers

— stationery
— toys
— gifts

keywords keywords keywords

panificio
pa-nee-fee-cho
baker's

macelleria
ma-chel-lay-ree-a
butcher's

fruttivendolo
froot-tee-ven-do-lo
fruit shop

alimentari
a-lee-men-ta-ree
grocer's

pasticceria
pas-tee-cher-ee-a
cake shop

supermercato
soo-per-mer-ka-to
supermarket

pescheria
pes-kay-ree-a
fishmonger's

giornalaio
jor-nal-a-yo
newsagent's

Pharmacies sell baby products such as nappies and baby food, but they cost more than in supermarkets.

An *enoteca* sells wine. Look out for local specialities.

Supermarkets are generally open all day (until 9 pm) seven days a week. You can find other services within large supermarkets such as dry-cleaning and shoe repairs as well as a café serving fast food.

Supermarkets are becoming more widespread with smaller food shops harder to find.

Giovedì e Venerdì aperto fino alle 22.00
Thu and Fri open until 10pm

Fruit and veg must be weighed and stickered (the weighing machine has pictures so you can identify the produce) before getting to the checkout. Sometimes you have to do this; other times an assistant does it. You will also have to ask for and pay for plastic bags.

change machine at entrance

You need a coin for the trolley.

pay for 2 — **paghi 2**
take 3 — **prendi 3**

---

talking

where can I buy...?	some	batteries	a tin-opener
dove posso comprare...?	delle	pile	un apriscatole
do-vay pos-so komp-ra-ray...	*del-lay*	*pee-lay*	*oon ap-ree-ska-to-lay*

do you have...?
avete...?
a-vay-tay...

how much is it?
quanto costa?
kwan-to kos-ta

I am looking for...	a present	a good wine
cerco...	un regalo	un buon vino
cher-ko...	*oon ray-ga-lo*	*oon bwon vee-no*

can I pay with this card?
posso pagare con questa carta?
pos-so pa-ga-ray kon kwes-ta kar-ta

4 plastic bags
quattro borse di plastica
kwat-tro bor-say dee plas-tee-ka

> *Quantities are expressed in kilos and grams. For those who are more used to pounds and ounces, 1 kilo is roughly equivalent to 2lb, half a kilo is equivalent to 1lb, 250g is equivalent to a half pound and an ounce is equivalent to about 30g. You will also hear the word **etto** used, which is 100g. So 250g could be expressed either **duecentocinquanta grammi** or **due etti e mezzo**, i.e. two and a half **etti**.*

Bread is sold by weight, or if you are buying rolls (**panini**) by number. Large wholemeal loaves are cut up and you can ask for a piece. Bread is eaten with meals. Italians don't usually put butter on their bread, so you won't find it on the dining table. Italian butter is unsalted.

Markets are held in the morning, either daily in large towns or weekly in smaller places. They generally have a great variety of stalls: cheese, bread, meat and fish. It is the best place to buy your fruit and vegetables. Markets will also have stalls selling hardware, clothes, shoes, etc. If you feel confident, in markets you can ask for a discount on anything other than food.

Ham is either cured, such as Parma ham, and known as **prosciutto crudo**. Cooked ham is **prosciutto cotto**. When you ask for **prosciutto**, you may hear the shop assistant asking whether you want **crudo** or **cotto**. It is sliced very finely. **Un etto di prosciutto** should generously fill a couple of bread rolls.

is there a market?	**which day?**
c'è un mercato?	quale giorno?
*che oon mer-**ka**-to*	***kwa**-lay **jor**-no*
it's a bit too much	**would you give me a discount?**
è un po' troppo caro	mi fa uno sconto?
*e oon po **trop**-po **ka**-ro*	*mee fa **oo**-no **skon**-to*

talking

da consumarsi entro
to be consumed by

Milk is generally colour-coded. Here blue is for whole milk (**intero**), pink for semi-skimmed (**parzialmente scremato**). It is sold by the half litre (**mezzo litro**) or litre (**litro**).

Mineral water is sparkling (**frizzante**) or still (**naturale**). Look out for the colour coding: red for sparkling and blue/grey for still.

surgelati

frozen foods

ingetrale

wholemeal

SENZA COLORANTI

free of colouring

SENZA ZUCCHERO

sugar-free

typical nutritional info per 100ml

LATTE INTERO OMOGENEIZZATO
VALORI NUTRITIVI MEDI per 100 ml

energy — ENERGIA	65 kcal / 273 kJ
protein — PROTEINE	3,2 g
carbohydrates — CARBOIDRATI	5,0 g
fat — GRASSI	3,6 g
calcium — CALCIO	120 mg

biologico

organic

talking talking talking

a piece of that cheese
un pezzo di quel formaggio
*oon **pet**-so dee kwel for-**mad**-jo*

that's fine thanks
basta così grazie
*bas-ta ko-**zee grats**-yay*

a litre of milk
un litro di latte
*oon **leet**-ro dee **lat**-tay*

mineral water
acqua minerale
*ak-wa mee-nay-**ra**-lay*

a tin of...
una scatola di...
*oo-na **ska**-to-la dee...*

a packet of...
un pacchetto di...
*oon pak-**ket**-to dee...*

a little more
ancora un po'
*an-**ko**-ra oon po*

8 slices of ham
otto fette di prosciutto
*ot-to **fet**-tay dee pro-**shoot**-to*

a bottle of...
una bottiglia di...
*oo-na bot-**teel**-ya dee...*

still
naturale
*na-too-**ra**-lay*

a jar of...
un vaso di...
*oon **va**-zo dee...*

that's all thanks
è tutto grazie
*e toot-to **grats**-yay*

a little less
un po' meno
*oon po **may**-no*

fizzy
gassata
*gas-**za**-ta*

Here is a list of everyday foods you might need.

Everyday Foods alimentari *a-lee-men-ta-ree*

biscuits i biscotti *bees-kot-tee*
bread il pane *pa-nay*
bread roll il panino *pa-nee-no*
bread (sliced) il pancarrè *pan-kar-ray*
butter il burro *boor-ro*
cheese il formaggio *for-mad-jo*
chicken il pollo *pol-lo*
coffee il caffè *kaf-fe*
cream la panna *pan-na*
crisps le patatine *pat-a-tee-nay*
eggs le uova *wov-a*
fish il pesce *pay-shay*
flour la farina *fa-ree-na*
fruit juice il succo di frutta
    sook-ko dee froot-ta
ham (cooked) il prosciutto cotto
    pro-shoot-to kot-to
ham (cured) il prosciutto crudo
    pro-shoot-to kroo-do
herbal tea la tisana *tee-za-na*
honey il miele *myay-lay*
jam la marmellata *mar-mel-la-ta*

margarine la margarina *mar-ga-ree-na*
marmalade la marmellata d'arance
    mar-mel-la-ta da-ran-chay
meat la carne *kar-nay*
milk il latte *lat-tay*
oil l'olio *ol-yo*
orange juice il succo d'arancia
    sook-ko da-ran-cha
pasta la pasta *pas-ta*
pepper il pepe *pep-ay*
rice il riso *ree-zo*
salt il sale *sa-lay*
sausage la salsiccia *sal-see-cha*
sugar lo zucchero *tsook-kay-ro*
stock cubes i dadi da brodo
    da-dee da bro-do
tea il tè *te*
tomatoes (tin) i pelati *pay-la-tee*
tuna il tonno *ton-no*
vinegar l'aceto *a-chay-to*
yoghurt lo yogurt *yo-goort*

The market is the best place to buy fresh fruit and vegetables.
*A greengrocer's is called **il fruttivendolo**.*

Vegetables verdura ver-**doo**-ra

artichokes i carciofi kar-**cho**-fee
aubergines le melanzane
  may-lant-**sa**-nay
asparagus gli asparagi as-**pa**-ra-jee
carrots le carote ka-**ro**-tay
cauliflower il cavolfiore ka-volf-**yor**-ay
celery il sedano **sed**-a-no
courgettes le zucchine tsook-**kee**-nay
cucumber il cetriolo chay-tree-**yo**-lo
french beans i fagiolini fa-jo-**lee**-nee
garlic l'aglio **al**-yo
leeks i porri **por**-ree
lettuce la lattuga lat-**too**-ga
mushrooms i funghi **foong**-ee
onions le cipolle chee-**pol**-lay
peas i piselli pee-**zel**-lee
peppers i peperoni pay-pay-**ro**-nee
potatoes le patate pa-**ta**-tay
radishes i ravanelli ra-va-**nel**-lee
spinach gli spinaci spee-**na**-chee
spring onions le cipolline
  chee-pol-**lee**-nay

tomatoes i pomodori po-mo-**do**-ree
turnip la rapa **ra**-pa

Fruit frutta **froot**-ta

apples le mele **may**-lay
apricots le albicocche al-bee-**kok**-kay
bananas le banane ba-**na**-nay
cherries le ciliege cheel-**yay**-jay
figs i fichi **fee**-kee
grapefruit il pompelmo pom-**pel**-mo
grapes l'uva **oo**-va
lemon il limone lee-**mo**-nay
melon il melone may-**lo**-nay
nectarines le peschenoci
  pes-kay-**no**-chee
oranges le arance a-**ran**-chay
peaches le pesche **pes**-kay
pears le pere **pay**-ray
pineapple l'ananas a-na-**nas**
plums le prugne **proon**-yay
raspberries i lamponi lam-**po**-nee
strawberries le fragole **fra**-go-lay
watermelon l'anguria an-**goo**-ree-a

*Look out for **Upim** and **Standa**, Italy's two main chains of department stores. In Milan there is **la Rinascente**. The stores are generally not open on Sundays.*

Italy is the land of style and you can find lots of small boutiques.

sciarpe scarves **pantaloni** trousers **camicie** shirts

silk

Italians take their seasons very seriously. You may get a boiling-hot day in April, but this does not mean that you will see people stripping off into shorts and bare legs. Summer clothes won't be worn until the end of May.

sales

Saldi Sconti fino al 50%
nel reparto abbigliamento e calzature

discounts up to 50% in department clothing and shoes

negozio
nay-**gots**-yo
shop

seminterrato
say-meen-ter-**ra**-to
basement

pianterreno
pee-an-ter-**ray**-no
ground floor

primo piano
pree-mo pee-**a**-no
first floor

reparto
ray-**par**-to
department

giocattoli
jo-**kat**-to-lee
toys

gioielleria
jo-yel-lay-**ree**-a
jewellery

donne
don-nay
ladies'

uomini
wo-mee-nee
men's

bambini
bam-**bee**-nee
children's

keywords keywords keywords keywords

on which floor can I find...?
a che piano si trova...?
a kay pee-**a**-no see **tro**-va...

lingerie
la biancheria intima
la bee-an-kay-**ree**-a **een**-tee-ma

swimsuits
costumi da bagno
kos-**too**-mee da **ban**-yo

shoes
le scarpe
lay **skar**-pay

talking

Women's clothes sizes

UK/Australia	8	10	12	14	16	18	20	22
Europe	36	38	40	42	44	46	48	50
US/Canada	6	8	10	12	14	16	18	20

Men's clothes sizes (suits)

UK/US/Canada	36	38	40	42	44	46
Europe	46	48	50	52	54	56
Australia	92	97	102	107	112	117

Shoes

UK/Australia	2	3	4	5	6	7	8	9	10	11
Europe	35	36	37	38	39	41	42	43	45	46
US/Canada women	4	5	6	7	8	9	10	11	12	-
US/Canada men	3	4	5	6	7	8	9	10	11	12

Children's Shoes

UK/US/Canada	0	1	2	3	4	5	6	7	8	9	10	11
Europe	15	17	18	19	20	22	23	24	26	27	28	29

talking talking

do you have this in my size?
c'è nella mia taglia?
*che **nel**-la **mee**-a **tal**-ya*

can I try this on?
posso provarlo?
*po-so pro-**var**-lo*

where are the changing rooms?
dove sono i camerini?
*do-vay **so**-no ee ka-mer-**ee**-nee*

I take size 42
la mia taglia è la quarantadue
*la **mee**-a **tal**-ya è la kwa-**ran**-ta-**doo**-ay*

it is too big
è troppo grande
*e **trop**-po **gran**-day*

it is too small
è troppo piccolo
*e **trop**-po **peek**-ko-lo*

I need a larger/smaller size
ho bisogno di una taglia più grande/più piccola
*o bee-**zon**-yo dee **oo**-na **tal**-ya pyoo **gran**-day/pyoo **peek**-ko-la*

I take shoe size 39
io porto il numero trentanove
*ee-yo **por**-to eel **noo**-may-ro tren-ta-**no**-vay*

do you have this in...?
c'è in...?
che een...

black/brown
nero/marrone
***nay**-ro/mar-**ro**-nay*

other colours
altri colori
***al**-tree ko-**lo**-ree*

*Post offices are open 8.30am to 2pm Monday to Friday. On Saturdays they are open until 12pm. Main post offices in large towns will stay open all day until 7pm. Stamps can also be bought at **tabacchi** or shops selling postcards.*

Post Office

Post Office logo

POSTA PRIORITARIA
Priority Mail

To ensure a fast, reliable delivery, you can pay extra and send your cards or letters **posta prioritaria**. Post letters and cards stamped **prioritaria** in the postbox with the blue sticker.

ultimo ritiro

last collection

The blue sticker indicates priority mail. In theory letters take 2 days to be delivered within Italy and 3 days for abroad. However, the Italian mail can sometimes be erratic.

where is the post office?
dov'è la posta?
*do-**ve** la **pos**-ta*

do you have stamps?
avete dei francobolli?
*a-**vay**-tay day fran-ko-**bol**-lee*

10 stamps
dieci francobolli
*dee-**ay**-chee fran-ko-**bol**-lee*

for postcards
per cartoline
*payr kar-to-**lee**-nay*

for letters
per lettere
*payr **let**-tay-ray*

to Europe
per l'Europa
*payr lay-oo-**ro**-pa*

to America
per gli Stati Uniti
*payr lee **sta**-tee oo-**nee**-tee*

to Australia
per l'Australia
*payr low-**stra**-lee-a*

I want to send this registered
voglio spedire questo raccomandato
***vol**-yo spay-**dee**-ray **kwes**-to rak-ko-man-**da**-to*

priority
posta prioritaria
***pos**-ta pree-o-ree-**tar**-ya*

I want to send this parcel
voglio spedire questo pacco
***vol**-yo spay-**dee**-ray **kwes**-to **pak**-ko*

surface
via normale
*vee-a nor-**ma**-lay*

airmail
via aerea
*vee-a a-**ay**-ree-a*

talking talking talking

You can find photobooths at photo shops, shopping centres and stations. If you want to buy film, look out for 3 for 2 offers.

keywords keywords keywords

rullino
rool-lee-no
film

pile
pee-lay
batteries

opache
o-pa-kay
mat

lucide
loo-chee-day
glossy

videocamera
vee-day-o-ka-may-ra
camcorder

fuoco
fwo-ko
focus

You can find photobooths in train stations.

your photos ready in 30 minutes

Photography is not allowed in art galleries, museums and churches.

VIETATO FOTOGRAFARE

no photography

SERVIZI FOTOGRAFICI

photographic services available

a colour film	24	36	exposures
un rullino a colori	ventiquattro	trentasei	pose
oon rool-lee-no a ko-lo-ree	*ven-tee-kwat-tro*	*tren-ta-say*	*po-zay*

talking

can you develop this film?
può svilupparmi questo rullino?
pwo svee-loop-par-mee kwes-to rool-lee-no

can we take pictures?
si possono fare foto?
see pos-so-no fa-ray fo-to

can you take a picture of us?
ci può fare una foto?
chee pwo fa-ray oo-na fo-to

Phones

*There is no shortage of public phones in Italy taking coins and phonecards (**scheda telefonica**) available from **tabacchi** and newsagents. Cheaper times to phone are between 10pm and 8am Monday-Saturday and all day Sunday. Italy is awash with mobile phones. If you take your own, ensure that you contact your service provider to enable you to use it abroad.*

Vending machine selling phonecards.

Phonecards will be on sale where you see the words **scheda telefonica**.

do you have phonecards?
avete delle schede telefoniche?
*a-**vay**-tay **del**-lay **sked**-ay te-le-**fo**-nee-kay*

a phonecard
una scheda telefonica
*oo-na **sked**-ay te-le-**fo**-nee-ka*

a 5-euro card
una scheda da cinque euro
*oo-na **sked**-ay da **cheen**-kway ay-**oo**-ro*

can I make a phone call?
posso fare una chiamata?
*pos-so fa-ray oo-na kee-a-**ma**-ta*

Signor Grandi please
Il Signor Grandi per favore
*eel seen-**yor gran**-dee payr fa-**vo**-ray*

extension number...
interno numero...
*een-**ter**-no **noo**-may-ro...*

can I speak to Paul?
posso parlare con Paul?
*pos-so par-**la**-ray kon paul*

this is Caroline
qui è Caroline
kwee e caroline

it's Anna
sono Anna
*so-no **An**-na*

can I have an outside line please?
posso avere la linea per favore?
*pos-so a-**vay**-ray la **lee**-nay-a payr fa-**vo**-ray*

hello
pronto
***pron**-to*

I'd like to make a reverse-charge call
vorrei fare una chiamata a carico del destinatario
*vor-**ray** fa-ray oo-na kee-a-**ma**-ta a ka-**ree**-ko del des-tee-na-**tar**-yo*

what is you phone number?
qual è il suo numero di telefono?
*kwal e eel **soo**-o **noo**-may-ro dee te-**le**-fo-no*

my phone number is...
il mio numero è...
*eel **mee**-o **noo**-may-ro e...*

keywords keywords keywords

scheda telefonica
skay-da te-le-fo-nee-ka
phonecard

cellulare
chel-loo-la-ray
mobile phone

prefisso
pray-fees-so
code

elenco telefonico
ay-len-ko te-le-fo-nee-ko
phonebook

pagine gialle
pa-jee-nay jal-lay
yellow pages

Note the pictogram across the top of the phonebox. It takes
monete – coins
schede – phonecards
carte – credit cards

UK	00 44
USA	00 1
Australia	00 61

International dialling codes from Italy.

To use phonecards you must tear off the perforated corner.
strappare = tear off

Phonecards come in 5-euro units
(**da cinque euro** da **cheen**-kway ay-**oo**-ro)
and 10-euro units
(**da dieci euro** da dee-**ay**-chee ay-**oo**-ro)

Numero verde literally means *green number*. It is freephone, so no money is needed.

talking

I'll call back...
richiamo...
reek-ya-mo...

later
più tardi
pyoo tar-dee

tomorrow
domani
do-ma-nee

do you have a mobile phone?
ha un cellulare?
a oon chel-loo-la-ray

is it switched on?
è acceso?
e ach-ay-zo

what is your mobile number?
qual è il suo numero di cellulare?
kwal e eel soo-o noo-may-ro dee che-loo-la-ray

*Internet cafés are becoming more and more widespread. If you know where you are going to be staying in Italy, check in advance at www.cybercafes.com if there is a local internet café nearby. The suffix for Italian websites is **.it**.*

The word for 'at' is **chiocciola** (*kee-o-cho-la*).

WWW.

www. is
voo voo voo punto.

Allegato.........Attachment
Invio...............Send

Many English terms are used for e-mail and the internet.

Internet café

There are internet access points at airports. You insert your credit card to pay for time online.

what is your e-mail address?
qual è il suo indirizzo e-mail?
*kwal e eel **soo**-o een-dee-**reet**-so ee-mail*

my e-mail address is...
il mio indirizzo e-mail è...
*eel **mee**-o een-dee-**reet**-so ee-mail e...*

caroline.smith@anywhere.co.uk
caroline punto smith chiocciola anywhere punto co punto uk
*caroline **poon**-to smith kee-**och**-lo-la anywhere **poon**-to ko **poon**-to oo **kap**-pa*

can I send an e-mail?
posso mandare un'e-mail?
***po**-so man-**da**-ray oon ee-mail*

did you get my e-mail?
ha ricevuto la mia e-mail?
*a ree-chay-**voo**-to la **mee**-a ee-mail*

can you send it by e-mail?
può mandarlo via e-mail?
*pwo man-**dar**-lo **vee**-a ee-mail*

as an attachment
allegato
*al-lay-**ga**-to*

how much does an hour of netsurfing cost?
quanto costa un'ora in internet
***kwan**-to **kos**-ta oon **o**-ra een **een**-ter-net*

talking talking

photocopy and fax here

National and local tourist and what's-on information
can be accessed via the internet.

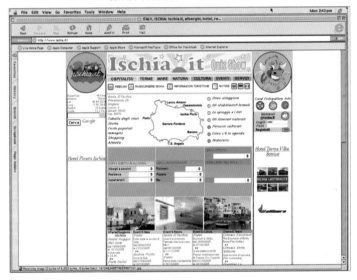

I want to send a fax voglio mandare un fax ***vol**-yo man-**da**-ray oon faks*	**do you have a fax?** avete un fax? *a-**vay**-tay oon faks*
can I send a fax from here? posso mandare un fax da qui? ***pos**-so man-**da**-ray oon faks da kwee*	**can I receive a fax here?** posso ricevere un fax qui? ***pos**-so ree-**chev**-ay-ray oon faks kwee*
how much is it to send a fax? quanto costa mandare un fax? ***kwan**-to **kos**-ta man-**da**-ray oon faks*	**it has … pages** ha … pagine *a … **pa**-jee-nay*
what is your fax number? qual è il suo numero di fax? *kwal e eel **soo**-o **noo**-may-ro dee faks*	**can you confirm the number** può confermare il numero *pwo kon-fer-**ma**-ray eel **noo**-may-ro*
did you get my fax? ha ricevuto il mio fax? *a ree-chay-**voo**-to eel **mee**-o faks*	

talking talking talking

Out & About

Local tourist offices have free maps and brochures. They can generally help with booking accommodation and advise on local attractions and excursions. Museum opening hours are very variable so it is best to check before you visit. If you are visiting churches or religious sites you should remember that these are primarily places of worship, so dress appropriately: no shorts or bare shoulders.

Most Italian cities, towns and small villages have a tourist information office, known officially as *l'Azienda di Promozione Turistica*, but they can usually be identified with the *i* sign.

Places of interest such as museums and art galleries are signposted in brown.

Churches are signposted in yellow. Opening hours can vary, particularly in smaller places. Churches are places of worship and visitors should take care to dress appropriately. If a Mass is taking place, you should disturb worshippers as little as possible.

Collezioni Comunali d'Arte — Municipal art collection

Museo Morandi

Museo Archeologico — Archeological museum

Museo Medievale — Medieval museum

Archiginnasio

Pinacoteca Nazionale — National Art Gallery

Museo Patrimonio Industriale — Industrial Heritage Museum

Piazza means square, *Duomo* means cathedral.

keywords keywords keywords keywords keywords

spettacolo
spet-**ta**-ko-lo
show

esposizione
es-po-zeets-**yo**-nay
exhibition

passeggiata
pas-sed-**ja**-ta
walk

divertimenti
dee-ver-tee-**men**-tee
attractions

fiera
fee-**ay**-ra
fair

chiesa
kee-**ay**-za
church

duomo
dwo-mo
cathedral

isola
ee-zo-la
island

municipio
moo-nee-**cheep**-yo
town hall

VILLA VALMARANA « AI NANI »
INGRESSO — **entrance ticket** — entrance
alla **PALAZZINA**
ed alla **FORESTERIA** — to the Palazzina and the Foresteria
Ricevuta per l'utente
Nº 4499 singoli €5 — single ticket

ENTE CONCESS. VILLA CARLOTTA
TREMEZZO
Biglietto d'ingresso
PER LA VISITA DEI GIARDINI
E DEL MUSEO
STUDENTI Serie 5
5770
DA CONSERVARE PER CONTROLLO
Il visitatore sprovvisto del presente tagliando dovrà
corrispondere il prezzo dell'ingresso.
Esente da I.V.A. Nº 10
Art. 10 D.P.R. 26-10-72 n. 633

An international student card will get reductions into many museums and sites.

scenic walk — **passeggiata panoramica**

public beach — **lido pubblico**

The opera season in cities runs Oct–June (though the season at **La Scala** starts in

Dec). Theatre performances in Italy generally start at 9pm. Concert tickets are sold in music stores, kiosks or at the place of performance, prior to it.

talking talking talking

excuse me, where is the tourist office?
scusi, dov'è l'ufficio turistico?
skoo-zee do-**ve** loof-**fee**-cho too-**rees**-tee-ko

do you have...?
avete...?
a-**vay**-tay...

a town guide
una guida della città
oo-na **gwee**-da **del**-la cheet-**ta**

leaflets
degli opuscoli
del-yee o-**poos**-ko-lee

we want to visit...
vogliamo visitare...
vol-**ya**-mo vee-zee-**ta**-ray...

are there any excursions?
ci sono delle gite?
chee **so**-no **del**-lay **jee**-tay

when can we visit the...?
quando si può visitare...?
kwan-do see pwo vee-zee-**ta**-ray...

when does it close?
quando chiude?
kwan-do kee-**oo**-day

how much is it to get in?
quanto costa l'ingresso?
kwan-to **kos**-ta leen-**gres**-so

is there a guided tour?
c'è una visita guidata?
che **oo**-na **vee**-zee-ta gwee-**da**-ta

Many beaches in Italy are private or attached to a hotel and you will have to pay to hire a sunbed and sunshade.

— sports centre

— swimming pool

It is obligatory to wear a swimming cap in pools. Check locally for pool times.

sports centre

— ice rink
— pool – solarium
— gym

The local tourist office will have brochures on many sporting and leisure activities. If you are interested in hiking, ask for brochures on any local hikes.

HIKING ON THE VIA DEI MONTI LARIANI

1	CERNOBBIO - VAL D'INTELVI
2	VAL D'INTELVI - VAL MENAGGIO
3	VAL MENAGGIO - VALLE ALBANO
4	VALLE ALBANO - SORICO

---

where can we...?
dove si può...?
do-vay see pwo...

play tennis
giocare a tennis
jo-ka-ray a ten-nees

play golf
giocare a golf
jo-ka-ray a golf

how much is it...?
quanto costa...?
kwan-to kos-ta...

to hire bikes
noleggiare le bici
no-led-ja-ray lay bee-chee

to fish
pescare
pes-ka-ray

go riding
andare a cavallo
an-da-ray a ka-val-lo

per hour
all'ora
al-lo-ra

per day
al giorno
al jor-no

is there a swimming pool?
c'è una piscina?
che oo-na pee-shee-na

is dangerous to swim here?
è pericoloso nuotare qui?
e pay-ree-ko-lo-zo nwo-ta-ray kwee

where can we go...?
dove si può...?
do-vay see pwo...

windsurfing
fare windsurf
fa-ray windsurf

waterskiing
fare sci nautico
fa-ray shee now-tee-ko

how do we hire a beach umbrella?
come si noleggia un ombrellone?
ko-may see no-led-ja oon om-brel-lo-nay

talking talking talking

The football season in Italy runs from end August to early June. Matches are usually played on Sunday afternoons. Italians are passionate about the game.

stadium

If you do go to a match, be prepared for fireworks being set off (it may be worth wearing a scarf to cover your mouth).

main stand seats —— TRIBUNA € 35,00
CENTRALE

reductions —— RIDOTTI € 30,00
disabled-military-retired INVAIDI-MILITARI-PENSIONATI

Tickets to football matches can be bought at the stadiums.

football ground prices

Curva —— **Curva** seats are at each end of the ground. The most expensive tickets are **tribuna** in the main stand.

---

we'd like to see a football match
ci piacerebbe vedere una partita di calcio
*chee pya-chay-**reb**-bay ved-**ay**-ray **oo**-na par-**tee**-ta dee **kal**-cho*

where can we get tickets?
dove si prendono i biglietti?
***do**-vay see **pren**-do-no ee beel-**yet**-tee*

how much are they?
quanto costano?
*kwan-to **kos**-ta-no*

how do we get to the stadium?
come si arriva allo stadio?
***ko**-may see ar-**ree**-va **al**-lo **stad**-yo*

what time is the match?
quando comincia la partita?
*kwan-do ko-**meen**-cha la par-**tee**-ta*

talking

The Italian word for hotel is **albergo**, but you will often find the word hotel.

Italian hotels are star rated.

Booking in advance

You can phone up the hotel of your choice and book a room. They generally require a fax to confirm the booking and your credit card number. Smaller places generally don't take bookings very far in advance, particularly if there is perhaps a trade fair on, when they are likely to be busy.

I would like to book a room
vorrei prenotare una camera
vor-**ray** pray-no-**ta**-ray oo-na **ka**-may-ra

single/double
singola/doppia
seen-go-la/**dop**-pya

for ... nights
per ... notti
payr ... **not**-tee

from ... to ...
dal ... al ...
dal ... al ...

my name is...
il mio nome è...
eel **mee**-o **no**-may e...

I'll fax to confirm
confermo con un fax
kon-**fer**-mo kon oon faks

my credit card number is...
il numero della mia carta di credito è...
eel **noo**-may-ro **del**-la **mee**-a **kar**-ta dee **kray**-dee-to e...

expiry date...
data di scadenza...
da-ta dee ska-**dent**-sa...

PENSIONE

agriturist

There is little difference between a *pensione* and a 1- or 2-star hotel.

Agriturism is popular.
You get away from it all on a farm,
visit *www.agriturist.it.*

sighignola

albergo

Guardia di Finanza

skilift

centro ortopedico
e fisioterapico

completo

full – no rooms/spaces

Hotels are generally signposted.
The busiest time outside the
cities is August, particularly the
weekend nearest 15 August,
known as *ferragosto*.

---

do you have a room?
avete una camera?
a-**vay**-tay **oo**-na **ka**-may-ra

with ensuite bath
con bagno
kon **ban**-yo

for tonight
per stanotte
payr sta-**not**-tay

how much is it?
quanto costa?
kwan-to **kos**-ta

how much is half board?
quanto costa mezza pensione?
kwan-to **kos**-ta **med**-za pens-**yo**-nay

I would like to see the room
vorrei vedere la camera
vor-**ray** ved-**ay**-ray la **ka**-may-ra

a single/double room
una camera singola/doppia
oo-na **ka**-may-ra **seen**-go-la/**dop**-pya

a family room
una camera per una famiglia
oo-na **ka**-may-ra payr **oo**-na fa-**meel**-ya

with shower
con doccia
kon **doch**-cha

for just one night
per una notte sola
payr **oo**-na **not**-tay **so**-la

for ... nights
per ... notti
payr ... **not**-tee

is breakfast included?
comprende la colazione?
com-**pren**-day la ko-lats-**yo**-nay

full board
la pensione completa
la pens-**yo**-nay kom-**play**-ta

talking talking talking talking talking

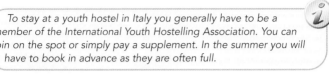

To stay at a youth hostel in Italy you generally have to be a member of the International Youth Hostelling Association. You can join on the spot or simply pay a supplement. In the summer you will have to book in advance as they are often full.

signs for a youth hostel

Ostello per la gioventù

RACCOLTA   CARTA

Paper recyling bank
You will also come across bottle banks. In smaller villages there is a refuse point where you leave your rubbish. The times of the collection should be posted next to it.

Italian plugs are two-pin and you should take an adapter with you if you are taking any of your own electrical appliances such as hairdryer or iron. The electric current is 220V.

how do we get to the youth hostel?
come si arriva all'ostello per la gioventù?
ko-may see ar-ree-va al-los-tel-lo payr la jov-en-too

how much is it to become a member?
quanto costa diventare socio?
kwan-to kos-ta dee-ven-ta-ray so-cho

talking

detersivo per i piatti
day-ter-see-vo payr ee pee-a-tee
washing-up liquid

carta igienica
kar-ta ee-jay-nee-ka
toilet paper

sapone
sa-po-nay
soap

apriscatole
ap-ree-ska-to-lay
tin-opener

candele
kan-day-lay
candles

fiammiferi
fee-am-mee-fay-ree
matches

bombola del gas
bom-bo-la del gaz
gas cylinder

annuario alberghi e campeggi

lago di como

AMMINISTRAZIONE PROVINCIALE DI COMO
Assessorato Turismo

Edizione

Local tourist offices provide annual guides to self-catering, hotel and camping accommodation in their area. They should also be able to assist you with booking.

Camere

rooms

COMPLETO

full up

there is/are no...
non c'è/non ci sono...
non che/chee so-no...

how does ... work?
come funziona...?
ko-may foonts-yo-na...

can you show us how it works?
può farci vedere come funziona?
pwo far-chee ved-ay-ray ko-may foonts-yo-na

the cooker
la cucina
la koo-chee-na

the dishwasher
la lavastoviglie
la la-va-sto-veel-yay

the washing machine
la lavatrice
la la-va-tree-chay

the microwave
il forno a microonde
eel for-no a mee-kro-on-day

who do I contact if there is a problem?
con chi parlo se c'è un problema?
kon kee par-lo say che oon prob-lay-ma

where do we leave the rubbish?
dove lasciamo la spazzatura?
do-vay lash-am-o la spats-sa-too-ra

can we have another key?
possiamo avere un'altra chiave?
poss-ya-mo a-vay-ray oon-alt-ra kee-a-vay

The local tourist office will provide information about local campsites. Off-site camping is allowed in Italy provided you have the permission of the landowner on whose land you are camping – otherwise it is illegal. Official campsites are open mainly from April to September and are well equipped.

campsite
The local tourist information office will provide a list of sites.

no parking from 1 Jun to 30 Sep for lorries and campers

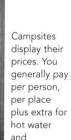

Campsites display their prices. You generally pay per person, per place plus extra for hot water and electricity.

A car towing a caravan or trailer must not exceed 50kph in built-up areas, 70kph outside built-up areas and 80kph on motorways.

is there a campsite near here?
c'è un campeggio qui vicino?
*che oon kam-**ped**-jo kwee vee-**chee**-no*

have you any vacancies?
avete dei posti?
*a-**vay**-tay day **pos**-tee*

we want to stay for ... nights
vogliamo restare per ... notti
*vol-**ya**-mo res-**ta**-ray payr ... **not**-tee*

how much is it...?
quanto costa...?
kwan-to kos-ta...

per tent
per tenda
*payr **ten**-da*

per caravan
per roulotte
*payr roo-**lot***

where are...?
dove sono...?
*do-**vay so**-no...*

the showers
le docie
*lay **doch**-chay*

the toilets
le toilette
*lay twa-**let***

is there a restaurant on the campsite?
c'è un ristorante nel campeggio?
*che oon rees-to-**ran**-tay nel kam-**ped**-jo*

is there a more sheltered site?
c'è un posto più riparato?
*che oon **pos**-to pyoo ree-pa-**ra**-to*

dry-cleaners

trousers
skirts
jackets
coats
jumpers

There are not many coin-operated launderettes in Italy outside
large campsites. Larger supermarkets have cleaning services
which take 1 to 2 hours and are good value. At the dry-cleaners
it may take from 1 to 3 days, but it is generally better value
and service.

is there a launderette?
c'è una lavanderia automatica?
che oon la-van-day-ree-a ow-to-ma-tee-ka

where can I do some washing?
dove posso lavare questi panni?
do-vay pos-so la-va-ray kwes-tee pan-nee

is there an iron?
c'è un ferro da stiro?
che oon fer-ro da stee-ro

is there a laundry service?
c'è il servizio lavanderia?
che eel ser-veets-yo la-van-day-ree-a

when will my things be ready?
quando saranno pronti?
kwan-do sa-ran-no pron-tee

where is the nearest dry-cleaner's?
dov'è la tintoria più vicina?
do-ve la teen-to-ree-a pyoo vee-chee-na

talking

Special Needs

Disabled facilities are gradually improving in Italy with some museums and churches providing wheelchair-accessible entrances.

Some service stations offer facilities for the disabled.

Disabled parking is usually available and indicated by the orange wheelchair sign.

Trains marked with this blue disabled badge are equipped to carry wheelchairs. These are mainly the newer intercity trains.

are there any toilets for the disabled?
ci sono le toilette per i disabili?
chee so-no lay twa-let payr ee dee-za-bee-lee

is there an entrance for wheelchairs?
c'è l'accesso per la sedia a rotelle?
che la-ches-so payr la sed-ya a ro-tel-lay

is it possible to visit ... with a wheelchair?
si può visitare ... con la sedie a rotelle?
see pwo vee-zee-ta-ray ... kon la sed-ya a ro-tel-lay

is there a reduction for the disabled?
c'è una riduzione per i disabili?
che oo-na ree-doots-yo-nay payr ee dee-za-bee-lee

I need a bedroom on the ground floor
ho bisogno di una camera al pian terreno
o bee-zon-yo dee oo-na ka-may-ra al pee-an ter-ray-no

can I take the train to ... with a wheelchair?
si può prendere il treno per ... con la sedia a rotelle?
see pwo pren-day-ray eel tray-no payr ... kon la sed-ya a ro-tel-lay

I'm in a wheelchair
sono in una sedia a rotelle
so-no een oo-na sed-ya a ro-tel-lay

is there a lift?
c'è un ascensore?
che oon a-shen-so-ray

talking talking talking talking talking

With Kids

A small child is bambino(a); an older child is ragazzo(a). Children are welcome everywhere.

keywords keywords keywords

bambino(a)
bam-bee-no(a)
child

seggiolino
sed-jo-lee-no
baby seat

seggiolone
sed-jo-lo-nay
high chair

lettino
let-tee-no
cot

parco giochi
par-ko jo-kee
play park

pannolini
pan-no-lee-nee
nappies

On most public transport children under 5 travel free. Between 5 and 12 years old they can get a 50% discount on their ticket.

Navigazione Lago di Como
P.IVA 00802050153

Biglietteria di Menaggio

21-07-06 | 17:35 | 36841 | 22/ 1

Da MENAGGIO   a TREMEZZO

A —>

1 - ORDINARIO BATTELLO
Vale giorni 1

Euro 9,00

Adulti 2 Ragazzi 1 ← 2 adults, 1 child

Non sono ammesse fermate intermedie
This ticket is valid for a direct jour ney to your destination

what is there for children to do?
cosa c'è da fare per i bambini?
ko-za che da fa-ray payr ee bam-bee-nee

where can I change the baby?
dove posso cambiare il bambino?
do-vay pos-so kamb-ya-ray eel bam-bee-no

do you have...?
avete...?
a-vay-tay...

a high chair
un seggiolone
oon sed-jo-lo-nay

a cot
un lettino
oon let-tee-no

nappies
panolini
pa-no-lee-nee

baby wipes
salviettine
sal-vyet-tee-nay

baby food
alimenti per bambini
a-lee-men-tee payr bam-bee-nee

is there a children's menu?
c'è un menù per bambini?
che oon me-noo payr bam-bee-nee

a half portion
una mezza porzione
oo-na med-za ports-yo-nay

is there a play park near here?
c'è un parco giochi qui vicino?
che oon par-ko jo-kee kwee vee-chee-no

Health

The old E111 form has been replaced with a new European Health Insurance Card – apply at the Post Office or online at www.dh.gov.uk.

Each pharmacy must display the list of duty chemists open at night or on Sunday.

Facilities in towns are usually well signposted.

pharmacy—

first aid—

Pharmacies are open during shopping hours. If you are feeling unwell (and it is not an emergency), your first point of call should be the pharmacy, especially if you have an idea of what is wrong. They are usually helpful and know which products would suit.

where is there a chemist?
dove c'è una farmacia?
do-vay che oo-na far-ma-chee-a

have you something for...?
avete qualcosa per...?
a-vay-tay kwal-ko-za payr...

indigestion
l'indigestione
leen-dee-jest-yo-nay

sunburn
la scottatura solare
la skot-ta-too-ra so-la-ray

diarrhoea
la diarrea
la dee-a-ray-a

a cough
la tosse
la tos-say

I need...
ho bisogno di...
o bee-zon-yo dee...

a painkiller
un analgesico
oon a-nal-jay-zee-ko

antibiotics
antibiotici
an-tee-bee-o-tee-chee

talking

talking talking talking talking talking talking

I am not well
mi sento male
mee **sen**-to **ma**-lay

... doesn't feel well
... si sente male
... see **sen**-tay **ma**-lay

I need a doctor
ho bisogno di un dottore
o bee-**zon**-yo dee oon dot-**to**-ray

please call the doctor
mi chiami il dottore
mee kee-**a**-mee eel dot-**to**-ray

my son/my daughter is ill
mio figlio/mia figlia sta male
mee-o **feel**-yo/**mee**-a **feel**-ya sta **ma**-lay

I have a pain here
ho un dolore qui
o oon do-**lor**-ay kwee

I am on this medication
sto prendendo queste medicine
sto pren-**den**-do **kwes**-tay may-dee-**chee**-nay

I'm pregnant
sono incinta
so-no een-**cheen**-ta

I am on the pill
prendo la pillola
pren-do la **peel**-lo-la

I'm breastfeeding
sto allattando al seno
sto al-lat-**tan**-do al **say**-no

I have cystitis
ho la cistite
o la chees-**tee**-tay

I'm diabetic
sono diabetico(a)
so-no dee-a-**bet**-ee-ko(a)

I am allergic to...
sono allergico(a) a...
so-no al-**ler**-jee-ko(a) a...

I have high blood pressure
ho la pressione alta
o la pres-**yo**-nay **al**-ta

my blood group is...
il mio gruppo sanguigno è...
eel **mee**-yo **groop**-po san-**gween**-yo e...

can I have a receipt for my insurance?
mi dà una ricevuta per l'assicurazione?
mee da **oo**-na ree-chay-**voo**-ta payr las-see-koo-rats-**yo**-nay

I need a dentist
ho bisogno di un dentista
o bee-**zon**-yo dee oon den-**tees**-ta

I have toothache
ho mal di denti
o mal dee **den**-tee

I need a temporary filling
ho bisogno di un'otturazione provvisoria
o bee-**zon**-yo dee oon ot-too-rats-**yo**-nay prov-vee-**sor**-ya

can you repair my dentures?
può riparare la mia dentiera?
pwo ree-pa-**ra**-ray la **mee**-a dent-**yer**-a

my filling has come out
è uscita l'otturazione
e oo-**shee**-ta lot-too-rats-**yo**-nay

Sign to local hospital.

You are entering a hospital zone in 150m.

*If you need emergency treatment, you should go directly to the **Pronto Soccorso** (A & E) in the nearest hospital. You should present them with your E111 card and your passport.*

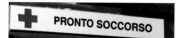

accident & emergency

admissions

— X-Ray
— ultrasound

visitors' entrance — Ingresso Visitatori

A & E — Pronto Soccorso

parking & laundry — Parcheggio Lavanderia

general services — Servizi Generali

If you need to go to hospital

will he/she have to go to hospital?
deve andare all'ospedale?
day-vay an-da-ray al-los-ped-a-lay

where is the hospital?
dov'è l'ospedale?
do-ve los-ped-a-lay

where is the nearest A & E department?
dov'è il pronto soccorso più vicino?
do-ve eel pron-to sok-kor-so pyoo vee-chee-no

please take me to the hospital
per favore mi porti all'ospedale
payr fa-vo-ray mee por-tee al-los-ped-a-lay

I need to go to casualty
devo andare al pronto soccorso
day-vo an-da-ray al pron-to sok-kor-so

when are visiting hours?
qual è l'orario delle visite?
kwal e lor-ar-yo del-lay vee-zee-tay

which ward?
quale reparto?
kwa-lay ray-par-to

can you explain what is the matter?
può spiegare cos'è il problema?
pwo spyay-ga-ray ko-ze eel prob-lay-ma

Emergency

i If you are robbed or suffer a crime, you should make a report to the police (either **Polizia** or **Carabinieri**, both perform more or less the same function) at the police station, **Questura**. You will need a copy of the report to present to your insurance company if you want to make a claim. All the emergency services can be reached via the police on 113 though each has its own number: Carabinieri, 112; Medical emergency 118; Fire brigade 115.

CARABINIERI
localita' via statale regina
indirizzo **LENNO**
telefoni **57073**

Address of the local police.

Police car

help!
aiuto!
a-**yoo**-to

can you help me?
può aiutarmi?
pwo a-yoo-**tar**-mee

please call...
per favore chiamate...
payr fa-**vo**-ray kee-a-**ma**-tay...

the police
la polizia
la po-leet-**see**-a

an ambulance
un'ambulanza
oon am-boo-**lant**-sa

help! Fire!
aiuto! Aluoco!
a-**yoo**-to alfwo-ko

please call the fire brigade!
per favore chiamate i vigili del fuoco!
payr fa-**vo**-ray kee-a-**ma**-tay ee **vee**-jee-lee del **fwo**-ko

my ... has been stolen
mi hanno rubato...
mee **an**-no roo-**ba**-to...

I want to report a theft
voglio denunciare un furto
vol-yo den-oon-**cha**-ray oon **foor**-to

here are my insurance details
ecco i dati della mia assicurazione
ek-ko ee **da**-tee **del**-la **mee**-a as-see-koo-rats-**yo**-nay

please give me your insurance details
mi dia i suoi dati di assicurazione
mee **dee**-a ee swoy **da**-tee dee as-see-koo-rats-**yo**-nay

where is the police station?
dov'è la questura?
do-**ve** la kwes-**too**-ra

I would like to phone...
vorrei telefonare...
vor-**ray** te-le-fo-**na**-ray...

my car has been broken into
hanno svaligiato la mia macchina
an-no sva-lee-**ja**-to la **mee**-a **mak**-kee-na

I need a report for my insurance
ho bisogno di un verbale per la mia assicurazione
o bee-**zon**-yo dee oon ver-**ba**-lay payr la **mee**-a as-see-koo-rats-**yo**-nay

Food
&
Drink

Italian Food

*Italians enjoy good food and to do this they make sure that they cook with the best ingredients available. In the north of Italy traditionally the main meal of the day is lunch, **il pranzo**. In the south of Italy, because of the heat, it is dinner, **la cena**. However with working habits changing and people working further away from their homes, a large lunch is not always possible except at weekends. **La prima colazione** (breakfast) is often eaten standing at a bar and is usually an **espresso** (small strong black coffee) or **cappuccino** and **brioche** (sweet bun). Otherwise at home it is generally milky coffee and biscuits. However, cereals are becoming more common. A traditional full Italian meal consists of **antipasto** (often finely sliced ham, salami, and other cold meats), **primo** (pasta or risotto) and **secondo** (meat or fish) served with a salad or French fries or vegetables. Cheese and a dessert normally follow.*

Many bars and **caffès** serve food: generally salads, sandwiches, pasta dishes and pizzas. Check where the bar is situated: if it is in a very touristy area, it may be expensive. It is worth checking side streets to see if you can find a quieter bar. If Italians are eating there, take that as a recommendation.

MENÙ TURISTICO

Many restaurants offer set price meals (sometimes including wine). Although generally good value, the food is aimed mainly at the tourist market.

As well as a tobacconist, a **tabaccaio** is often a bar and may serve meals. There are no frills, but the food should be good.

A **rosticceria** sells spit-roasted chicken and food to be eaten there (generally standing) or to take away. The food should be good and well-worth sampling.

Italians are more interested in their food than the decor, so most restaurants are quite similar, with crisp linen tablecloths and unfussy surroundings.

Trattoria

Traditionally, a **trattoria** was a family-run restaurant, usually with less choice than a restaurant. There may be no menu and you will be told what is available that day.

Hamburger chains are appearing in Italy, but with a slight Italian flavour in that Italians don't like queuing, so you may find them trying to sneak ahead!

Tavola Calda

Self-service type restaurant; good for a quick meal.

cucina casalinga

home cooking

where can we get a snack?
dove possiamo fare uno spuntino?
do-vay pos-ya-mo fa-ray oo-no spoon-tee-no

can you recommend a good restaurant?
ci può consigliare un buon ristorante?
chee pwo kon-seel-ya-ray oon bwon rees-to-ran-tay

are there any vegetarian restaurants?
ci sono ristoranti vegetariani?
chee so-no rees-to-ran-tee vay-jay-tar-ya-nee

do we need to book a table?
dobbiamo prenotare un tavolo?
dob-ya-mo pray-no-ta-ray oon ta-vo-lo

what do you recommend?
che cosa ci consiglia?
kay ko-za chee kon-seel-ya

how do we get to the restaurant?
come si arriva a questo ristorante?
ko-may see ar-ree-va a kwes-to rees-to-ran-tay

talking talking

i If you want a snack rather than a full meal, bars generally have things such as **pizza**, **toast** (toasted sandwiches) and **panini** (sandwiches). They may also serve pasta dishes such as **spaghetti**, **lasagne**, etc.

keywords

formaggio
*for-**mad**-jo*
cheese

prosciutto
*pro-**shoot**-to*
ham

pomodoro
*po-mo-**do**-ro*
tomato

farcito(a)
*far-**chee**-to(a)*
stuffed with titbits

liscio(a)
lee-sho(a)
plain

food on offer

RISO FREDDO

PIZZA FREDDA

FOCACCIA DI RECCO

PANINI IMBOTTITI

riso freddo =
cold rice dish

pizza fredda =
cold pizza

focaccia di Recco =
cheese focaccia
Ligurian style

panini imbottiti =
filled rolls/
sandwiches

These are sandwiches made with soft white bread.

tramezzini

talking talking talking

I'd like ... please
vorrei ... per favore
*vor-**ray** ... payr fa-**vo**-ray*

we'd like...
vorremmo...
*vor-**rem**-mo...*

a cappuccino
un cappuccino
*oon kap-poo-**chee**-no*

a large black coffee
un caffè americano
*oon kaf-**fe** a-mer-ee-**ka**-no*

decaffeinated
decaffeinato
*day-kaf-fay-**na**-to*

a hot chocolate
una cioccolata calda
*oo-na chok-ko-**la**-ta **kal**-da*

a tea with milk
un tè al latte
*oon te al **lat**-tay*

an orange juice
un succo d'arancia
*oon **sook**-ko da-**ran**-cha*

a peach juice
un succo di pesca
*oon **sook**-ko dee **pes**-ka*

with ice
con giacchio
*kon gee-**ach**-cho*

without ice
senza giacchio
*sent-sa gee-**ach**-cho*

a bottle of mineral water
una bottiglia di acqua minerale
*oo-na bot-**teel**-ya dee **ak**-wa mee-nay-**ra**-lay*

fizzy
gassata
*gas-**sa**-ta*

still
naturale
*na-too-**ra**-lay*

Paninoteca sandwich bar

cono	1.40
cono grande	1.70
coppa piccola	1.40
coppa media	2.00
coppa grande	2.90
supplemento panna	0.30
brioches con gelato	2.00
frappè	2.20
frullati	2.5

cono = cone
cono grande = large cone
coppa piccola = small tub
coppa media/grande = medium/large tub
supplemento panna = extra cost for cream
brioches con gelato = bun with ice cream
frappè = milkshake
frullati = fruit smoothies

A *gelateria* is a bar selling ice cream where you can also get drinks. Italy has a mouth-watering variety of ice creams which can be almost a meal in themselves.

bibite

soft drinks

ice-creams

chocolate	CIOCCOLATO
vanilla	VANIGLIA
hazelnut	NOCCIOLA
lemon	LIMONE
strawberry	FRAGOLA
banana	BANANA
apricot	ALBICOCCA

If you buy a cono, **un cono**, you will be asked what flavours you want (**che gusti?**). If you want all chocolate, say **tutto cioccolato**, if you want lemon and chocolate, say **limone e cioccolato**. If you prefer it in a tub, ask for **una coppa**.

can we eat here?
si può mangiare qui?
see pwo man-ja-ray kwee

what can we eat?
cosa si può mangiare?
ko-za see pwo man-ja-ray

is there a dish of the day?
c'è un piatto del giorno?
che oon pee-at-to del jor-no

what is the dish of the day?
qual è il piatto del giorno?
kwal e eel pee-at-to del jor-no

what sandwiches do you have?
quali panini avete?
kwa-lee pa-nee-nee a-vay-tay

I'd like an icecream
vorrei un gelato
vor-ray oon jay-la-to

what flavours do you have?
che gusti ci sono?
kay goos-tee chee so-no

talking

Italy is the home of the pizza. They are thin based and cooked in wood-fired ovens. You won't find the wide range of deep-pan options that originated in America. Nor will you find combinations such as ham and pineapple, though new additions are gradually finding their way into the classic pizza repertoire.

PIZZE

tomato, mozzarella, oregano — Margherita (pom, mozz, origano)

Siciliana (pom, acciughe, olive, origano) — tomato, anchovies, olives, oregano

tomato, mozzarella, onion, olives — Pugliese (pom, mozz, cipolle, olive)

Marinara (pom, aglio, origano) — tomato, garlic, oregano

tomato, mozzarella, anchovies — Napoletana (pom, mozz, acciughe)

Romana (pom, mozz, acciughe, capperi, olive) — tomato, mozzarella, anchovies, capers, olives

tomato, mozzarella, ham — Prosciutto (pom, mozz, prosciutto)

Prosciutto e Funghi (pom, mozz, prosciutto, funghi) — tomato, mozzarella, ham, mushroom

tomato, mozzarella, mushroom — Funghi (pom, mozz, funghi)

Gorgonzola — blue-veined Gorgonzola cheese

with 4 cheeses: mozzarella, fontina, gorgonzola, gruyère — Ai 4 Formaggi

Ai Frutti di Mare — seafood

Quattro Stagioni — 4-section (or season) pizza: with tomato, ham, onion, pepper, artichokes & whatever is available

tomato, mozzarella, pickled vegetables — Capricciosa (pom, mozz, capricciodi verdure)

tomato, mozzarella, spicy salami — Diavola (pom, mozz, salame piccante)

Al Tonno (pom, mozz, tonno, cipolla) — tomato, mozzarella, tuna, onion

tomato, mozzarella, grilled vegetables — Vegetariana (pom, mozz, verdure grigliate)

Rustica (pom, mozz, speck) — tomato, mozzarella & a type of bacon

tomato, wild mushroom — Funghi Porcini

folded-over pizza with tomato, mozzarella, ham, mushroom & pickles — Calzone liscio (pom, mozz, prosciutto)

Calzone farcito (pom, mozz, prosciutto, funghi, farcitura) — folded-over pizza with tomato, mozzarella, ham

one pizza please
una pizza per favore
oo-na **peet**-sa payr fa-**vo**-ray

2 pizzas please
due pizze per favore
doo-ay **peet**-say payr fa-**vo**-ray

I'd like a pizza
vorrei una pizza
vor-**ray** *oo*-na **peet**-sa

what is there to drink?
cosa c'è da bere?
ko-za che da **ber**-ay

When you ask for a **birra** in Italy, you will be served lager. If you want an ale or bitter, you should ask for **birra scura** or **birra rossa**. Draught beer will come either **piccola** (half pint approx.) or **media** (just under a pint). If you want to drink beer, look out for bars which call themselves pubs. They may be quite expensive.

keywords keywords keywords

piccolo(a)
peek-ko-lo(a)
half pint

medio(a)
med-yo(a)
pint

birra
beer-ra
lager

birra rossa
beer-ra ros-sa
ale

alla spina
al-la spee-na
draught

in bottiglia
een bot-teel-ya
bottled

half a pint of lager
una birra piccola
oo-na beer-ra peek-ko-la

draught
alla spina
al-la spee-na

do you have any ales?
avete delle birre rosse?
a-vay-tay del-lay beer-ray ros-say

a pint of lager
una birra media
oo-na beer-ra med-ya

an Italian lager
una birra nazionale
oo-na beer-ra nats-yo-na-lay

talking

Restaurants tend to shut one day a week. As a rule, eating places (including restaurants) have a menu with prices outside, so you will be prepared for the cost before going in.

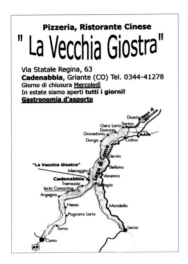

Pizzeria, Ristorante Cinese
" La Vecchia Giostra"

Via Statale Regina, 63
Cadenabbia, Griante (CO) Tel. 0344-41278
Giorno di chiusura <u>Mercoledì</u>
In estate siamo aperti **tutti i giorni!**
<u>Gastronomia d'asporto</u>

menu of combined pizzeria and Chinese restaurant
Italians are conservative in their eating habits so you will not find a great variety of foreign restaurants as you do in London, for instance. However, Chinese and Indian restaurants are gradually appearing.

A pizza is often a cheaper option than a full meal.

I would like to book a table
vorrei prenotare un tavolo
vor-ray pray-no-ta-ray oon ta-vo-lo

for 4 people
per quattro persone
payr kwat-tro per-so-nay

for tonight
per stasera
payr sta-say-ra

for tomorrow night
per domani sera
payr do-ma-nee say-ra

for lunch
per pranzo
payr prant-so

for 12.30
per le dodici e mezza
payr lay do-dee-chee e med-za

for 7.30
per le sette e mezza
payr lay set-tay ay med-za

for 8 o'clock
per le otto
payr lay ot-to

in the name of...
a nome di...
a no-may dee...

In the countryside there is a type of rustic restaurant known as a **crotto**. These serve the real traditional food of the region, often homegrown and prepared. At harvest time (around the start of September) there are festivals, **sagre**, where you can sample the produce of the harvest.

The typical Italian dining table will have a basket of bread rolls, **grissini** (breadsticks), salt and pepper, toothpicks, oil and vinegar to dress your salad, a jug or bottle of wine and mineral water.

> formaggio nostrano

local cheese

the menu please
il menù per favore
eel me-noo payr fa-vo-ray

the wine list please
la lista dei vini per favore
la lees-ta day vee-nee payr fa-vo-ray

is there a set-price menu?
c'è un menù turistico?
che oon me-noo too-rees-tee-ko

for a starter I will have...
per antipasto prendo...
payr an-tee-pas-to pren-do...

for a main dish I will have...
per secondo prendo...
payr se-kon-do pren-do...

do you have any vegetarian dishes?
avete dei piatti vegetariani?
a-vay-tay day pyat-tee ve-jay-ta-ree-a-nee

what desserts do you have?
cosa c'è per dolce?
ko-za che payr dol-chay

I'll have this
prendo questo
pren-do kwes-to

a glass of water
un bicchiere di acqua semplice
oon beek-yer-ay dee ak-wa semp-lee-chay

some more bread
ancora un po' di pane
an-ko-ra oon po dee pa-nay

the bill please
il conto per favore
eel kon-to payr fa-vo-ray

we'd like separate bills
ci fa il conto separato
chee fa eel kon-to sep-a-ra-to

talking talking talking talking

*Most restaurants charge **pane e coperto** (cover charge). Service is generally 10% and is often automatically charged. If not, tipping of 10% is an acceptable amount.*

Restaurant bill listing exactly what has been consumed.

receipt for fiscal purposes —
bill/invoice —

information about client —
firm —
residence or home address —
VAT —
number of people —
bread & cover charge —
wine —
other drinks —
starter —
first course —
main course —
side dishes —
cheeses —
dessert —
fruit —
coffee —
liqueurs —

RICEVUTA FISCALE - FATTURA (Legge 30 Dicembre 19991 n. 413)

taverna antico agnello s.r.l.
ristorante
via olina n. 18
28016 Orta S. Giulio (no)
tel. 0322 90259
partita i.v.a. 01130970039

☐ RICEVUTA FISCALE
☐ FATTURA - RICEVUTA FISCALE   N. ATTRIBUTO

DATA   XNR N° 04079 /2006

Dati identificativi del Cliente

DITTA

Residenza o domicilio

P. IVA

Per N. ____ pasti . . . .
Pane - Coperto . . . .
Vino . . . .
Altre bevande . . . .
Antipasti . . . .
Primi . . . .
Secondi . . . .
Contorni . . . .
Formaggi . . . .
Dolce . . . .
Frutta . . . .
Caffè . . . .
Liquori . . . .

ALIQ. IVA	IMPONIBILE	IMPOSTA	CORRISPETTIVO PAGATO
%			CORRISPETTIVO NON PAGATO
%			
TOTALE			TOTALE DOCUMENTO

☐ PAGATO   A TITOLO DI: ☐ ANTICIPO ☐ ACCONTO
☐ R.F. EMESSA ALL'ATTO DELLA PRESTAZIONE O CONSEGNA (CORRISPETTIVO GIÀ SALDATO ANTICIPATAMENTE)
☐ SALDO DI R.F. GIÀ EMESSA ☐ RIFERIM. PREC. DOCUM. R.F. _____ DEL _____

Tipolitografia Esperia snc – Novara - Autorizzazione del Ministero delle Finanze VI-12-1095/94 del 31-01-94

Menù a prezzo fisso (solo pranzo) €10,00

fixed price menu (lunch only)

*You don't have to have all the courses, you could skip **antipasto**
and just have the first and second courses. Or you could have
antipasto and the second course. Or you can just have one course.*

MENU *menu*

ANTIPASTI *starters*

antipasto misto *sliced ham, salami and other sliced meats*

PRIMI *first courses*

SECONDI *main dishes*

carne *meat* **vitello** *veal* **manzo** *beef* **maiale** *pork* **pollo**
chicken **agnello** *lamb* **pesce** *fish*

CONTORNI *side dishes*

FORMAGGI *cheeses*

DOLCI *dessert*

FRUTTA *fruit*

*IL PIATTO DEL GIORNO
CON
POLENTA
Brasato o Coniglio
o Ossobuco*

€ 13,00

dish of the day *with **polenta** – beef stew or rabbit or veal stew*

A scelta

choice of
There may be a
couple of options
to choose from.

nostrano

local

stagione

in season

cucina casalinga

home cooking

enjoy your meal!
buon appetito!
bwon ap-pay-**tee**-to

thanks, and you too!
grazie, e altrettanto!
grats-yay ay al-tret-**tan**-to

talk

Wine

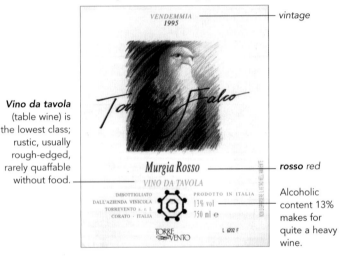

i The classic Italian wine is a red, made for food, light, cherryish, dry, sharp. But things are changing. Not only are better, richer white wines emerging now, but fruitier, deeper-flavoured, more international reds. The best of them still retain that signature Italian twist, a hint of cherrystone and of herb dryness.

Italian classification of wine is a rough guide to quality but there are bad and good wines in every grade.

VENDEMMIA
1995 — vintage

Vino da tavola
(table wine) is
the lowest class;
rustic, usually
rough-edged,
rarely quaffable
without food.

Murgia Rosso — **rosso** red
VINO DA TAVOLA

IMBOTTIGLIATO   PRODOTTO IN ITALIA
DALL'AZIENDA VINICOLA   13% vol
TORREVENTO s. r. l.   750 ml e
CORATO - ITALIA

TORRE
VENTO   L 6202 F

Alcoholic
content 13%
makes for
quite a heavy
wine.

Cantine del Borgo Reale

VERDICCHIO
DEI CASTELLI DI JESI
DENOMINAZIONE DI ORIGINE CONTROLLATA
CLASSICO
1997
75cl e   CANTINE DEL BORGO REALE - ITALIA   11,5% VOL
IMBOTTIGLIATO DA F.G. S.p.A - DIANO D'ALBA - ITALIA

DOC (*Denominazione di Origine Controllata*) operates like AC in France, with tight controls on wine production. The higher classification of DOCG does not necessarily promise a better wine, despite its adding of **Garantita** (guaranteed). Some DOC quality wines can also appear as IGT (*Indicazione Geograficha Tipica*).

Indicazione Geograficha Tipica is the equivalent of French *vin de pays*; it can be rustic, can be superb.

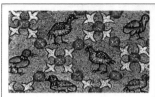

FALANGHINA

SANNIO BENEVENTANO
INDICAZIONE GEOGRAFICA TIPICA

FEVDI
DISAN
GREGORIO

keywords keywords keywords

bianco(a)
bee-an-ko(a)
white

rosso(a)
ros-so(a)
red

rosato(a)
ro-za-to(a)
rosé

secco(a)
sek-ko(a)
dry

dolce
dol-chay
sweet

un quarto
oon kwar-to
a quarter litre

un mezzo
oon med-so
half a litre

un litro
oon leet-ro
a litre

---

talking talking

the wine list please
la lista dei vini per favore
la lees-ta day vee-nee payr fa-vo-ray

what wines do you have?
quali vini avete?
kwa-lee vee-nee a-vay-tay

is there a local wine?
c'è un vino locale?
che oon vee-no lo-ka-lay

can you recommend a good wine?
ci può consigliare un buon vino?
chee pwo kon-seel-ya-ray oon bwon vee-no

a glass of red wine
un bicchiere di vino rosso
oon beek-yer-ay dee vee-no ros-so

a quarter litre of white wine
un quarto di vino bianco
oon kwar-to dee vee-no bee-an-ko

a bottle of wine
una bottiglia di vino
oo-na bot-teel-ya dee vee-no

red
rosso
ros-so

white
bianco
bee-an-ko

half a litre of wine
mezzo litro di vino
med-zo leet-ro dee vee-no

a litre of wine
un litro di vino
oon leet-ro dee vee-no

Flavours of Italy

burrida
famous Genoese fish soup
pesto
*sauce made from basil, olive oil,
parmesan and pine-nuts*
focaccia
*flat bread brushed with garlic, salt
and olive oil*
cappon magro
cold seafood and vegetable salad

baccalà alla milanese
*Milanese salt cod fritters, served
with lemon*
cotoletta alla milanese
*fried veal cutlet dressed in
breadcrumbs*
risotto alla milanese
rich saffron-coloured risotto
ossobuco
*shin of veal cooked in tomato
sauce*
wines: Sassella, Grumello, Inferno

acqua cotta
*traditional soup made from
onions, peppers, celery and
tomato. Beaten eggs and
parmesan are added on serving.*
bistecca alla fiorentina
large thick grilled T-bone steak
stracotto
braised beef cooked in red wine
trippa
tripe with tomatoes and onions
fagioli all'uccelletto
*haricot beans in tomato, garlic
and sage*
**wines: Chianti, Vernaccia,
Brunello di Montalcino**

ALTO
ADIGE

FRIULI-
VENEZIA
GIULIA

VALLE
D'AOSTA

• Milano
LOMBARDIA

• Verona   Venezia •
VENETO

• Torino
PIEMONTE

LIGURIA
Genova •

• Parma
EMILIA-ROMAGNA

Rimini •
• Firenze   LE
• Pisa   MARCHE
TOSCANA
Perugia •

UMBRIA

abbacchio
suckling lamb
coda alla vaccinara
oxtail stewed with tomatoes and herbs
spaghetti all'amatriciana
spaghetti in a tomato and bacon sauce
gnocchi alla romana
*oven-baked dumplings made from
semolina, butter and parmesan*
carciofi alla Giudia
flattened, deep-fried globe artichokes
saltimbocca alla romana
finely sliced veal with ham and sage
wines: frascati, Est! Est! Est!

SARDEGNA

Cagliari •

bottarga
*preserved tuna or mullet roes,
sprinkled over pasta*
cinghiale
wild boar
porceddu
suckling pig

risotto alle seppie
risotto cooked with squid
fegato alla veneziana
*calf's liver slices fried in butter
with onions*
baccalà alla vicentina
salt cod simmered in milk
polenta
corn or maize meal porridge
**wines: Soave, Valpolicella,
Bardolino**

pasta
*fresh pasta: tagliatelle, pappardelle,
ravioli, etc*
ragù alla Bolognese
*finely minced steak and tomato
sauce served with pasta and in
lasagne and cannelloni*
Parmigiano
*Parmesan cheese, grated over
pasta dishes*
Prosciutto di Parma
cured ham which is finely sliced
cotechino
*spicy pork sausage often served
with lentils*
wines: Sangiovese, Trebbiano

pizza
Naples is the home of the pizza
parmigiana di melanzane
*layers of finely sliced aubergines cooked in the
oven with olive oil, tomato and parmesan*
wines: Greco di Tufo, Taurasi, Limoncello
(lemon liqueur served as an aperitif)

agnello
*lamb is a main
ingredient*

ABRUZZI

Roma MOLISE

PUGLIA Bari

CAMPANIA

Napoli

BASILICATA

CALABRIA

Palermo

SICILIA

**Campania, Basilicata & Calabria
mozzarella di bufala**
*mozzarella made from buffalo milk
and stored in a buttermilk bath*

involtini di pescespada
herb-stuffed swordfish
triglie alla siciliana
red mullet cooked in white wine and orange peel
caponata
aubergines cooked in a sweet and sour sauce
farsu magru
veal stuffed and rolled up, cooked in wine
cannoli
*fried pastries stuffed with ricotta, candied fruits
and dark chocolate*
wines: Marsala *(dark dessert wine)*

There are times when you cannot eat some things. It is as well to warn the waiter before making your choice.

I'm vegetarian
sono vegetariano(a)
so-no ve-jay-ta-ree-ya-no(a)

I don't eat meat/pork
non mangio carne/carne di maiale
non man-jo kar-nay/kar-nay dee ma-ya-lay

I don't eat fish/shellfish
non mangio pesce/i frutti di mare
non man-jo pay-shay/ee froot-tee dee ma-ray

I'm allergic to shellfish
sono allergico(a) ai frutti di mare
so-no al-ler-jee-ko(a) a-ee froot-tee dee ma-ray

I am allergic to peanuts
sono allergico(a) alle arachidi
so-no al-ler-jee-ko(a) al-lay a-ra-kee-dee

I can't eat raw eggs
non posso mangiare le uova non cotte
non pos-so man-ja-ray lay wo-va non kot-tay

I can't eat liver
non posso mangiare il fegato
non pos-so man-ja-ray eel fay-ga-to

I am on a diet
sono a dieta
so-no a dee-ay-ta

I don't drink alcohol
non bevo alcool
non bay-vo al-kol

what is in this?
cosa c'è dentro?
ko-za che den-tro

is it raw?
è crudo?
e kroo-do

is it made with unpasteurised milk?
è fatto con latte non pastorizzato?
e fat-to kon lat-tay non pas-to-reed-za-to

fritto(a)
freet-to(a)
fried

bollito(a)
bol-lee-to(a)
boiled

alla brace
al-la bra-chay
barbecued

arrosto(a)
ar-ros-to(a)
roast

allo spiedo
al-lo spyay-do
on a spit

ripieno(a)
ree-pyay-no(a)
stuffed

alla griglia
al-la greel-ya
grilled

affumicato(a)
af-foo-mee-ka-to(a)
smoked

al sangue
al sang-way
rare

cotto(a)
kot-to(a)
cooked

crudo(a)
kroo-do(a)
raw

al dente
al den-tay
firm

al forno
al for-no
baked

brasato(a)
bra-za-to(a)
stewed

Menu Reader

abbacchio *suckling or milk-fed lamb, usually eaten at Easter. Roasted with garlic and rosemary*
abbacchio alla cacciatora *lamb cooked in olive oil, garlic and rosemary*

acciughe *anchovies: fresh, salted or in olive oil*
acciughe ripiene *fresh anchovies filled with salted anchovy fillets and cream cheese and fried in oil*

aceto *vinegar*
aceto balsamico *balsamic vinegar*

acqua brillante *tonic water*

acqua cotta *traditional Tuscan soup made from onions, peppers, celery and tomato. Beaten eggs and parmesan are added just before serving*

acqua minerale *mineral water; this can be still (**naturale**), with gas (**effervescente naturale**), or with added gas (**gassata**)*

affettato misto *selection of cold meats: ham, salami, mortadella, etc*

affogato *poached*

affogato al caffè *vanilla ice cream with hot espresso coffee poured over it*

affumicato *smoked*

aglio *garlic*

albicocche

aglio, olio e peperoncino *garlic, olive oil and hot chilli served on pasta*

agnello *lamb*
agnello al forno *roast lamb*
agnello arrosto *roast lamb*

agnolotti *pasta squares filled with white meat and cheese, usually served with bolognese sauce*

agoni *small fresh-water fish, usually marinated in vinegar and herbs*

agrodolce *sweet and sour sauce made from sugar, water, vinegar, wine, pine-nuts and sultanas; served with vegetables or meat such as rabbit or duck*

ai ferri *grilled*

al, alla *etc means with, or in the style of: e.g. **pasta al sugo** is pasta with tomato sauce, and **pollo alla cacciatora** is chicken hunter-style*

albicocche *apricots*
albicocche ripiene *stuffed apricots*

alici *fresh anchovies, often served dipped in flour and fried*

alloro *bayleaf*

amarene *sour cherries*

amaretti *macaroons, biscuits with a strong almond flavour*

Amaretto di Saronno *almond liqueur*

amaro *bitter liqueur drunk as a digestivo (to aid digestion)*

amatriciana, ...all' *bacon, tomato and onion sauce*

analcolico *non-alcoholic, slightly bitter drink served as an aperitif*

ananas *pineapple*

anatra *duck*
  anatra in porchetta *roast duck stuffed with its liver and ham*

anguilla *eel*
  anguille alla comácchio *stewed eels with tomato and vinegar*
  anguille carpionate *fried eels in a vinegar sauce*
  anguille in umido *stewed eels*

anguria *watermelon*

anguria

anice *aniseed*

anisetta *powerful aniseed liqueur*

antipasto *starter/appetizer*
  antipasto misto *selection of cold starters such as ham, salami and pickles*

aperitivo *aperitif*

Aperol *type of slightly alcoholic aperitif*

aragosta *lobster*

arance *oranges*

aranciata *orangeade*

arancini di riso *rice croquettes filled with minced veal and peas*

arrabbiata, ...all' *tomato sauce with bacon, onion, tomatoes and hot chillies*

arrosto *roast meat, usually cooked in casserole with wine and herbs*
  arrosto di maiale *roast pork*
  arrosto di manzo *roast beef*
  arrosto di vitello *roast veal*

asparagi *asparagus*
  asparagi alla parmigiana *lightly boiled asparagus sprinkled with parmesan*

asparagi

astice *crayfish*

baccalà *salt cod*
  baccalà fiorentina *salt cod cooked in tomato sauce*
  baccalà alla vicentina *salt cod cooked in milk with anchovies, garlic and parsley*
  baccalà alla livornese *salt cod cooked in a tomato sauce*

bagna cauda *hot garlic and anchovy dip*

banana *banana*

basilico *basil*

Bel Paese *soft mild cheese*

ben cotto *well done*

besciamella *béchamel sauce*

bianco, in *literally it means white,*

pasta or rice served with butter or olive oil and parmesan cheese

bietola beetroot

birra lager-type beer; draught beer is **birra alla spina**

biscotti biscuits

bistecca steak
bistecca fiorentina thickly cut, charcoal-grilled T-bone steak

bistecchini di cinghiale wild boar steaks

bitter non-alcoholic, bitter drink served as an aperitif

bocconcini di vitello pieces of veal cooked in wine and butter

bollito boiled
bollito misto different kinds of meat and vegetables boiled together

bolognese, ...alla tomato and minced meat sauce, served with parmesan

bomba doughnut with custard filling

bonet alla Piemontese chocolate pudding made with biscuits, macaroons and rum

budino chocolate or vanilla pudding

borlotti dried red haricot beans

boscaiola, ...alla with mushroom and ham sauce

bistecca alla fiorentina

bottarga preserved mullet roes, grated and sprinkled on pasta dishes, or served in thin slices as a starter (Sardinian speciality)

brace, ...alla grilled

braciola rib steak/chop

brasato beef stew

bresaola dried cured beef, finely sliced and served with black pepper, lemon and olive oil

broccoli broccoli

brodetto di pesce fish soup made with different kinds of fish

brodo bouillon or broth often served with meat-stuffed pasta such as ravioli (**in brodo**)

bruschetta thickly-sliced grilled bread rubbed with garlic and olive oil, often served topped with tomato

bucatini thick spaghetti-like pasta with hole running through it

budino a blancmange-type pudding, usually chocolate or vanilla

baccalà alla fiorentina

burro *butter*
  burro, ...al *fried in butter, usually wih garlic and sage*
  burro e salvia *butter and sage sauce*

busecca *rich tripe and cheese soup*

cacciatora, ...alla *meat or game, hunter-style – cooked with tomato, herbs, garlic and wine*

cachi *persimmons*

caciocavallo *cow's cheese, quite strong when mature*

caffè *coffee – if you ask for* **un caffè** *you'll be served* **un espresso** *(small, strong and black)*
  caffè americano *black filter coffee*
  caffè corretto *coffee laced with* **grappa** *or any strong spirit*
  caffè doppio *a large coffee (twice normal size)*
  caffèllatte *milky coffee*

calamaretti imbottiti *baby squid stuffed with breadcrumbs and anchovies*

calamari *squid*
  calamari fritti *squid rings dipped in batter and fried*

calzone *folded over pizza with filling. There are lots of local variations*

camomilla *camomile tea*

Campari *bitter-tasting aperitif made with herbs and fruit*

carciofo

canederli tirolesi *Tyrolean dumplings made with smoked cured ham and bread*

cannella *cinnamon*

cannellini *small white beans*

cannelloni *meat-filled pasta tubes covered with béchamel sauce and baked. Vegetarian options are filled with spinach and ricotta*

cannoli *fried pastries stuffed with ricotta, candied fruit and bitter chocolate from Sicily*

cantucci *nutty biscuits*

caponata *Sicilian dish of aubergines, potatoes and peppers, cooked in a sweet and sour sauce*

cappelletti *literally 'little hats' filled with cheese or meat filling, can be served with bolognese meat sauce or in broth*

capperi *capers*

cappon magro *an elaborate salad of cold seafood, fish and cooked vegetables*

cappuccino *frothy white coffee*

caprese *tomato and mozzarella salad with basil*

capretto *baby goat (kid)*
  capretto arrosto *oven-roasted kid with vegetables and wine*

caponata

caprino *soft goat's cheese, usually eaten with a sprinkling of olive oil and freshly ground black pepper*

caramelle *sweets*

carbonara, ...alla *smoked bacon, egg, cream and parmesan*

carciofi *artichokes*

carciofi alla Giudia *young artichokes, flattened and deep-fried*

carciofi alla romana, carciofi ripieni *artichokes stuffed with breadcrumbs, parsley and anchovies*

cardi *cardoons (similar to fennel)*

carne *meat*

carote *carrots*

carpaccio *raw sliced lean beef eaten with lemon juice, olive oil and thickly grated parmesan cheese*

carpa *carp*

carpione, in *pickled in vinegar, wine and lemon juice. Fried fish is often served this way*

casalinga, ...alla *home-made*

cassata *layers of ice cream with candied fruits*

ciliege

cassata alla siciliana *sponge dessert with ricotta and candied fruits*

cassola *pork, cabbage and vegetable casserole*

castagnaccio *chestnut cake*

castagne *chestnuts*

cavolfiore *cauliflower*

cavolo *cabbage*

ceci *chickpeas*

céfalo *grey mullet*

cena *dinner*

Centerbe *herbal liqueur*

cervella *calves' brains, usually fried*

cetriolo *cucumber*

China *bittersweet liqueur*

chinotto *fizzy, bitter-orange soft drink*

cialzons alla carnia *pasta squares filled with spinach, chocolate and cinnamon*

ciambella *ring-shaped fruit cake*

ciambellini *ring-shaped aniseed biscuits*

cicoria *chicory*

ciliege *cherries*

cime di rapa *leafy, green vegetable similar to turnip tops, often served with **orecchiette***

carpaccio

cipolle

cinghiale *wild boar*

Cinzano *popular aperitif*

cioccolata calda *rich hot chocolate, often served with cream*

cioccolatini *chocolates*

cioccolato *chocolate*

cipolle *onions*

cocco *coconut*

cocomero *watermelon*

coda di bue *oxtail*
  coda alla vaccinara *famous Roman dish of oxtail stewed with tomatoes and herbs*

Colomba *bird-shaped cake with orange peel, topped with sugared almonds, eaten at Easter*

conchiglie *shell-shaped pasta*

confetti *sugared almonds*

congelato *frozen*

coniglio *rabbit*
  coniglio in umido *rabbit stew*

contorni *vegetable side dishes*

cornetto *ice-cream cone; a croissant filled with jam, custard or chocolate*

cosciotto d'agnello all'abruzzese *braised leg of lamb with garlic, tomatoes, rosemary and wine*

cotechino *spicy pork sausage boiled and served with lentils*

cotoletta *cutlet/chop*
  cotoletta al prosciutto *veal cutlet with a slice of Parma ham*
  cotoletta alla bolognese *veal cutlet topped with ham and cheese*
  cotoletta alla milanese *veal cutlet dipped in egg and breadcrumbs then fried*
  cotoletta alla valdostana *breaded veal chop topped with Fontina cheese and ham*
  cotoletta di vitello *veal cutlet*
  cotolette di abbacchio *lamb chops*
  cotolette di agnello alla brace *marinated, grilled lamb chops*

cotto *cooked*

cozze *mussels*

crema di... *cream soup or sauce/custard*

crêpe *pancake*

crespella *stuffed pancake*

crocchette di patate *potato croquettes*

crodino *slightly bitter, non-alcoholic aperitif*

crostata *tart, usually filled with jam*
  crostata di frutta *tart filled with fruit and glazed*

crostini di fegatini *chicken liver pâté on toast*

crudo *raw*

cotechino

fichi

cuori di carciofo *artichoke hearts*

Cynar *bitter aperitif (made from artichokes)*

dente, ...al *pasta cooked so it is still quite firm*

dèntice *sea bream*

digestivo *bitter, herb-flavoured liqueur to aid digestion*

dolce *dessert*

dolcelatte *soft, creamy blue cheese*

dragoncello *tarragon*

entrecote *steak*

fagiano *pheasant*
  fagiano con funghi *pheasant with porcini mushrooms*
  fagiano in salmì *pheasant stewed in wine*

fagioli *beans*
  fagioli al tonno *haricot beans with tuna fish in olive oil*
  fagioli con cotiche *bean stew with pork rinds*
  fagioli nel fiasco *haricot beans cooked in a flask*

fagiolini *runner beans*

faraona *guinea fowl*

farcito *stuffed*

farfalle *butterfly-shaped pasta*

farsu magru *veal stuffed and rolled up, cooked in wine (Sicilian speciality)*

fave *broad beans*
  fave al guanciale *broad beans cooked with bacon and onion*

fegatini di pollo *chicken livers*

fegato *liver (mainly calves')*
  fegato alla veneziana *calves' liver fried in butter and onion*

ferri, ...ai *grilled without oil*

fettuccine *fresh ribbon pasta*

fichi *figs*
  fichi d'India *prickly pears*
  filetto *fillet steak*
  filetto di tacchino alla bolognese *turkey breast served with a slice of ham and cheese*

Filu Ferru *very strong grappa from Sardinia*

finanziera, ...alla *mince of chicken livers, mushrooms and wine sauce*

finocchio *fennel*

fiori di zucchini *courgette flowers, often served fried in batter*

focaccia *flat bread brushed with salt and olive oil, sprinkled with herbs or onions*

fonduta *cheese fondue made with Fontina cheese, eggs,*

focaccia

fritto misto di mare

butter and truffles. Eaten with crusty bread

Fontina *mild to strong cow's milk cheese (from the Val d'Aosta)*

formaggio *cheese*

forno, ...al *cooked in the oven*

fragole *strawberries*

frittata *omelette, usually with different ingredients*

fritto *fried*
  fritto misto *selection of fried seafood*

frullato di frutta *fruit smoothie*

frutta *fruit*

frutti di mare *shellfish/seafood*

funghi *mushrooms – very popular and varied in Italy. In autumn many Italians take to the woods in search of the prized* **porcini**
  funghi trifolati *sliced mushrooms fried with garlic and parsley*

Fuoco dell'Etna *very strong liqueur from Sicily*

fusilli *spiral-shaped pasta*

gamberi *prawns*

gamberoni *giant prawns*

gazzosa *fizzy bottled lemonade*

gelato *ice cream*
  gelato misto *a selection of different flavoured ice creams*

girasole *sunflower*

gnocchi *small dumplings made from potato and flour. Boiled and served with tomato sauce or ragù*
  gnocchi alla romana *dumplings made from semolina, butter and parmesan, oven-baked*
  gnocchi verdi *spinach and potato dumplings, usually cooked in butter, garlic and sage*

Gorgonzola *a strong blue cows'-milk cheese*

granchio *crab*

grana *hard cows'-milk cheese; generic name given to Parmesan cheese*

granita *slush puppy, crushed ice drink*
  granita al caffè *cold coffee with crushed ice*
  granita al limone *lemon drink with crushed ice sorbet*

granseola *large crab*

grappa *strong spirit from grape pressings, often added to coffee*

grattugiato *grated*

griglia, ...alla *grilled*

grigliata di cervo *grilled venison steaks*

grigliata mista *mixed grill consisting of various barbecued meats*

lamponi

grissini *breadsticks*
guanciale *streaky bacon made from pig's cheek*
gulasch *spicy beef stew*
impepata di cozze *peppery mussels*
insalata *salad*
 insalata caprese *tomato, basil and mozzarella salad*
 insalata di mare *mixed seafood salad*
 insalata di pomodori *tomato salad*
 insalata di riso *rice salad*
 insalata mista *mixed salad*
 insalata russa *cold diced vegetables seved with mayonnaise*
 insalata verde *green salad*
involtini *rolls of veal or pork stuffed in various ways*
lamponi *raspberries*
lasagne *layers of pasta with bolognese and béchamel sauces, baked*
 lasagne verdi *layers of green pasta filled with bolognese (or ricotta) and béchamel sauces.*
latte *milk*
lattuga *lettuce*
lemonsoda *fizzy lemon drink*
lenticchie *lentils*
lepre *hare*
 lepre in salmì *hare stewed in wine*
lesso *boiled*
limonata *bottled lemon drink*
limone *lemon*
limoncello *lemon liqueur*
lingua *tongue*
linguine *flat spaghetti*
lombata di maiale *pork chop*

melanzane

lonza *type of pork fillet*
luccio *pike*
lumache *snails*
maccheroni *macaroni*
 maccheroni ai quattro formaggi *pasta with four cheeses*
macedonia (con gelato) *fresh fruit salad (with ice cream)*
macinata *mince*
magro, di *a meatless dish (often a fish alternative)*
maiale *pork*
 maionese *mayonnaise*
 mandorle *almonds*
 manzo *beef*
 marmellata *jam*
 Marsala *dark dessert wine from Sicily*
 Martini *famous Italian aperitif*
mascarpone *rich cream cheese used in desserts such as **tiramisù***
 mela *apple*
 melagrana *pomegranate*
 melanzane *aubergines*

ossobucco

melanzane alla Parmigiana *layers of fried aubergine baked with tomato sauce, ham, parmesan and mozzarella*

melanzane ripiene *stuffed aubergines*

melone *melon*

menta *mint*

meringata *meringue and ice cream dessert*

merluzzo *cod*

miele *honey*

milanese, ...alla *normally applied to veal cutlets dipped in egg and breadcrumbs before frying*

minestra *soup*

minestrone *vegetable soup (with either pasta or rice)*

missultin *grilled dried fish, often eaten with* **polenta**

misto di funghi *mushroom stew*

more *blackberries*

mortadella *type of salami*

mostarda *pickled fruit. Served with* **bollito** *(boiled meats)*

mozzarella *fresh cheese preserved in whey, used in pizzas*

mozzarella di bufala *mozzarella made with buffalo milk*

mozzarella in carrozza *mozzarella sandwiched in bread, dipped in egg and breadcrumbs and fried*

mugnaia, ...alla *usually fish dusted in flour then fried in butter*

nocciole *hazelnuts*

noci *walnuts*

norma, ...alla *tomato and fried aubergine Sicilian sauce*

olio *oil*

olio d'oliva *olive oil*

olive *olives*

orecchiette *ear-shaped pasta, served with either tomoato sauce or* **cime di rapa** *(type of broccoli)*

orecchiette ai broccoli *pasta with broccoli*

origano *oregano*

orzata *cool, milky drink made from barley*

ossobuco *marrow-bone veal steak cooked in tomato and wine sauce*

ostriche *oysters*

panettone

pasta e fagioli

paglia e fieno *green and plain ribbon pasta*

pan pepato *sweet loaf with mixed nuts and spices*

pancetta *streaky bacon*

pandoro *soft cork-shaped yeast cake sprinkled with icing-sugar, traditionally eaten at Christmas*

pane *bread*
  pane e coperto *cover charge*
  pane integrale *wholemeal bread*

panettone *cork-shaped yeast cake with orange peel and raisins, traditionally eaten at Christmas*

panforte *a hard, dried-fruit and nut cake*

panino *bread roll or sandwich*

panna *cream*

pansotti *pasta squares filled with herbs and cheese and served in a walnut and parmesan sauce*

panzerotti *folded pizza dough stuffed with mozzarella, salami and ham, usually fried*

pappardelle *wide ribbon-shaped pasta*
  pappardelle al sugo di lepre *wide ribbon pasta with hare, wine and tomato sauce*

parmigiana di melanzane *aubergine layers, oven-baked with tomato sauce and parmesan cheese*

parmigiano *parmesan cheese. A hard cow's milk cheese used extensively in Italian cooking*

pasta *the dry variety takes 10–15 minutes to cook, the fresh just 3 or 4*
  pasta al forno *pasta baked with minced meat, eggs, tomato and cheese*
  pasta all'uovo *fresh pasta made from flour and eggs*
  pasta asciutta *pasta served with a sauce, such as* **spaghetti al sugo,** *and not in a soup form, such as* **ravioli in brodo** *(ravioli in bouillon)*
  pasta e fagioli *pasta with beans*
  pasta fresca *fresh pasta*

pasticcio *pie*

pastina in brodo *pasta pieces in clear broth*

patate *potatoes*
  patate fritte *chips*

patatine *crisps*
  patatine fritte *french fries*

pecorino *hard tangy cheese made from sheep's milk*

penne *quill-shaped pasta*
  penne rigate *ribbed quill-shaped pasta*

pesca

pepe *pepper*

peperonata *sweet peppers cooked with tomatoes and olive oil*

peperoncino *hot chilli pepper*

peperoni *peppers*
  peperoni ripieni *stuffed peppers*

pere *pears*

pesca *peach*
  pesca noce *nectarine*

pesce *fish*
  pesce arrosto *baked fish*
  pesce persico *perch*
  pesce spada *swordfish, often grilled or served in a tomato sauce*

pesto *sauce of pounded basil, garlic, pine-nuts, olive oil and Parmesan cheese*

petto di pollo *chicken breast*

piatto *dish*
  piatto del giorno *dish of the day*
  piatti tipici *regional dishes*

piccata al limone *tender thinly sliced veal in butter and lemon*

pietanze *main courses*

pinoli *pine nuts*

piselli *peas*

pistacchio *pistachio*

pizza *originally from Naples, cooked in wood-burning ovens*

pizza ai funghi *mushroom pizza*

pizza alla Siciliana *pizza with tomato, anchovy, black olives and capers*

pizza capricciosa *pizza with baby artichoke, ham and egg*

pizza ai frutti di mare *pizza with seafood*

pizza margherita *named after the first queen of a united Italy, symbolising the colours of the Italian flag: red (tomatoes), green (basil) and white (mozzarella)*

pizza marinara *tomato and garlic pizza*

pizza Napoli/Napoletana *pizza with tomato, cheese, anchovy, olive oil and oregano*

pizza quattro formaggi *a pizza divided into four sections, each with a different cheese topping*

pizza quattro stagioni *pizza divided into four sections with a selection of toppings on each*

pizzaiola, ...alla *cooked with tomatoes, garlic and herbs*

polenta e peperoni

pizzetta *small cheese and tomato pizza*

pizzoccheri *buckwheat pasta noodles, cooked with cabbage, potatoes and cheese and dressed with fried butter and garlic*

polenta *coarse corn or maize meal solidified porridge. A perfect accompaniment to stews. Can also be fried*
 polenta uncia *polenta baked with butter, garlic and cheese*

pollame *poultry/fowl*

pollo *chicken*
 pollo alla diavola *chicken grilled with herbs and chilli pepper*
 pollo alla romana *chicken with tomatoes and peppers*
 pollo arrosto *roast chicken*

polpette *beef meatballs made with parmesan and parsley*

polpo *octopus, served in salad (cold) or tomato sauce*
 polpo affogato *octopus cooked in tomato sauce*

pomodoro *tomato*
 pomodoro, ...al *tomato sauce (same as **sugo**)*
 pomodori da sugo *plum tomatoes*
 pomodori ripieni *stuffed tomatoes*

pompelmo *grapefruit*

porceddu *roast suckling pig (Sardinian style)*

porchetta *roast suckling pig*

porcini *prized cep mushrooms, often dried*

porri *leeks*

pranzo *lunch*

prezzemolo *parsley*

prima colazione *breakfast*

primo *first course*

prosciutto *ham*

prosciutto cotto *boiled ham*

prosciutto crudo *cured Parma ham which is sliced off the bone*

prosciutto di cinghiale *cured ham made from wild boar*

prosciutto e melone *Parma ham and melon slices*

Prosecco *sparkling dry white wine*

provolone *cow's milk cheese, mild to strong*

prugne *plums*

puttanesca, ...alla *tomato, garlic, hot chilli, anchovies and capers*

quaglie *quails*

radicchio *red-leaf lettuce*

ragù, ...al *minced meat, tomato and garlic (same as **bolognese**)*

pomodori

rana pescatrice *monkfish*

rane *frogs (only the legs are eaten)*

ravioli *pasta cushions filled with meat or cheese and spinach*

ribes *blackcurrants*

riccio di mare *sea urchin*

ricotta *soft white cheese often used as filling for pasta as well as in desserts*

rigatoni *ribbed tubes of pasta*

ripieno *stuffed*

risi e bisi *thick rice and pea soup (almost liquid risotto) cooked with bacon*

risotto alla milanese

riso *rice*

risotto *rice cooked in broth with different ingredients added*
risotto ai funghi *risotto with porcini mushrooms*
risotto al nero di seppia *risotto made with squid and its ink*
risotto alla milanese *rich yellow risotto flavoured with saffron, parmesan and butter, and cooked in meat broth*

risotto alla pescatora *seafood rice*
robiola *creamy cheese with a mild taste*
rognone *kidney*
rosmarino *rosemary*
rucola *rocket (in Rome: **rughetta**)*
salame *salami (there are many types)*
sale *salt*
salmone *salmon*
salsa *sauce*
  salsa verde *sauce made of olive oil, anchovies, hard boiled egg and parsley, usually served with boiled meat or fish*
salsicce *sausages: there are many regional variations but they are mainly thick pork sausages which can be boiled or grilled*
saltimbocca alla romana *veal cooked in white wine with parma ham*
salvia *sage*
Sambuca *aniseed liqueur, served with coffee beans and set alight*
sampietro *John Dory (type of fish)*
sangue, ...al *rare*

scaloppine al marsala

scaloppine alla milanese

sarde *sardines*
  sarde al beccafico *sardines marinated and stuffed with breadcrumbs, Pecorino cheese, garlic and parsley, then fried*
  sarde in saor *fried sardines marinated in vinegar, onions, sultanas and pine nuts*
sartù di riso *rice and meat timbale (rather like a pie)*
scaloppine *veal escalopes*
  scaloppine al limone *veal escalopes cooked in lemon juice*
  scaloppine al marsala *veal escalopes cooked in marsala*
  scaloppine alla milanese *veal escalopes dipped in egg, breadcrumbs and fried in butter, served with wedges of lemon*
  scaloppine alla pizzaiola *thinly sliced steak fried in a tomato and herb sauce*
scamorza *a soft cow's milk cheese (type of dried mozzarella)*
  scamorza affumicata *smoked scamorza*
scampi *scampi*

secondo *second course, usually meat or fish*
sedano *celery*
selz *soda water*
semifreddo *chilled dessert made with ice cream*
senape *mustard*
seppia *cuttlefish*
servizio compreso *service included*
sfogliatelle *puff pastry cakes*
sgombro *mackerel*
soffritto *sliced onion and/or garlic fried in olive oil, generally used to prepare sauces or meat dishes*
sogliola *sole*
soppressata *type of salami, with pistachio*
sott'olio *in olive oil*
spaghetti *spaghetti*
  spaghetti aglio, olio e peperoncino *spaghetti with garlic, chilli pepper and olive oil*
spaghetti alla chitarra *square-shaped pasta*

spaghetti alle vongole

spaghetti all'amatriciana *spaghetti with bacon, onion and tomato sauce*

spaghetti alle vongole *spaghetti with clams*

speck *type of smoked cured ham from mountain regions*

spezzatino *stew*

spiedini *meat kebabs*

spiedo, ...allo *spit-roasted, or on skewer*

spinaci *spinach*

spremuta *freshly squeezed fruit juice*

spremuta di pompelmo *fresh grapefruit juice*

spumante *sparkling wine*

stoccafisso *dried stockfish which requires lots of soaking before cooking*

stracciatella *consommé with egg stirred in and grated parmesan; or ice-cream with chocolate chips*

stracotto *braised beef slow-cooked with vegetables. Often served with polenta*

Strega *strong herb-flavoured liqueur*

succo di frutta *bottled fruit juice*

sugo *sauce, often refers to the basic tomato, basil and garlic sauce (same as al pomodoro)*

surgelato *frozen*

tacchino *turkey*

spinaci

tagliata *thinly-sliced meat, briefly cooked on a griddle and served with herbs or parmesan chips*

tagliata di pesce spada *thinly-sliced swordfish, served raw with lemon juice and olive oil*

tagliatelle *ribbon-like pasta often served in cream sauce*

Taleggio *soft, creamy cheese similar to Camembert*

tartine *canapés*

tartufo *truffles: black (nero) and white (bianco) are used extensively in risotto and game dishes*
   tartufo di cioccolato *rich chocolate ice cream shaped like a truffle*

tè *tea. Normally served with lemon (**al limone**). If you want it with milk you must ask for **tè al latte***

timballo *a baked pie*

timo *thyme*

tinca *tench*

tiramisù *dessert made with mascarpone, sponge, coffee and marsala*

tónica *tonic water*

tonno *tuna fish*
   tonno, ...al *tuna sauce*
   tonno e fagioli *tuna and bean salad*

torrone *nougat, traditionally eaten at Christmas*

torta *cake/flan/tart*

tortellini *meat-filled pasta cushions*

tortellini panna e prosciutto *tortellini served with cream and ham*

tramezzini *sliced white bread with mixed fillings*

trenette *long thin strips of pasta, traditionally served with pesto sauce*

triglie *red mullet*
   triglie alla livornese *red mullet fried with chillies in tomato sauce*

trippa *tripe, often cooked with tomatoes and onions*

trota *trout*

uccelli scappati *pork kebabs*

umido, in *stewed*

uova *eggs*
   uova alla fiorentina *poached eggs on spinach tarts*

uva *grapes*

uva passa *raisins*

vaniglia *vanilla*

Vecchia Romagna *Italian cognac*

verdure *vegetables*

vermicelli *very thin pasta*
   Vermut *very popular aperitif made from herbs and wine*
   verza *Savoy (green) cabbage*
   vino *wine*
   vin brûlé *mulled wine*
   vino bianco *white wine*
   vino dolce *sweet wine*
   vino frizzante *sparkling wine*
   vino rosato *rosé wine*
   vino rosso *red wine*
   vino secco *dry wine*

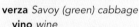

uva

vitello *veal*

vongole *clams*
  vongole, ...alle *clam, parsley, garlic and olive oil*

wurstel *Frankfurter sausages*

yogurt *yoghurt*

zabaglione *frothy dessert made with egg yolks and sugar beaten with marsala over heat*

zafferano *saffron, used in* **risotto alla milanese**

zampone *pig's trotter filled with spicy sausage, sliced and served hot*

zola *soft cheese similar to gorgonzola but sweeter*

zucca *marrow, pumpkin*

zucchero *sugar*

zucchini *courgettes*

zuccotto *rich cream, coffee and nut pudding*

zuppa *soup*
  zuppa di cozze *mussel soup*
  zuppa di fagioli *bean soup*
  zuppa di pesce *seafood soup with many delicious regional variations*
  zuppa inglese *dessert similar to trifle laced with whisky or* **Vermut**
  zuppa pavese *a bread soup with broth and poached eggs, topped with grated cheese*

zucchini

A

a(n) un/una/uno
abbey l'abbazia (f)
able: to be able (to) essere capace (di)
abortion l'aborto (m)
about su ; circa
  a book about... un libro su...
  about ten o'clock circa le dieci
above sopra
abroad all'estero (m)
  to go abroad andare all'estero
abscess l'ascesso (m)
accelerator l'acceleratore (m)
accent l'accento (m)
to accept accettare
access l'accesso (m)
  wheelchair access accesso per disabili
accident l'incidente (m)
accident & emergency department il pronto soccorso
accommodation l'alloggio (m)
to accompany accompagnare
account (bill) il conto
  (in bank) il conto in banca
account number il numero di conto
to ache fare male
  it aches fa male
acid l'acido (m)
actor (m/f) l'attore/l'attrice
adaptor (electrical appliance) il riduttore
address l'indirizzo (m)
  what is the address? qual è l'indirizzo?
address book la rubrica
admission charge/fee il biglietto d'ingresso
to admit (to hospital) ricoverare
adult l'adulto(a)
  for adults per adulti
advance: in advance in anticipo
advertisement la pubblicità
  (in newspaper) l'annuncio (m)
to advise consigliare
A&E il pronto soccorso
aeroplane l'aeroplano (m)
aerosol l'aerosol (m)
afraid: to be afraid avere paura
after dopo
afternoon il pomeriggio
  this afternoon oggi pomeriggio
  tomorrow afternoon domani pomeriggio
  in the afternoon di pomeriggio

aftershave il dopobarba
again ancora ; di nuovo
against contro
age l'età (f)
agency l'agenzia (f)
ago fa
  a week ago una settimana fa
to agree essere d'accordo
agreement l'accordo (m)
AIDS l'AIDS (m)
air ambulance l'elisoccorso (m)
airbag l'airbag (m)
airbed il materassino gonfiabile
air-conditioning l'aria condizionata (f)
air freshener il deodorante per l'ambiente
airline la linea aerea
air mail: by air mail per via aerea
airplane l'aeroplano (m)
airport l'aeroporto (m)
airport bus l'autobus per aeroporto (m)
air ticket il biglietto d'aereo
aisle il corridoio
alarm l'allarme (m)
alarm clock la sveglia
alcohol l'alcool (m)
alcohol-free analcolico(a)
alcoholic alcolico(a)
all tutto(a)
allergic to allergico(a) a
  I'm allergic to... sono allergico(a) a...
allergy l'allergia (f)
to allow permettere
all right (agreed) va bene
  are you all right? sta bene?
almost quasi
alone solo(a)
Alps le Alpi
already già
also anche
altar l'altare (m)
aluminium foil la carta stagnola
always sempre
a.m. del mattino
am: I am sono
amber (light) il giallo
ambulance l'ambulanza (f)
America l'America (f)
American americano(a)
anaesthetic l'anestetico (m)
  local anaesthetic l'anestetico locale
  general anaesthetic l'anestetico generale
anchor l'ancora (f)
ancient antico(a)

and e
angina l'angina pectoris (f)
angry arrabbiato(a)
animal l'animale (m)
ankle la caviglia
anniversary l'anniversario (m)
to announce annunciare
announcement l'annuncio (m)
annual annuale
another un altro/un'altra
   another beer un'altra birra
   another coffee un altro caffè
answer la risposta
to answer rispondere
answerphone la segreteria telefonica
antacid l'antiacido (m)
antibiotic l'antibiotico (m)
antifreeze l'antigelo (m)
antihistamine l'antistaminico (m)
antiques i pezzi d'antiquariato
antique shop il negozio d'antiquariato
antiseptic l'antisettico (m)
any dei/delle/degli (di)
   I haven't any money non ho soldi
   have you any apples? ha delle mele?
anyone qualcuno ; chiunque
anything qualcosa ; qualsiasi cosa
apartment l'appartamento (m)
appendicitis l'appendicite (f)
apple la mela
application form il modulo di domanda
appointment l'appuntamento (m)
   I have an appointment ho un
   appuntamento
approximately circa
apricots le albicocche
April aprile
architect m/f l'architetto
architecture l'architettura (f)
arm il braccio
armbands (swimming) i braccioli
armchair la poltrona
to arrange sistemare
to arrest arrestare
arrivals (plane, train) gli arrivi
to arrive arrivare
art l'arte (f)
art gallery la galleria d'arte ;
   la pinacoteca
arthritis l'artrite (f)
artificial finto(a) ; artificiale
artist m/f l'artista
ashtray il portacenere
to ask (question) domandare
   (for something) chiedere

asleep: *he/she is asleep* dorme
asparagus gli asparagi
aspirin l'aspirina (f)
asthma l'asma (f)
   I have asthma ho l'asma
at a
   at home a casa
   at 8 o'clock alle otto
   at once subito
   at night di notte
ATM il Bancomat®
to attack aggredire
attractive attraente
aubergine la melanzana
auction l'asta (f)
audience il pubblico
August agosto
aunt la zia
au pair la ragazza alla pari
Australia l'Australia (f)
Australian australiano(a)
author m/f l'autore/l'autrice
automatic automatico(a)
automatic car la macchina con cambio
   automatico
auto-teller il Bancomat®
autumn l'autunno (m)
available disponibile
avalanche la valanga
avenue il viale
average medio(a)
to avoid evitare
awake: *to be awake* essere sveglio(a)
away via
awful terribile
awning (for caravan etc) il tendalino
axle (car) l'asse (m)

B

baby il/la bambino(a)
baby food gli alimenti per bambini
baby milk il latte per bambini
baby wipes le salviettine per bambini
baby's bottle il biberon
babyseat (in car) il seggiolino per
   bambini
babysitter il/la babysitter
back (of body) la schiena
backpack lo zaino
bacon la pancetta
bad (weather, news) brutto(a)
   (food) andato(a) a male
badminton il badminton
bag la borsa

baggage i bagagli
baggage allowance il peso consentito di bagaglio
baggage reclaim il ritiro bagagli
bait *(for fishing)* l'esca *(m)*
baked al forno
baker's la panetteria ; il panificio
balcony il balcone
bald *(person)* calvo(a)
  (tyre) liscio(a)
ball *(large)* il pallone
  (small) la pallina
ballet il balletto
balloon il palloncino
banana la banana
band *(musical)* la banda
bandage la benda
bank la banca
  (river) la riva
bank account il conto in banca
banknote la banconota
bankrupt fallito(a)
bar il bar
bar of chocolate la tavoletta di cioccolato
barbecue il barbecue
  to have a barbecue fare il barbecue
barber il barbiere
to bark abbaiare
barn il granaio
barrel *(wine/beer)* il barile
basement il seminterrato
basil il basilico
basket il cestino
basketball la pallacanestro
bat *(baseball, etc)* la mazza
bath il bagno
  to have a bath fare un bagno
bathing cap la cuffia
bathroom il bagno
  with bathroom con bagno
battery *(radio, etc)* la pila
  (car) la batteria
  (rechargeable) la batteria ricaricabile
bay *(along coast)* la baia
B&B la pensione familiare
to be essere
beach la spiaggia
  private beach la spiaggia privata
  sandy beach la spiaggia con sabbia
  naturist beach la spiaggia per nudisti
beach hut la cabina
bean il fagiolo
beard la barba
beautiful bello(a)

beauty salon l'istituto di bellezza *(m)*
because perché
to become diventare
bed il letto
  double bed il letto matrimoniale
  single bed il letto a una piazza
  sofa bed il divano letto
  twin beds i letti gemelli
bed and breakfast la pensione familiare
bed clothes le coperte e lenzuola
bedroom la camera da letto
bee l'ape *(f)*
beef il manzo
beer la birra
  draught beer la birra alla spina
before prima di
  before breakfast prima di colazione
to begin cominciare
behind dietro
beige beige
to believe credere
bell *(church)* la campana
  (doorbell) il campanello
to belong to appartenere a
  it belongs to... appartiene a…
below sotto
belt la cintura
bend *(in road)* la curva
berth *(train, ship)* la cuccetta
beside *(next to)* accanto a
  beside the bank accanto alla banca
best: the best il/la migliore
bet la scommessa
to bet scommettere
better (than) meglio (di)
between fra
to beware of stare attento(a) a
beyond oltre
bib *(baby's)* il bavaglino
bicycle la bicicletta ; la bici
  by bicycle in bicicletta
bicycle pump la pompa da bicicletta
bicycle repair kit il kit per riparare la bici
bidet il bidet
big grande
  bigger (than) più grande (di)
bike *(pushbike)* la bici
  (motorbike) la moto
bike lock il lucchetto della bici
bikini il bikini
bill *(hotel, restaurant)* il conto
  (for work done) la fattura
  (gas, telephone) la bolletta
bin *(dustbin)* il bidone

bin liner il sacco della spazzatura
binoculars il binocolo
bird l'uccello *(m)*
biro la biro
birth la nascita
birth certificate il certificato di nascita
birthday il compleanno
  happy birthday! auguri! buon compleanno
  my birthday is on... il mio compleanno è il...
birthday card il biglietto d'auguri di compleanno
birthday present il regalo di compleanno
biscuits i biscotti
bit il pezzo
  a bit un po'
bite *(of insect)* la puntura
  (of dog) la morsicatura
  a bite to eat qualcosa da mangiare
to bite *(animal)* mordere
  (insect) morsicare
bitten morso(a)
  (by insect) punto(a)
bitter *(taste)* amaro(a)
black nero(a)
black ice il ghiaccio sulla strada
blank *(adjective) [disk, tape]* vuoto(a); vergine
blanket la coperta
bleach la candeggina
to bleed sanguinare
blender il frullatore
blind *(person)* cieco(a)
blind *(window)* la veneziana ; la tapparella
blister la vescica
block of flats il palazzo ; il condominio
blocked *(pipe, sink)* tappato(a)
  (road) bloccato(a)
blond *(person)* biondo(a)
blood il sangue
blood group il gruppo sanguigno
blood pressure la pressione sanguigna
blood test l'analisi del sangue *(f)*
blouse la camicetta
blowout *(noun) [of tyre]* lo scoppio (di pneumatico)
to blow-dry asciugare con il fon
blue *(light)* azzurro(a)
  dark blue blu scuro
  light blue azzurro(a)
blunt *(knife, blade)* non taglia
boar il cinghiale

to board *(plain, train, etc)* imbarcarsi su
boarding card/pass la carta d'imbarco
boarding house la pensione
boat la barca ; il battello
  (rowing) la barca a remi
boat trip la gita in battello
body il corpo
  (dead) il cadavere
to boil bollire
boiler la caldaia
boiled bollito(a)
bomb la bomba
bone l'osso *(m)*
  fish bone la spina di pesce
bonfire il falò
bonnet *(car)* il cofano
book il libro
  book of tickets il blocchetto di biglietti
to book prenotare
booking la prenotazione
booking office *(train)* la biglietteria
bookshop la libreria
boot *(of car)* il bagagliaio
boots *(long)* gli stivali
  (ankle) gli stivaletti
border *(of country)* la frontiera
boring noioso(a)
born: to be born essere nato(a)
to borrow prendere in prestito
boss il capo
both tutti e due
bottle la bottiglia
  a bottle of wine una bottiglia di vino
  a half-bottle una mezza bottiglia
bottle opener l'apribottiglie
bowl *(cereal, soup)* la scodella
bow tie la cravatta a farfalla
box la scatola
box office il botteghino
boxer shorts i boxer
boy *(young child)* il bambino
  (teenage) il ragazzo
boyfriend il ragazzo
bra il reggiseno
bracelet il braccialetto
brain il cervello
to brake frenare
brake cable il cavo del freno
brake fluid il liquido dei freni
brake light il fanalino dello stop
brake pads le pastiglie dei freni
brakes i freni
branch *(of tree)* il ramo
  (of bank, etc) la succursale

brand *(make)* la marca
brass l'ottone *(m)*
brave coraggioso(a)
bread il pane
  brown bread il pane integrale
  French bread il filoncino
  sliced bread il pancarré
bread roll il panino
to break rompere
breakable fragile
breakdown *(car)* il guasto
  (nervous) l'esaurimento nervoso *(m)*
breakdown van il carro attrezzi
breakfast la (prima) colazione
breast il seno
to breast-feed allattare
to breathe respirare
brick il mattone
bride la sposa
bridegroom lo sposo
bridge il ponte
briefcase la cartella
Brillo-pad la paglietta
to bring portare
Britain la Gran Bretagna
British britannico(a)
broadband *(noun)* la banda larga
broccoli i broccoli
brochure l'opuscolo *(m)*
broken rotto(a)
broken down *(car, etc)* guasto(a)
bronchitis la bronchite
bronze il bronzo
brooch la spilla
broom *(brush)* la scopa
brother il fratello
brother-in-law il cognato
brown marrone
bruise il livido
brush la spazzola
bubble bath il bagnoschiuma
bucket il secchiello
buffet car il vagone ristorante
to build costruire
building l'edificio *(m)*
bulb *(lightbulb)* la lampadina
bumbag il marsupio
bumper *(on car)* il paraurti
bunch *(of flowers)* il mazzo di fiori
  (of grapes) il grappolo d'uva
bungee jumping il bungee jumping
bureau de change l'agenzia di cambio *(f)*
burger l'hamburger *(m)*

burglar il/la ladro(a)
burglar alarm l'antifurto *(m)*
to burn bruciare
  (CD) masterizzare
bus l'autobus *(m)*
bus pass la tessera dell'autobus
bus station la stazione delle autolinee
bus stop la fermata (dell'autobus)
bus ticket il biglietto d'autobus
business gli affari
  on business per affari
business card il biglietto da visita
business centre il centro affari
business class la business class
businessman/woman l'uomo/la donna
  d'affari
business trip il viaggio d'affari
busy occupato(a) ; impegnato(a)
but ma ; però
butcher's il macellaio
butter il burro
button il bottone
to buy comprare
by *(next to)* accanto a
  by bus in autobus
  by car in macchina
  by train in treno
  by ship in battello
bypass *(road)* la circonvallazione

C

cab *(taxi)* il taxi
cabaret il cabaret
cabin *(on boat)* la cabina
cabin crew l'equipaggio di bordo *(m)*
cablecar la funivia
café il bar
  internet café il cyber-café
cafetière la caffettiera
cake *(big)* la torta
  (small) il pasticcino
cake shop la pasticceria
calculator la calcolatrice
calendar il calendario
call *(phone call)* la chiamata
to call chiamare
  (phone) chiamare per telefono
calm calmo(a)
camcorder la videocamera
camera la macchina fotografica
  digital camera la fotocamera digitale
camera case la custodia della macchina
  fotografica
camera phone il videofonino

to camp campeggiare
camping gas il gas da campeggio
camping stove il fornellino da campeggio
campsite il campeggio
can il barattolo ; la scatola
can *(to be able)* potere
  I can posso
  we can possiamo
  I cannot non posso
  we cannot non possiamo
  can I...? posso...?
  can we...? possiamo...?
Canada il Canada
Canadian canadese
canal il canale
to cancel cancellare ; annullare
cancellation la cancellazione
cancer il cancro
candle la candela
canoe la canoa
to canoe andare in canoa
can opener l'apriscatole *(m)*
cap *(hat)* il berretto
  (diaphragm) il diaframma
capital *(city)* la capitale
car la macchina ; l'auto *(m)*
car alarm l'antifurto *(m)*
car ferry il traghetto
car hire l'autonoleggio *(m)*
car insurance l'assicurazione della macchina *(f)*
car keys le chiavi della macchina
car park il parcheggio
car parts i pezzi di ricambio
car port il ricovero per auto
car radio l'autoradio *(f)*
car seat *(for children)* il seggiolino per bambini
carrots le carote
carwash l'autolavaggio *(m)*
carafe la caraffa
caravan la roulotte
carburettor il carburatore
card *(greetings)* il biglietto d'auguri
  (business) il biglietto da visita
  (playing cards) le carte da gioco
cardboard il cartone
cardigan il cardigan
careful attento(a)
  to be careful fare attenzione
carpet *(fitted)* la moquette
  (rug) il tappeto
carriage *(railway)* il vagone
carrots le carote

to carry portare
carton il cartone
case *(suitcase)* la valigia
cash i contanti
to cash *(cheque)* incassare
cash desk la cassa
cash machine il Bancomat®
cashier il/la cassiere(a)
cashpoint il Bancomat®
casino il casinò
casserole dish la casseruola
cassette la cassetta
cassette player il registratore
castle il castello
casualty department il pronto soccorso
cat il gatto
cat food il cibo per gatti
catacombs le catacombe
catalogue il catalogo
to catch *(train, etc)* prendere
cathedral il duomo
Catholic cattolico(a)
cauliflower il cavolfiore
cave la grotta
cavity *(in tooth)* la carie
CD il CD
  (blank) il CD vuoto
CD player il lettore CD
ceiling il soffitto
celery il sedano
cellar la cantina
cellphone il cellulare
cemetery il cimitero
cent *(euro)* il centesimo
centimetre il centimetro
central centrale
central heating il riscaldamento
central locking *(car)* la chiusura centralizzata
centre il centro
century il secolo
ceramics la ceramica
cereal *(for breakfast)* i cereali
certificate il certificato
chain la catena
chair la sedia
chairlift la seggiovia
chalet lo chalet
challenge la sfida
chambermaid la cameriera
Champagne lo Champagne
change il cambio
  (small coins) gli spiccioli
  (money returned) il resto

to change: to change money cambiare soldi
  to change clothes cambiarsi
  to change train cambiare treno
changing room lo spogliatoio
Channel (English) la Manica
chapel la cappella
charcoal il carbone
charge (fee) la tariffa
charge (for mobile, etc) la carica
  I've run out of charge mi si è scaricata la batteria
  to charge (mobile, etc) **(ri)caricare**
  I need to charge my phone devo ricaricare il telefonino
to charge addebitare
  charge it to my account lo metta sul mio conto
charge card carta di credito (del supermercato?)
charger (for battery) il caricabatterie
charter flight il volo charter
chatroom (internet) il chatroom
cheap economico(a)
  cheaper più economico(a)
cheap rate (phone) la tariffa economica
to check controllare
to check in (airport) fare il check-in
  (at hotel) firmare il registro
check-in il check-in
cheek la guancia
cheers! salute! ; cin-cin!
cheese il formaggio
chef il cuoco
chemist's la farmacia
cheque l'assegno (m)
cheque book il libretto degli assegni
cheque card la carta assegni
cherries le ciliegie
chess gli scacchi
chest (of body) il petto
chewing gum la gomma da masticare
chicken il pollo
chicken breast il petto di pollo
chickenpox la varicella
chilli il peperoncino
child il/la bambino(a)
children (small) i bambini
  (older children) i ragazzi
  for chidren per bambini
child safety seat (car) il seggiolino di sicurezza per bambini
chimney il camino
chin il mento
china la porcellana

chips (french fries) le patatine fritte
chiropodist il podologo
chocolate la cioccolata
chocolates i cioccolatini
choir il coro
choice la scelta
to choose scegliere
chop (meat) la costoletta
chopping board il tagliere
christening il battesimo
Christian name il nome di battesimo
Christmas il Natale
  Merry Christmas! Buon Natale!
Christmas card il biglietto d'auguri natalizi
Christmas Eve la vigilia di Natale
church la chiesa
cigar il sigaro
cigarette la sigaretta
cigarette lighter l'accendino
cigarette papers le cartine
cinema il cinema
circle (theatre) la galleria
circuit breaker il salvavita
circus il circo
cistern la cisterna
  (of toilet) il serbatoio dell'acqua
city la città
city centre il centro città
class: first class prima classe
  second class seconda classe
clean pulito(a)
to clean pulire
cleaner (person) l'addetto(a) alle pulizie
cleanser il detergente
clear chiaro(a)
client il/la cliente
cliff (on coast) la scogliera
  (mountain) la rupe
to climb scalare
climbing l'alpinismo (m)
climbing boots gli scarponi da montagna
Clingfilm® la pellicola per alimenti
clinic la clinica
cloakroom il guardaroba
clock l'orologio (m)
to close chiudere
closed (shop, etc) chiuso(a)
cloth il panno
clothes i vestiti
clothes peg la molletta
clothes shop il negozio d'abbigliamento
cloudy nuvoloso(a)

club il club
clutch (car) la frizione
coach il pullman
coach station la stazione dei pullman
coach trip la gita in pullman
coal il carbone
coast la costa
coastguard il guardacoste
coat il cappotto
coat hanger la gruccia
cockroach lo scarafaggio
cocktail il cocktail
cocktail bar il cocktail bar
cocoa il cacao
code il codice
coffee (espresso) il caffè
  black coffee il caffè americano
  white coffee il caffellatte
  instant coffee il caffè solubile
  cappuccino il cappuccino
  decaffeinated coffee il decaffeinato
coil (IUD) la spirale
coin la moneta
Coke® la Coca®
colander lo scolapasta
cold freddo(a)
  I'm cold ho freddo
  it's cold fa freddo
cold (illness) il raffreddore
  I have a cold ho il raffreddore
cold sore l'herpes (m)
Coliseum il Colosseo
collar il colletto
collar bone la clavicola
colleague il/la collega
to collect raccogliere
  (to collect someone) andare a prendere
  qualcuno
collection (of stamps) la collezione
  (of letters) la levata
  (of rubbish) la rimozione
colour il colore
colour-blind daltonico(a)
colour film (for camera) la pellicola
  a colori
comb il pettine
to come venire
  (to arrive) arrivare
to come back tornare
to come in entrare
  come in! avanti!
comedy la commedia
comfortable comodo(a)
company (firm) la ditta
compartment lo scompartimento

compass la bussola
to complain fare un reclamo
complaint il reclamo
complete completo(a)
to complete (finish) finire
  (form) riempire
compulsory obbligatorio(a)
computer il computer
computer disk il dischetto
computer game il videogioco
computer program il programma di
  computer
concert il concerto
concert hall la sala da concerti
concession la riduzione
concussion la commozione cerebrale
condensed milk il latte condensato
conditioner il balsamo
condoms i preservativi
conductor (on bus) il bigliettaio
cone il cono
conference il congresso
to confirm confermare
confirmation (of flight, etc) la conferma
confused confuso(a)
congratulations le congratulazioni
connection (train, etc) la coincidenza
constipated stitico(a)
consulate il consolato
to consult consultare
to contact mettersi in contatto con
contact lens cleaner il liquido per lenti
  a contatto
contact lenses le lenti a contatto
to continue continuare
contraceptive l'anticoncezionale
contract il contratto
convenient: is it convenient? va bene?
convulsions le convulsioni
to cook cucinare
cooked cotto(a)
cooker la cucina
cookies i biscotti
cool fresco(a)
cool-box (picnic) la borsa termica
copper il rame
copy la copia
to copy copiare
cordless phone il cordless
cork il tappo
corkscrew il cavatappi
corner l'angolo (m)
cornflakes i cornflakes
corridor il corridoio
cosmetics i cosmetici

to cost costare
  how much does it cost? quanto costa?
costume *(swimming)* il costume
  da bagno
cot il lettino
cottage il cottage
cotton il cotone
cotton bud il cotton fioc®
cotton wool il cotone idrofilo
couchette la cuccetta
cough la tosse
to cough tossire
cough mixture lo sciroppo per la tosse
cough sweets le pasticche per la tosse
counter *(in shop, etc)* il banco
country *(not town)* la campagna
  (nation) il paese
countryside la campagna
couple *(two people)* la coppia
  a couple of... un paio di...
courgettes gli zucchini
courier service il corriere
course *(of meal)* il piatto
  (of study) il corso
cousin il/la cugino(a)
cover charge il coperto
cow la mucca
crafts l'artigianato *(m)*
craft fair la fiera dell'artigianato
craftsperson l'artigiano(a)
cramps i crampi
crash *(car)* lo scontro
to crash *(car)* avere un incidente
crash helmet il casco
cream *(lotion)* la crema
  (dairy) la panna
  soured cream la panna acida
  whipped cream la panna montata
credit *(noun) (on mobile phone)* credito
credit card la carta di credito
crime il reato
crisps le patatine
croissant la brioche
to cross *(road)* attraversare
cross la croce
cross-country skiing lo sci di fondo
crossing *(sea, lake)* la traversata
crossroads l'incrocio *(m)*
crossword puzzle il cruciverba
crowd la folla
crowded affollato(a)
crown la corona
cruise la crociera
crutches le grucce
to cry *(weep)* piangere

crystal *(made of)* di cristallo
cucumber il cetriolo
cufflinks i gemelli
cul-de-sac il vicolo cieco
cup la tazza
cupboard l'armadio *(m)*
curlers i bigodini
currant l'uva sultanina
current la corrente
curtain la tenda
cushion il cuscino
custom *(tradition)* il costume
customer il/la cliente
customs *(duty)* la dogana
cut il taglio
to cut tagliare
cutlery le posate
to cycle andare in bicicletta
cycle track la pista ciclabile
cycling il ciclismo
cyst la cisti
cystitis la cistite

D

daily *(each day)* ogni giorno ;
  quotidiano(a)
dairy produce i latticini
dam la diga
damage il danno
damp umido(a)
dance il ballo
to dance ballare
danger il pericolo
dangerous pericoloso(a)
dark *(colour)* scuro(a)
  (night) buio(a)
  after dark a notte fatta
date la data
date of birth la data di nascita
daughter la figlia
daughter-in-law la nuora
dawn l'alba *(f)*
day il giorno
  per day al giorno
  every day ogni giorno
  (span of time) la giornata
dead morto(a)
deaf sordo(a)
dear caro(a)
debts i debiti
debit card la carta di addebito
decaffeinated decaffeinato(a)
  have you decaff coffee? ha del
  decaffeinato?

December dicembre
deckchair la sedia a sdraio
to declare dichiarare
  nothing to declare niente da dichiarare
deep profondo(a)
deep freeze il surgelatore
deer il cervo
to defrost scongelare
to de-ice sbrinare
delay il ritardo
  how long is the delay? di quant'è il ritardo?
delayed: to be delayed *(flight)* subire un ritardo
delicatessen il negozio di specialità gastronomiche
delicious delizioso(a)
demonstration la manifestazione
dental floss il filo interdentale
dentist il/la dentista
dentures la dentiera
deodorant il deodorante
to depart partire
department il reparto
department store il grande magazzino
departure la partenza
departure lounge la sala partenze
deposit il deposito
to describe descrivere
description la descrizione
desk la scrivania
  (information, etc) il banco
dessert il dolce
details i dettagli
detergent il detersivo
detour la deviazione
to develop *(photos)* sviluppare
diabetes il diabete
diabetic diabetico(a)
  I'm diabetic sono diabetico(a)
to dial fare il numero
dialect il dialetto
dialling code il prefisso telefonico
dialling tone il segnale di libero
diamond il diamante
diapers i pannolini
diaphragm il diaframma
diarrhoea la diarrea
diary l'agenda *(f)*
dice il dado
dictionary il dizionario ; il vocabolario
to die morire
diesel il gasolio

diet la dieta
  I'm on a diet sono a dieta
  special diet una dieta specifica
different diverso(a)
difficult difficile
digital camera la fotocamera digitale
to dilute diluire
dinghy *(rubber)* il canotto
dining room la sala da pranzo
dinner *(evening meal)* la cena
  to have dinner cenare
dinner jacket lo smoking
direct *(train, etc)* diretto(a)
directions le indicazioni
  to ask for directions chiedere la strada
directory *(telephone)* l'elenco telefonico *(m)*
directory enquiries il servizio informazioni
dirty sporco(a)
disability l'handicap *(m)*
disabled *(person)* disabile ; handicappato(a)
to disagree non essere d'accordo
to disappear scomparire
disaster il disastro
disco la discoteca
discount lo sconto
to discover scoprire
disease la malattia
dishtowel lo strofinaccio dei piatti
dishwasher la lavastoviglie
disinfectant il disinfettante
disk *(floppy disk)* il disco
to dislocate *(joint)* lussarsi
disposable *(camera)* usa e getta
distance la distanza
distilled water l'acqua distillata *(f)*
district *(of town)* il quartiere
to disturb disturbare
to dive tuffarsi
diversion la deviazione
diving i tuffi
divorced divorziato(a)
DIY shop il negozio di bricolage
dizzy: to be dizzy avere capogiri
to do fare
doctor il medico/la dottoressa
documents i documenti
dog il cane
dog food il cibo per cani
dog lead il guinzaglio
doll la bambola
dollars i dollari

domestic (flight) nazionale
donor card la tessera dell'A.I.D.O.
door la porta
doorbell il campanello
double doppio(a)
double bed il letto matrimoniale
double room la camera doppia
down: *to go down* scendere
Down's syndrome il sindrome di Down
  he/she has Down's syndrome è Down
downstairs giù ; dabbasso
drain lo scarico
draught (of air) la corrente (d'aria)
  there's a draught c'è corrente
draught lager la birra alla spina
drawer il cassetto
drawing il disegno
dress il vestito
to dress (oneself) vestirsi
dressing (for food) il condimento
  (for wound) la fasciatura
dressing gown la vestaglia
drill (tool) il trapano
drink (soft) la bibita
to drink bere
drinking water l'acqua potabile (f)
to drive guidare
driver (of car) l'autista (m/f)
driving licence la patente
drought la siccità
to drown affogare
drug (medicine) il farmaco
  (narcotics) la droga
drunk ubriaco(a)
dry secco(a) ; asciutto(a)
to dry asciugare
dry-cleaner's la tintoria ; il lavasecco
dummy (for baby) la tettarella
during durante
dust la polvere
duster lo straccio
dustpan and brush la paletta e lo
  scopino
duty-free esente da dogana
duvet il piumino
duvet cover il copripiumone
DVD il DVD
DVD player il lettore DVD
dye la tinta
dynamo la dinamo

E

each ogni
ear l'orecchio (m)

earache il mal d'orecchi
earlier più presto
early presto
to earn guadagnare
earphones le cuffie
earplugs i tappi per le orecchie
earrings gli orecchini
earth la terra
earthquake il terremoto
east l'est (m)
Easter la Pasqua
  Happy Easter! Buona Pasqua!
easy facile
to eat mangiare
ecological ecologico(a)
economy (class) la classe turistica
eco-tourism l'ecoturismo (m)
egg l'uovo (m)
  eggs le uova
  fried egg l'uovo fritto
  hard-boiled egg l'uovo sodo
  scrambled eggs le uova strapazzate
  soft-boiled egg l'uovo alla coque
either ... or o ... o
elastic band l'elastico (m)
Elastoplast il cerotto
elbow il gomito
electric elettrico(a)
electric blanket la coperta elettrica
electrician l'elettricista (m/f)
electricity l'elettricità (f)
electricity meter il contatore
  dell'elettricità
electric razor il rasoio elettrico
electric shock la scossa
electric toothbrush lo spazzolino da
  denti elettrico
electronic elettronico(a)
electronic organizer l'agenda
  elettronica (f)
elevator l'ascensore (m)
e-mail la posta elettronica ; l'e-mail (f)
  to e-mail s.o. mandare un'e-mail a
  qualcuno
e-mail address l'indirizzo di posta
  elettronica (m)
embassy l'ambasciata (f)
emergency l'emergenza (f)
emergency exit l'uscita d'emergenza (f)
emery board la limetta per le unghie
empty vuoto(a)
end la fine
engaged (to be married) fidanzato(a)
  (phone, toilet, etc) occupato(a)
engine il motore

England l'Inghilterra *(f)*
English inglese
  (language) l'inglese *(m)*
to enjoy divertirsi
  (to like) piacere
  I enjoyed the trip la gita mi è piaciuta
  I enjoy swimming mi piace nuotare
  enjoy your meal! buon appetito!
enough abbastanza
  that's enough basta così
enquiry desk il banco informazioni
to enter entrare
entertainment il divertimento
entrance l'entrata *(f)* ; l'ingresso *(m)*
entrance fee il biglietto d'ingresso
envelope la busta
epileptic epilettico(a)
epileptic fit la crisi epilettica
equal uguale ; pari
equipment l'attrezzatura *(f)*
eraser la gomma da cancellare
error l'errore *(m)*
eruption l'eruzione *(f)*
escalator la scala mobile
to escape fuggire
essential essenziale
estate agent's l'agenzia immobiliare *(f)*
euro l'euro *(m)*
euro cent il centesimo
Europe l'Europa *(f)*
European europeo(a)
European Union l'Unione Europea *(f)*
eve la vigilia
evening la sera
  this evening stasera
  tomorrow evening domani sera
  in the evening la sera
evening dress l'abito da sera *(m)*
evening meal la cena
every ogni ; ciascuno ; tutti
everyone tutti
everything tutto
everywhere dappertutto
examination l'esame *(m)*
example: for example per esempio
excellent ottimo(a)
except salvo
excess baggage il bagaglio in
  eccedenza
to exchange cambiare
exchange rate il cambio
exciting emozionante
excursion l'escursione *(f)*
to excuse scusare

excuse me! *(sorry)* mi scusi!
  (when passing) permesso!
exercise l'esercizio *(m)*
exhaust pipe il tubo di scappamento
exhibition la mostra
exit l'uscita *(f)*
expenses le spese
expensive costoso(a) ; caro(a)
expert l'esperto(a)
to expire *(ticket, etc)* scadere
to explain spiegare
explosion l'esplosione *(f)*
to export esportare
express *(train)* l'espresso *(m)*
express *(parcel, etc)* espresso(a)
extension *(phone)* l'interno *(m)*
  (electrical) la prolunga
extra *(spare)* in più
  (more) supplementare
  an extra bed un letto in più
eye l'occhio *(m)*
eyebrows le sopracciglia
eye drops il collirio
eyelashes le ciglia
eye shadow l'ombretto *(m)*

F

fabric la stoffa
face la faccia
face cloth il guanto di spugna
facial la pulizia del viso
facilities *(leisure facilities)* le attrezzature
factor *(sunblock)* fattore di protezione
factory la fabbrica
to fail fallire
to faint svenire
fainted svenuto(a)
fair *(just)* giusto(a)
  (blond) biondo(a)
fair *(trade)* la fiera
  (funfair) il luna park
fake falso(a)
fall *(autumn)* l'autunno *(m)*
to fall cadere
  he/she has fallen è caduto(a)
false teeth la dentiera
family la famiglia
famous famoso(a)
fan *(hand-held)* il ventaglio
  (electric) il ventilatore
  (football) il/la tifoso(a)
fan belt la cinghia della ventola
fancy dress il costume ; la maschera

far lontano(a)
  is it far? è lontano?
fare la tariffa
farm la fattoria
farmer l'agricoltore *(m)*
farmhouse la fattoria
fashionable alla moda
fast veloce
  too fast troppo veloce
to fasten *(seatbelt, etc)* allacciare
fat grasso(a)
  (noun) il grasso
  saturated fats i grassi saturi
  unsaturated fats i grassi insaturi
father il padre
father-in-law il suocero
fault *(defect)* il difetto
  it's not my fault non è colpa mia
favour il favore
favourite preferito(a)
fax il fax
  by fax per fax
to fax mandare un fax
February febbraio
to feed dare da mangiare
to feel sentire ; sentirsi
  I don't feel well non mi sento bene
  I feel sick ho la nausea
feet i piedi
felt-tip pen il pennarello
female femmina ; femminile
ferry il traghetto
festival la festa
to fetch *(bring)* portare
  (to go and get) andare a prendere
fever la febbre
few pochi
  a few alcuni
fiancé(e) il/la fidanzato(a)
field il campo
to fight combattere ; lottare
file *(folder)* il raccoglitore
  (computer) l'archivio *(m)*
to fill riempire
to fill in *(form)* compilare
fill it up! *(petrol)* il pieno!
fillet il filetto
filling *(dental)* l'otturazione *(f)*
film *(at cinema)* il film
  (for camera) la pellicola
Filofax® l'agenda *(f)*
filter il filtro
to find trovare

fine *(to be paid)* la multa
finger il dito
to finish finire
finished finito(a)
fire il fuoco ; l'incendio *(m)*
  fire! al fuoco!
fire alarm l'allarme antincendio *(m)*
fire brigade i vigili del fuoco
fire engine l'autopompa *(f)*
fire escape la scala antincendio
fire extinguisher l'estintore
fireplace il caminetto
fireworks i fuochi d'artificio
firm *(company)* l'azienda *(f)* ; la ditta
first primo(a)
first aid il pronto soccorso
first aid kit la cassetta di pronto
  soccorso
first class la prima classe
first name il nome di battesimo
fish il pesce
to fish pescare
fisherman il pescatore
fishing permit la licenza di pesca
fishing rod la canna da pesca
fishmonger's la pescheria
to fit *(clothes)* andare bene
  it doesn't fit non va bene
fit *(seizure)* l'attacco *(m)*
to fix riparare ; sistemare
  can you fix it? può ripararlo?
fizzy gassato(a)
flag la bandiera
flame la fiamma
flash *(for camera)* il flash
flashlight la pila
flask *(thermos)* il thermos
flat l'appartamento *(m)*
flat piatto(a)
  flat battery la batteria scarica
  flat tyre la gomma a terra
flavour il gusto
  what flavour? che gusto?
flaw il difetto
fleas le pulci
flesh la carne
flex il filo flessibile
flight il volo
flip flops gli infradito
flippers le pinne
floppy disk il floppy disk
flood l'alluvione *(f)*
  flash flood l'inondazione *(f)*

floor *(of building)* il piano
  (of room) il pavimento
  which floor? a che piano?
  on the ground floor al pianterreno
  on the first floor al primo piano
  on the second floor al secondo piano
floorcloth lo straccio per pavimenti
Florence Firenze
florist's shop il fioraio
flour la farina
flowers i fiori
flu l'influenza *(f)*
fly la mosca
to fly volare
flysheet *(tent)* la tenda da campo
fog la nebbia
foggy nebbioso(a)
foil *(silver paper)* la carta stagnola
to fold ripiegare
to follow seguire
food il cibo
food poisoning l'intossicazione
  alimentare *(f)*
foot il piede
  on foot a piedi
football il calcio ; il pallone
football match la partita di calcio
football pitch il campo di calcio
football player il calciatore
footpath il sentiero
for per
  for me/us per me/noi
  for him/her per lui/lei
  for you per te/lei/voi
forbidden proibito(a)
forehead la fronte
foreign straniero(a)
foreigner lo/la straniero(a)
forest la foresta
forever per sempre
to forget dimenticare
fork *(for eating)* la forchetta
  (in road) il bivio
form *(document)* il modulo
fortnight quindici giorni
forward avanti
foul *(football)* il fallo
fountain la fontana
four-wheel drive con quattro ruote
  motrici
fox la volpe
fracture la frattura
fragile fragile
fragrance la fragranza
frame *(picture)* la cornice
France la Francia

free *(not occupied)* libero(a)
  (costing nothing) gratis
free-range eggs le uova di polli
  ruspanti *(fpl)*
freezer il congelatore
French francese
  (language) il francese
French fries le patatine fritte
frequent frequente
fresh fresco(a)
fresh water l'acqua dolce *(f)*
Friday il venerdì
fridge il frigorifero
fried fritto(a)
friend l'amico(a)
friendly amichevole
frog la rana
from da
  from Scotland dalla Scozia
  from England dall'Inghilterra
front davanti
  in front of... di fronte a...
front door la porta d'ingresso
frost la brina
frozen *(food)* surgelato(a)
fruit la frutta
  dried fruit la frutta secca
fruit juice il succo di frutta
fruit salad la macedonia
to fry friggere
frying-pan la padella
fuel *(petrol)* la benzina
fuel gauge la spia della benzina
fuel pump la pompa
fuel tank il serbatoio della benzina
full pieno(a)
  (occupied) completo(a)
full board la pensione completa
fumes *(of car)* i gas di scarico
fun il divertimento
funeral il funerale
funfair il luna park
funny *(amusing)* divertente
fur il pelo
furnished ammobiliato(a)
furniture i mobili
fuse il fusibile
fuse box la scatola dei fusibili
future il futuro

G

gallery la galleria
game il gioco
  (meat) la selvaggina

garage (private) il garage
  (for repairs) l'autofficina (f)
  (for petrol) la stazione di servizio
garden il giardino
garlic l'aglio (m)
gas il gas
gas cooker la cucina a gas
gas cylinder la bombola del gas
gastritis la gastrite
gate il cancello
  (airport) l'uscita (f)
gay (person) gay
gear (car) la marcia
  first gear la prima
  second gear la seconda
  third gear la terza
  fourth gear la quarta
  neutral folle
  reverse la retromarcia
gearbox il cambio
gear cable il cavo del cambio
generous generoso(a)
gents' (toilet) la toilette (per uomini)
genuine (leather, silver) vero(a)
  (antique, etc) autentico(a)
German tedesco(a)
  (language) il tedesco
German measles la rosolia
Germany la Germania
to get (obtain) ottenere
  (to receive) ricevere
  (to fetch) prendere
to get in/on (vehicle) salire in/su
to get off (bus, etc) scendere da
gift il regalo
gift shop il negozio di souvenir
girl (young child) la bambina
  (teenage) la ragazza
girlfriend la ragazza
to give dare
to give back restituire
glacier il ghiacciaio
glass (substance) il vetro
  (for drinking) il bicchiere
  a glass of water un bicchiere d'acqua
  a glass of wine un bicchiere di vino
glasses (specs) gli occhiali
glasses case la custodia degli occhiali
gloves i guanti
glue la colla
gluten glutine
GM-free privo(a) di organismi
  geneticamente modificati (OGM)

to go andare
  I'm going to... vado a...
  we're going to... andiamo a...
to go back ritornare
to go in entrare in
to go out (leave) uscire
goat la capra
God Dio
goggles gli occhialini
  (for skiing) gli occhiali da sci
gold l'oro (m)
golf il golf
golf ball la pallina da golf
golf clubs le mazze da golf
golf course il campo di golf
good buono(a)
  (pleasant) bello(a)
  very good ottimo(a)
good afternoon buon giorno
  (after 5pm) buona sera
goodbye arrivederci
good day buon giorno
good evening buona sera
good morning buon giorno
good night buona notte
goose l'oca (f)
GPS (global positioning system) il Gps
gram il grammo
grandchild il/la nipote
granddaughter la nipotina
grandfather il nonno
grandmother la nonna
grandparents i nonni
grandson il nipotino
grapefruit il pampelmo
grapes l'uva (f)
grass l'erba (f)
grated grattugiato(a)
grater la grattugia
greasy grasso(a)
great (big) grande
  (wonderful) fantastico(a)
Great Britain la Gran Bretagna
green verde
green card (car insurance) la carta verde
greengrocer's il fruttivendolo
greetings card il biglietto d'auguri
grey grigio(a)
grill la griglia
to grill cuocere alla griglia
grilled alla griglia
grocer's il negozio di alimentari
ground la terra

ground floor il pianterreno
 on the ground floor a pianterreno
groundsheet il telone impermeabile
group il gruppo
guarantee la garanzia
guard *(on train)* il capotreno
guest *(house guest)* l'ospite *(m/f)*
 (in hotel) il/la cliente
guesthouse la pensione
guide *(tourist)* la guida
guidebook la guida
guided tour la visita guidata
guitar la chitarra
gun *(pistol)* la pistola
 (rifle) il fucile
gym *(place)* la palestra
gym shoes le scarpe da ginnastica
gynaecologist il/la ginecologo/a

H

haemorrhoids le emorroidi
hail la grandine
hair i capelli
hairbrush la spazzola per capelli
haircut il taglio di capelli
hairdresser il parrucchiere/la
 parrucchiera
hair dryer il fon
hair dye la tintura per capelli
hair gel il gel per capelli
hairgrip la molletta per capelli
hair mousse la spuma
hair spray la lacca per capelli
half la metà
 a half bottle of... una mezza bottiglia
 di...
 half an hour mezz'ora
half board mezza pensione
half fare il ridotto
half-price metà prezzo
ham *(cooked)* il prosciutto cotto
 (cured) il prosciutto crudo
hamburger l'hamburger *(m)*
hammer il martello
hand la mano
handbag la borsa
handicapped disabile ; handicappato(a)
handkerchief il fazzoletto
handle il manico
handlebars il manubrio
hand luggage il bagaglio a mano
hand-made fatto a mano
hands-free kit *(for phone)* il vivavoce
handsome bello(a)

hanger *(coat hanger)* la gruccia per abiti
hang gliding il volo con deltaplano
hangover i postumi della sbornia
to happen succedere
 what happened? cos'è successo?
happy felice
 happy birthday! buon compleanno!
harbour il porto
hard duro(a)
 (difficult) difficile
hardware shop il negozio di ferramenta
to harm nuocere
harvest il raccolto ; la vendemmia
hat il cappello
to have avere
 I have... ho...
 I don't have... non ho...
 we have... abbiamo...
 we don't have... non abbiamo...
 do you have...? ha/hai/avete...?
to have to dovere
hay fever il raffreddore da fieno
he egli ; lui
head la testa
headache il mal di testa
 I have a headache ho mal di testa
headlights i fari
headphones le cuffie
health la salute
health-food shop l'erboristeria *(f)*
healthy sano(a)
to hear sentire
hearing aid l'apparecchio acustico *(m)*
heart il cuore
heart attack l'infarto *(m)*
heartburn il bruciore di stomaco
to heat up *(food)* riscaldare
heater il termosifone
heating il riscaldamento
heavy pesante
heel il tallone
heel bar il banco del calzolaio
height l'altezza *(f)*
helicopter l'elicottero *(m)*
hello! salve! ; ciao!
 (on telephone) pronto
helmet il casco
help! aiuto!
to help aiutare
 can you help me? può aiutarmi?
hem l'orlo *(m)*
hepatitis l'epatite *(f)*
her il/la suo(a)
 her passport il suo passaporto
 her room la sua camera

herb l'erba aromatica *(f)*
herbal tea la tisana
here qui/qua
  here is... ecco...
  here is my passport ecco il mio
  passaporto
hernia l'ernia *(f)*
hi! ciao!
to hide nascondere
high alto(a)
  (speed) forte
high blood pressure la pressione alta
high chair il seggiolone
hill la collina
hill-walking il trekking
him lui ; lo ; gli
hip l'anca *(f)*
hip replacement la protesi dell'anca
hire il noleggio
  car hire il noleggio auto
  bike hire il noleggio bici
  boat hire il noleggio barche
  ski hire il noleggio sci
to hire noleggiare
hired car la macchina a noleggio
his il/la suo(a)
  his passport il suo passaporto
  his room la sua camera
historic storico(a)
history la storia
to hit colpire
to hitchhike fare l'autostop
hobby il passatempo
to hold tenere
  (to contain) contenere
hold-up *(traffic)* l'ingorgo *(m)*
hole il buco
holiday la festa
  on holiday in vacanza
holiday rep il/la rappresentante
  dell'agenzia di viaggio
home la casa
  at home a casa
homeopathic *(remedy etc)* omeopatico(a)
homeopathy l'omeopatia *(f)*
homesick: to be homesick avere
  nostalgia di casa
  I'm homesick ho nostalgia di casa
homosexual omosessuale
honest onesto(a)
honey il miele
honeymoon la luna di miele
hood *(on jacket)* il cappuccio
hook *(for fishing)* l'amo *(m)*

to hope sperare
  I hope so/not spero di sì/no
hors d'œuvre l'antipasto *(m)*
horse il cavallo
horse racing l'ippica *(f)*
to horse-ride andare a cavallo
hosepipe la canna dell'acqua
hospital l'ospedale *(m)*
hostel l'ostello *(m)*
hot caldo(a)
  I'm hot ho caldo
  it's hot *(weather)* fa caldo
hot-water bottle la borsa dell'acqua
  calda
hotel l'albergo *(m)* ; l'hotel *(m)*
hour l'ora *(f)*
  half an hour mezz'ora
  1 hour un'ora
  2 hours due ore
house la casa
housewife la casalinga
house wine il vino della casa
housework i lavori di casa
how? *(in what way)* come?
  how much? quanto(a)?
  how many? quanti(e)?
  how are you? come sta?
hungry: to be hungry avere fame
hunt la caccia
to hunt andare a caccia
hunting permit la licenza di caccia
hurry: I'm in a hurry ho fretta
to hurt fare male
  that hurts fa male
husband il marito
hut *(bathing/beach)* la cabina
  (mountain) la baita
hydrofoil l'aliscafo *(m)*
hypodermic needle l'ago ipodermico *(m)*

I

I io
ice il ghiaccio
  with ice con ghiaccio
  without ice senza ghiaccio
ice box il freezer
ice cream il gelato
iced coffee il caffè freddo
iced tea il tè freddo
ice lolly il ghiacciolo
ice rink la pista di pattinaggio su
  ghiaccio
to ice skate pattinare sul ghiaccio
ice skates i pattini da ghiaccio

idea l'idea *(f)*
identity card la carta d'identità
if se
ignition l'accensione *(f)*
ignition key la chiave dell'accensione
ill malato(a)
  I'm ill sto male
illness la malattia
immediately subito
immersion heater lo scaldabagno elettrico
immigration l'immigrazione *(f)*
immobilizer *(on car)* l'immobilizzatore *(m)*
immunisation l'immunizzazione *(f)*
to import importare
important importante
impossible impossibile
to improve migliorare
in in
  in 2 hours in due ore
  in London a Londra
in front of davanti a
included compreso(a) ; incluso(a)
inconvenient scomodo(a)
to increase aumentare
  to increase volume alzare il volume
indicator *(in car)* la freccia
indigestion l'indigestione *(f)*
indigestion tablets le compresse per digerire
indoors dentro ; al chiuso
infection l'infezione *(f)*
infectious contagioso(a)
informal *(clothes)* sportivo(a)
information le informazioni
ingredients gli ingredienti
inhaler l'inalatore *(m)*
injection l'iniezione *(f)* ; la puntura
to injure ferire
injured ferito(a)
injury la lesione
ink l'inchiostro *(m)*
inn la locanda
inner tube la camera d'aria
inquiries le informazioni
insect l'insetto *(m)*
insect bite la puntura d'insetto
insect repellent l'insettifugo
inside dentro
instant coffee il caffè solubile
instead of invece di
instructor l'istruttore/l'istruttrice
insulin l'insulina *(f)*
insurance l'assicurazione *(f)*

insurance certificate il certificato di assicurazione
to insure assicurare
insured: *to be insured* essere assicurato(a)
to intend to avere intenzione di
interesting interessante
international internazionale
internet l'internet *(m)*
internet access:
  do you have internet access? sei collegato a internet?
internet café il cyber-café
interpreter l'interprete *(m/f)*
interval l'intervallo *(m)*
interview l'intervista *(f)*
into in
  into town in città
  into the centre in centro
to introduce someone to presentare qualcuno a
invitation l'invito *(m)*
to invite invitare
invoice la fattura
iPod® l'iPod *(m)*
Ireland l'Irlanda *(f)*
Irish irlandese
iron *(for clothes)* il ferro da stiro
  (metal) il ferro
to iron stirare
ironing board l'asse da stiro
ironmonger's il negozio di ferramenta
is è
island l'isola *(f)*
it esse/essa ; lo/la
Italian italiano(a)
  (language) l'italiano *(m)*
Italy l'Italia *(f)*
to itch prudere
  my leg itches mi prude la gamba
  my eyes itch mi prudono gli occhi
item *(on bill)* la voce
itemised bill il conto dettagliato
IUD lo spirale ; l'IUD *(m)*

J

jack *(for car)* il cric
jacket la giacca
  waterproof jacket il giaccone impermeabile
jam *(food)* la marmellata
jammed bloccato(a)
January gennaio

jar (honey, jam, etc) il vaso
jaundice l'itterizia (f)
jaw la mascella
jealous geloso(a) ; invidioso(a)
jeans i blue jeans
jelly (dessert) la gelatina
jellyfish la medusa
jet ski l'acqua-scooter (m)
jetty il molo
jeweller's la gioielleria
jewellery i gioielli
Jewish ebreo(a)
job il lavoro
to jog fare jogging
to join (club) iscriversi a
to join in (game) partecipare a
joint (hip, etc) l'articolazione (f)
joke la barzelletta
    (practical) lo scherzo (m)
to joke scherzare
journalist il/la giornalista
journey il viaggio
judge il/la giudice (m/f)
jug la brocca
juice il succo
    a carton of juice un cartone di succo
    di frutta
    orange juice il succo d'arancia
July luglio
to jump saltare
jumper il maglione
jump leads (for car) i cavi per far partire
    la macchina
junction (road) l'incrocio (m)
June giugno
just: just two solamente due
    I've just arrived sono appena
    arrivato(a)

K

to keep (retain) tenere
    keep the change! tenga il resto
kennel il canile
kettle il bollitore
key la chiave
    card key il passe-partout
keyboard la tastiera
keycard la chiave elettronica
keyring il portachiavi
to kick dare calci a
kid (child) il bambino
kidneys (in body) i reni
to kill uccidere

kilo il chilo
    a kilo of apples un chilo di mele
    2 kilos due chili
kilogram il chilogrammo
kilometre il chilometro
kind (sort) il tipo
kind (person) gentile
king il re
kiosk l'edicola (f)
kiss il bacio
to kiss baciare
kitchen la cucina
kitchen paper la carta assorbente
    da cucina
kite l'aquilone (m)
kiwi fruit il kiwi
knee il ginocchio
knee highs i gambaletti
knickers le mutandine
knife il coltello
to knit lavorare a maglia
to knock (on door) bussare
to knock down (car) investire
to knock over (glass, vase) rovesciare
knot il nodo
to know (facts) sapere
    (to be acquainted with) conoscere
    I don't know non lo so
to know how to sapere
    to know how to swim saper nuotare
kosher kasher

L

label l'etichetta (f)
lace il pizzo
laces (shoe) i lacci
ladder la scala
ladies' (toilet) la toilette (per signore)
lady la signora
lager la birra (bionda)
lake il lago
lamb l'agnello (m)
lame zoppo(a)
lamp la lampada
lamppost il lampione
lampshade il paralume
land la terra
to land (plane) atterrare
landlady la padrona di casa
landlord il padrone di casa
landslide la frana
lane la stradina
    (of motorway) la corsia
language la lingua

language school la scuola di lingue
laptop il laptop
laptop bag la borsa per il computer portatile
large grande
last ultimo(a) ; scorso(a)
  the last bus l'ultimo autobus
  the last train l'ultimo treno
  last night ieri notte
  last week la settimana scorsa
  last year l'anno scorso
  last time l'ultima volta
late tardi
  the train's late il treno è in ritardo
  sorry we're late scusi il ritardo
later più tardi
to laugh ridere
launderette la lavanderia automatica
laundry il bucato
lavatory la toilette
lavender la lavanda
law la legge
lawn il prato inglese
lawyer *(m/f)* l'avvocato/l'avvocatessa
laxative il lassativo
layby la piazzola di sosta
lazy pigro(a)
lead *(electric)* il filo
lead *(metal)* il piombo
lead-free senza piombo
leaf la foglia
leak *(of gas, liquid)* la perdita
  (in roof) il buco
to leak: *it's leaking* perde
to learn imparare
learning disability:
  he/she has a learning disability ha difficoltà di apprendimento
lease *(rental)* l'affitto *(m)*
leather il cuoio ; la pelle
to leave *(leave behind)* lasciare
  (train, bus, etc) partire
  when does the bus leave? quando parte l'autobus?
  when does the train leave? quando parte il treno?
leeks i porri
left la sinistra
  on/to the left a sinistra
left-handed mancino(a)
left-luggage il deposito bagagli
left-luggage locker l'armadietto per depositare i bagagli *(m)*
leg la gamba
lemon il limone

lemonade la limonata
to lend prestare
length la lunghezza
lens *(camera)* l'obiettivo *(m)*
  (contact lens) la lente a contatto
lenses le lenti
lesbian lesbica
less meno
  less than meno di
lesson la lezione
to let *(allow)* permettere
  (to hire out) affittare
letter la lettera
letterbox la cassetta delle lettere
lettuce la lattuga
level crossing il passaggio a livello
library la biblioteca
licence il permesso
  (driving) la patente
lid il coperchio
to lie mentire
lie *(untruth)* la bugia
to lie down sdraiarsi
life belt il salvagente
lifeboat la scialuppa di salvataggio
lifeguard il bagnino
life insurance l'assicurazione sulla vita *(f)*
life jacket il giubbotto salvagente
life raft la zattera di salvataggio
lift *(elevator)* l'ascensore *(m)*
  (in car) il passaggio
light *(not heavy)* leggero(a)
  (colour) chiaro(a)
light la luce
  have you a light? ha da accendere?
light bulb la lampadina
lighter l'accendino *(m)*
lighthouse il faro
lightning il fulmine
like come
to like piacere
  I like coffee mi piace il caffè
  I don't like... non mi piace...
  I'd/we'd like... vorrei/ vorremmo...
lilo il materassino
lime *(fruit)* il lime
line *(row, queue)* la fila
  (telephone) la linea
linen il lino
lingerie la biancheria intima da donna
lip reading la labiolettura
lips le labbra
lip salve il burro di cacao
lipstick il rossetto
liqueur il liquore

list l'elenco (m) ; la lista
to listen (to) ascoltare
litre il litro
  a litre of milk un litro di latte
litter (rubbish) i rifiuti
little (small) piccolo(a)
  a little... un po' di...
to live vivere ; abitare
  I live in London vivo a Londra
  he lives in a flat abita in un
  appartamento
liver il fegato
living room il salotto
loaf of bread la pagnotta
local locale
to lock chiudere a chiave
lock la serratura
  the lock is broken la serratura è rotta
locker l'armadietto (m)
locksmith il fabbro
log book (for car) la carta di circolazione
  ; il libretto
log book (car) il libretto di circolazione
logs i ceppi
lollipop il lecca lecca
London Londra
  in/to London a Londra
long lungo(a)
  for a long time molto tempo
long-sighted presbite
to look after prendersi cura di
to look at guardare
to look for cercare
loose (not fastened) slegato(a)
  it's come loose (knot) si è allentato(a)
lorry il camion
to lose perdere
lost (object) perso(a)
  I've lost my... ho perso il/la...
  I'm lost mi sono smarrito(a)
  we're lost ci siamo smarriti(e)
lost property office l'ufficio oggetti
  smarriti (m)
lot: a lot molto
lottery la lotteria
loud forte
loudspeaker l'altoparlante (m)
lounge (in hotel) il salone
  (in house) la sala
  (in airport) la sala d'attesa
love l'amore (m)
to love (person) amare
  I love you ti amo
  I love swimming mi piace nuotare

lovely bellissimo(a)
low basso(a)
  (standard, quality) scadente
low-alcohol a basso contenuto alcolico
to lower volume abbassare il volume
low-fat magro(a)
luck la fortuna
lucky fortunato(a)
luggage i bagagli
luggage rack il portabagagli
luggage tag l'etichetta (f)
luggage trolley il carrello
lump (swelling) il gonfiore
lunch il pranzo
lunch break l'intervallo del pranzo (m)
lung il polmone
luxury di lusso

M

machine la macchina
mad (insane) matto(a)
  (angry) arrabbiato(a)
magazine la rivista
maggot il verme
magnet la calamita
magnifying glass la lente
  d'ingrandimento
maid (in hotel) la cameriera
maiden name il nome da ragazza
mail la posta
main principale
main course (meal) il secondo
main road la strada principale
to make (generally) fare
  (meal) preparare
make-up il trucco
male maschio ; maschile
mallet la mazza
man l'uomo (m)
to manage (be in charge of) dirigere
manager il direttore ; il gerente
mango il mango
manicure il manicure
manual (gear change) cambio manuale
many molti(e)
map (of country) la carta geografica
  (city) la piantina
marble il marmo
March marzo
margarine la margarina
marina il porticciolo
mark (stain) la macchia ; il segno
  (brand) la marca

market il mercato
  where is the market? dov'è il mercato?
  when is the market? quando c'è il mercato?
marmalade la marmellata d'arance
married sposato(a)
  I'm married sono sposato(a)
  are you married? è sposato(a)?
marry: to get married sposarsi
marsh la palude
mascara il mascara
mass *(in church)* la messa
massage il massaggio
mast l'albero della nave *(m)*
masterpiece il capolavoro
match *(game)* la partita
matches i fiammiferi
material il materiale
  (cloth) il tessuto
to matter importare
  it doesn't matter non importa
  what's the matter? cosa c'è?
mattress il materasso
May maggio
mayonnaise la maionese
mayor *(m/f)* il sindaco/la sindachessa
maximum il massimo
Mb *(megabyte)* il megabyte
  128 megabytes i 128 megabyte
me me ; mi
meal il pasto
to mean *(signify)* voler dire
  what does it mean? cosa vuol dire?
measles il morbillo
to measure misurare
meat la carne
mechanic il meccanico
medical insurance l'assicurazione medica *(f)*
medical treatment le cure mediche
medicine la medicina
Mediterranean il Mediterraneo
medium rare *(steak)* poco cotto(a)
to meet incontrare
  pleased to meet you! piacere!
meeting la riunione
  (by chance) l'incontro *(m)*
meeting point il meeting point
melon il melone
to melt sciogliere
member *(of club, etc)* il/la socio(a)
membership card la tessera
memory la memoria
  (memories) i ricordi

memory card *(for camera)* la memory card
memory stick *(for camera, etc)* la chiavetta di memoria
men gli uomini
to mend riparare
meningitis la meningite
menu il menù
  set menu il menù a prezzo fisso ; il menù turistico
  à la carte menu il menù alla carta
message il messaggio
metal il metallo
meter il contatore
metre il metro
metro *(underground)* la metropolitana
metro station la stazione del metrò
microwave oven il forno a microonde
microphone il microfono
midday il mezzogiorno
  at midday a mezzogiorno
middle il mezzo
middle-aged di mezz'età
midge il moscerino
midnight la mezzanotte
  at midnight a mezzanotte
migraine l'emicrania *(f)*
  I have a migraine ho l'emicrania
Milan Milano
mild dolce ; mite
milk il latte
  fresh milk il latte fresco
  hot milk il latte caldo
  long-life milk il latte a lunga conservazione
  powdered milk il latte in polvere
  whole milk il latte intero
  semi-skimmed milk il latte parzialmente scremato
  soya milk il latte di soia
  with/without milk con/senza latte
milkshake il frappé ; il frullato
millimetre il millimetro
mince *(meat)* la carne macinata
mind: do you mind? le dà fastidio?
  I don't mind non mi dà fastidio
mineral water l'acqua minerale *(f)*
minibar il minibar
minidisk il minidisk
minimum il minimo
minister *(church)* il sacerdote
  (political) il ministro
minor road la strada secondaria
mint *(herb)* la menta
mint tea il tè alla menta

minute il minuto
mirror lo specchio
to misbehave comportarsi male
miscarriage l'aborto spontaneo *(m)*
to miss *(train, etc)* perdere
Miss Signorina
missing *(thing)* smarrito(a)
  (person) scomparso(a)
mistake l'errore *(m)*
misty nebbioso(a)
misunderstanding il malinteso
to mix mescolare
mobile phone il cellulare
mobile mumber il numero di cellulare
modem il modem
modern moderno(a)
moisturizer l'idratante *(m)*
mole *(on skin)* il neo
moment: *just a moment* un momento
monastery il monastero
Monday il lunedì
money i soldi
  I have no money non ho soldi
money belt il marsupio
money order il vaglia
month il mese
  this month questo mese
  last month il mese scorso
  next month il mese prossimo
monthly mensilmente
monument il monumento
moon la luna
mooring l'ormeggio *(m)*
mop lo straccio da terra
moped il motorino
more (than) più (di)
  more than 3 più di tre
  more wine ancora un po' di vino
morning la mattina
  in the morning di mattina
  this morning stamattina
  tomorrow morning domani mattina
morning-after pill la pillola del giorno
  dopo
mosquito la zanzara
mosquito net la zanzariera
mosquito repellent lo zanzarifugo
most il/la più ; il massimo
moth *(clothes)* la tarma
mother la madre
mother-in-law la suocera
motor il motore
motorbike la moto
motorboat il motoscafo
motorway l'autostrada *(f)*

mould la muffa
mountain la montagna
mountain bike la mountain bike
mountain rescue il soccorso alpino
mountaineering l'alpinismo *(m)*
mouse il topo
  (computer) il mouse
moustache i baffi
mouth la bocca
mouthwash il colluttorio
move muoversi
  it isn't moving non si muove
movie il film
MP3 player il lettore di MP3
Mr Signor
Mrs Signora
Ms Signora
much molto
  too much troppo
muddy *(ground)* fangoso(a)
mugging lo scippo
mumps gli orecchioni
muscle il muscolo
museum il museo
mushrooms i funghi
music la musica
musical il musical
mussels le cozze
must *(to have to)* dovere
  I must devo
  we must dobbiamo
  I mustn't non devo
  we mustn't non dobbiamo
mustard la senape
my il/la mio(a)
  my passport il mio passaporto
  my room la mia camera

N

nail *(metal)* il chiodo
  (fingernail) l'unghia *(f)*
nailbrush lo spazzolino per le unghie
nail clipper il tagliaunghie
nail file la limetta per le unghie
nail polish/varnish lo smalto per le
  unghie
nail polish remover l'acetone *(m)*
nail scissors le forbicine
name il nome
  my name is... mi chiamo...
  what is your name? come si chiama?
nanny la bambinaia
napkin il tovagliolo
Naples Napoli

nappies i pannolini
narrow stretto(a)
national nazionale
national park il parco nazionale
nationality la nazionalità
natural naturale
nature la natura
nature reserve la riserva naturale
navy blue blu marino
near to vicino(a) a
  is it near? è vicino?
  near the bank vicino alla banca
necessary necessario(a)
neck il collo
necklace la collana
nectarine la nocepesca
to need avere bisogno di...
  I need... ho bisogno di...
  we need... abbiamo bisogno di...
needle l'ago *(m)*
  a needle and thread un ago e filo
negative *(photo)* il negativo
neighbour il/la vicino(a)
nephew il nipote
net la rete
  the Net l'Internet *(m)*
never mai
  I never drink wine non bevo mai il vino
new nuovo(a)
news le notizie
  (on television) il telegiornale
newsagent's il giornalaio
newspaper il giornale
newsstand l'edicola *(f)*
New Year il Capodanno
  happy New Year! buon Anno!
New Year's Eve la notte di San Silvestro ; l'ultimo dell'anno *(m)*
New Zealand la Nuova Zelanda
next prossimo(a)
  next to accanto(a) a
  next week la settimana prossima
  the next bus il prossimo autobus
  the next train il prossimo treno
  the next stop la prossima fermata
nice piacevole
  (person) simpatico(a)
niece la nipote
night la notte
  at night di notte
  last night ieri notte
  per night a notte
  tomorrow night domani sera
  tonight stasera

nightclub il nightclub
nightdress la camicia da notte
night porter il portiere notturno
no no
  no entry vietato l'ingresso
  no smoking vietato fumare
  no thanks no, grazie
  (without) senza
  no sugar senza zucchero
  no ice senza ghiaccio
  no problem non c'è problema
nobody nessuno
noise il rumore
noisy rumoroso(a)
  it's very noisy è molto rumoroso(a)
non-alcoholic analcolico(a)
none nessuno(a)
non-smoker non-fumatore
non-smoking per non-fumatori
north il nord
Northern Ireland l'Irlanda del Nord *(f)*
nose il naso
not non
  I do not know non lo so
note *(bank note)* la banconota
  (letter) il biglietto
note pad il bloc-notes
nothing niente
  nothing else nient'altro
notice l'avviso *(m)*
notice board la bacheca
novel il romanzo
November novembre
now adesso
nowhere da nessuna parte
nuclear nucleare
nudist beach la spiaggia nudista
number il numero
number plate *(car)* la targa
nurse l'infermiera/l'infermiere *(f/m)*
nursery *(children's)* l'asilo *(m)*
  (for plants) il vivaio
nursery slope la pista per principianti
nut *(to eat)* la noce
  (for bolt) il dado

O

oars i remi
oats l'avena *(f)*
to obtain ottenere
occupation *(work)* il lavoro
ocean l'oceano *(m)*
October ottobre
octopus il polpo

odd (strange) strano(a)
of di
  a bottle of wine una bottiglia di vino
  a glass of water un bicchiere d'acqua
  made of... fatto di...
off (machine, etc) spento(a)
  (milk, food) andato(a) a male
  this meat is off questa carne è andata
  a male
office l'ufficio (m)
often spesso
  how often? ogni quanto?
oil l'olio (m)
oil filter il filtro dell'olio
oil gauge l'indicatore del livello dell'olio
  (m)
ointment la pomata
OK! va bene!
old vecchio(a)
  how old are you? quanti anni ha?
  I'm ... years old ho ... anni
old age pensioner il/la pensionato(a)
olive oil l'olio d'oliva (m)
olives le olive
on (light, engine) acceso(a)
  (tap) aperto(a)
  on the table sulla tavola
  on time in orario
once una volta
  at once subito
one-way (street) a senso unico
onions le cipolle
only solo(a)
open aperto(a)
to open aprire
opera l'opera (f)
operation l'operazione (f)
operator (telephone) il/la centralinista
opposite di fronte a
  opposite the hotel di fronte
  all'albergo
  quite the opposite al contrario
optician's l'ottico (m)
or o
orange (colour) arancione
orange (fruit) l'arancia (f)
orange juice il succo d'arancia
orchestra l'orchestra (f)
order l'ordine (f)
  out of order fuori servizio
to order (food, etc) ordinare
oregano l'origano (m)
organic biologico(a)
to organize organizzare
ornament il soprammobile

other l'altro(a)
  the other one l'altro
  have you any others? ce ne sono
  altri?
our il/la nostro(a)
  our car la nostra macchina
  our hotel il nostro albergo
out (light) spento(a)
  he/she's out è fuori
  he's gone out è uscito
outdoor (pool, etc) all'aperto
outside: it's outside è fuori
oven il forno
ovenproof dish la pirofila
over (on top of) sopra
to overbook accettare troppe
  prenotazioni
to overcharge far pagare troppo
overdone (food) troppo cotto(a)
overdose l'overdose (f)
to overheat surriscaldare
to overload sovraccaricare
to oversleep non svegliarsi in tempo
to overtake sorpassare
to owe dover
  I owe you... le devo...
  you owe me... mi deve
owner il/la proprietario(a)
oxygen l'ossigeno (m)

P

pace il passo
pacemaker il pacemaker
to pack (suitcase) fare la valigia
package il pacco
package tour il viaggio organizzato
packet il pacchetto
padded envelope la busta imbottita
paddling pool la piscina per bambini
padlock il lucchetto
Padua Padova
page la pagina
paid pagato(a)
  I've paid ho pagato
pain il dolore
painful doloroso(a)
painkiller l'analgesico (m)
to paint (wall, etc) verniciare
  (picture) dipingere
painting (picture) il quadro
pair il paio
palace il palazzo
pale pallido(a)
palmtop il computer palmare

pan (saucepan) la pentola
(frying pan) la padella
pancake la crêpe
panties le mutandine
pants le mutande
panty liner il proteggislip
paper la carta
paper hankies i fazzolettini di carta
paper napkins i tovaglioli di carta
paragliding il parapendio
paralysed paralizzato(a)
paramedic il paramedico
parcel il pacco
pardon? scusi?
  I beg your pardon mi scusi
parents i genitori
park il parco
to park parcheggiare
parking disk il disco orario
parking meter il parchimetro
parking ticket (fine) la multa per sosta
vietata
parmesan il parmigiano
  grated parmesan il parmigiano
grattugiato
part la parte
partner (business) il/la socio(a)
(boy/girlfriend) il/la compagno(a)
party (celebration) la festa
(political) il partito
pass (mountain) il valico
(bus, train) la tessera
passenger il/la passeggero(a)
passport il passaporto
passport control il controllo passaporti
password la password ; la parola
d'ordine
pasta la pasta
pastry la pasta
(fancy cake) il pasticcino
path il sentiero
patient (in hospital) il/la paziente
pavement il marciapiede
to pay pagare
  I want to pay vorrei pagare
  where do I pay? dove pago?
payment il pagamento
payphone il telefono pubblico
PDA l'agenda elettronica (f)
peace la pace
peaches le pesche
peak rate la tariffa nelle ore di punta
peanut allergy l'allergia alle arachidi (f)
pearls le perle
pears le pere

peas i piselli
pedal il pedale
pedalo il pedalò
pedestrian il pedone
pedestrian crossing il passaggio
pedonale
to pee fare la pipì
to peel (fruit) sbucciare
peg (for clothes) la molletta
(for tent) il picchetto
pen la penna
pencil la matita
penfriend l'amico(a) di penna
penicillin la pennicillina
penis il pene
penknife il temperino
pension la pensione
pensioner il/la pensionato(a)
people la gente
pepper (spice) il pepe
(vegetable) il peperone
per per
  per day al giorno
  per hour all'ora
  per week alla settimana
  per person a persona
  100 km per hour 100 km all'ora
perfect perfetto(a)
performance la rappresentazione
perfume il profumo
perhaps forse
period (menstrual) le mestruazioni
perm la permanente
permit il permesso
person la persona
personal organizer l'agenda
elettronica (f)
personal stereo il walkman®
pet l'animale domestico (m)
pet food il cibo per gli animali
domestici
pet shop il negozio di animali domestici
petrol la benzina
  unleaded petrol la benzina senza
piombo
petrol cap il tappo del serbatoio
petrol tank il serbatoio della benzina
petrol pump la pompa della benzina
petrol station la stazione di servizio
PDA l'agenda elettronica (f)
pharmacy la farmacia
pharmacist il farmacista
phone il telefono
  by phone per telefono
to phone telefonare

phonebook l'elenco telefonico *(m)*
phonebox la cabina telefonica
phonecard la scheda telefonica
photocopier la fotocopiatrice
photocopy la fotocopia
  I need a photocopy mi serve una
  fotocopia
to photocopy fotocopiare
photograph la foto
  to take a photo fare una foto
phrase book il manuale di
  conversazione
piano il pianoforte
to pick *(fruit, flowers)* cogliere
  (to choose) scegliere
pickpocket il borseggiatore
pickle i sottaceti
picnic il picnic
  to have a picnic fare un picnic
picnic hamper il cestino per il picnic
picnic rug il plaid
picnic table il tavolo da picnic
picture *(painting)* il quadro
  (photo) la foto
pie *(sweet)* la torta
  (savoury) il pasticcio
piece il pezzo
pier il pontile
pig il maiale
pill la pillola
  to be on the pill prendere la pillola
pillow il guanciale ; il cuscino
pillowcase la federa
pilot il pilota
pin lo spillo
pink rosa
pipe *(water, etc)* il tubo
  (smoker's) la pipa
pitch *(place for tent/caravan)* il posto
  tenda/il posto per il caravan
pity: *what a pity!* che peccato!
pizza la pizza
place il luogo
place of birth il luogo di nascita
plain *(obvious)* chiaro(a)
  (unflavoured) naturale
plait la treccia
plan il piano
to plan progettare
plane l'aereo *(m)*
plant la pianta
plaster *(sticking)* il cerotto
  (for broken limb) l'ingessatura
plastic *(made of)* di plastica
plastic bag il sacchetto di plastica

plate il piatto
platform *(railway)* il binario
  from which platform? da quale
  binario?
play *(theatre)* la commedia
to play *(games)* giocare
play area l'area giochi *(f)*
playground il parco giochi
play park il parco giochi
playroom la stanza dei giochi
pleasant piacevole
please per favore ; prego
pleased: *pleased to meet you* piacere
plenty l'abbondanza *(f)*
pliers le pinze
plug *(electrical)* la spina
  (for sink) il tappo
to plug in attaccare
plum la prugna ; la susina
plumber l'idraulico *(m)*
plumbing l'impianto idraulico *(m)*
plunger lo sturalavandini
p.m. del pomeriggio
poached *(egg)* in camicia
  (fish) bollito(a)
pocket la tasca
point il punto
poison il veleno
poisonous velenoso(a)
police la polizia
policeman/woman il poliziotto/la donna
  poliziotto
police station il commissariato ;
  la questura
polish *(for shoes)* il lucido
  (for furniture) la cera
pollen il polline
polluted inquinato(a)
pony il pony
pony trekking le escursioni a cavallo
pool *(swimming)* la piscina
pool attendant il bagnino
poor povero(a)
pope il papa
pop socks i gambaletti
pork la carne di maiale
port *(seaport, wine)* il porto
porter il portiere
  (for luggage) il facchino
portion la porzione
Portugal il Portogallo
Portuguese portoghese
possible possibile
post: *by post* per posta
to post *(letters, etc)* imbucare

postbox la buca delle lettere
postcard la cartolina
postcode il codice postale
poster il poster
postman/woman il/la postino(a)
post office la posta ; l'ufficio postale *(m)*
to postpone rimandare
pot *(cooking)* la pentola
potato la patata
  baked potato la patata al forno
  boiled potatoes le patate lesse
  fried potatoes le patate fritte
  mashed potatoes il purè di patate
  roast potatoes le patate arrosto
potato masher lo schiacciapatate
potato peeler il pelapatate
potato salad l'insalata di patate *(f)*
pothole la buca
pottery la terracotta
pound *(money)* la sterlina
to pour versare
powder: *in powder form* in polvere
powdered milk il latte in polvere
power *(electricity)* l'elettricità
power cut l'interruzione di corrente *(f)*
pram la carrozzina
to pray pregare
to prefer preferire
pregnant incinta
  I'm pregnant sono incinta
to prepare preparare
to prescribe ordinare
prescription la ricetta
present *(gift)* il regalo
preservative il conservante
president il presidente
pressure: *tyre pressure* la pressione
  dei pneumatici
  blood pressure la pressione del
  sangue
pretty carino(a)
price il prezzo
price list il listino prezzi
priest il prete
print *(photo)* la foto
printer la stampante
printout la stampata
prison il carcere ; la prigione
private privato(a)
prize il premio
probably probabilmente
problem il problema
professor il professore/la professoressa
programme il programma
prohibited proibito(a)

promise la promessa
to promise promettere
to pronounce pronunciare
  how's it pronounced? come si
  pronuncia?
protein la proteina
Protestant protestante
to provide fornire
public pubblico(a)
public holiday la festa nazionale
pudding il dessert
to pull tirare
to pull over *(car)* accostare
pullover il pullover ; il maglione
pump la pompa
puncture la gomma a terra
puncture repair kit il kit per riparare le
  gomme
puppet il burattino
puppet show lo spettacolo di burattini
purple viola
purse il borsellino
to push spinger
pushchair il passeggino
to put *(to place)* mettere
to put back rimettere
pyjamas il pigiama

Q

quality la qualità
quantity la quantità
quarantine la quarantena
to quarrel litigare
quarter: *a quarter* un quarto
quay il molo
queen la regina
question la domanda
queue la coda
to queue fare la coda
quick veloce
quickly velocemente
quiet *(place)* tranquillo(a)
  a quiet room una stanza tranquilla
quilt la trapunta
quite *(rather)* piuttosto
  it's quite expensive è piuttosto caro(a)
  quite the opposite al contrario
quiz show il gioco a quiz

R

rabbit il coniglio
rabies la rabbia
race *(sport)* la gara

race course l'ippodromo *(m)*
racket *(tennis, etc)* la racchetta
radiator *(car)* il radiatore
  (heater) il termosifone
radio la radio
railcard la tessera di riduzione ferroviaria
railway station la stazione dei treni
rain la pioggia
to rain piovere
  it's raining piove
raincoat l'impermeabile *(m)*
rake il rastrello
rape lo stupro
raped violentata
  I've been raped sono stata violentata
rare *(unique)* raro(a)
  (steak) al sangue
rash *(skin)* l'orticaria *(f)*
raspberries i lamponi
rate *(cost)* la tariffa
rate of exchange il cambio
raw crudo(a)
razor il rasoio
razor blades le lamette
to read leggere
ready pronto(a)
  to get ready prepararsi
real vero(a)
to realize rendersi conto di
rearview mirror lo specchietto retrovisore
receipt la ricevuta
receiver *(phone)* il ricevitore
reception *(desk)* la reception
receptionist l'addetto(a)
to recharge ricaricare
recharger *(mobile)* il caricatelefono
  (battery) il caricabatterie
recipe la ricetta
to recognize riconoscere
to recommend raccomandare
to record *(programme)* registrare
to recover *(from illness)* rimettersi
to recycle riciclare
red rosso(a)
to reduce ridurre
reduction la riduzione
to refer to *(for information)* rivolgersi a
refill *(pen)* il ricambio
  (lighter) la bomboletta di gas
refund il rimborso
to refuse rifiutare
regarding riguardo a
region la regione

register il registro
to register *(letter)* assicurare
  (car) immatricolare
  (for class) iscriversi
registered letter la lettera raccomandata
registration form il modulo d'iscrizione
to reimburse rimborsare
relation *(family)* il/la parente
relationship il rapporto
to remain restare ; rimanere
to remember ricordare
  I don't remember non mi ricordo
remote control il telecomando
removal firm la ditta di traslochi
to remove togliere
rent l'affitto *(m)*
to rent *(house)* affittare
  (car) noleggiare
rental *(house)* l'affitto *(m)*
  (car) il nolo
repair la riparazione
to repair riparare
to repeat ripetere
to reply rispondere
report il resoconto
to report *(crime)* denunciare
request la richiesta
to request richiedere
to rescue salvare
reservation la prenotazione
to reserve prenotare
reserved prenotato(a)
resident residente
resort la località di vacanza
rest *(repose)* il riposo
  (remainder) il resto
to rest riposarsi
restaurant il ristorante
restaurant car il vagone ristorante
retired: *I'm retired* sono in pensione
to return *(go back)* ritornare
  (to give back) restituire
return ticket il biglietto di andata e ritorno
to reverse fare marcia indietro
to reverse the charges fare una telefonata a carico del destinatario
reverse charge call la chiamata a carico del destinatario
reverse gear la retromarcia
rheumatism il reumatismo
rib la costola
rice il riso
rich ricco(a)

ride *(in a car)* il giro in macchina
to ride a horse andare a cavallo
right *(correct)* giusto(a)
right la destra
  at/to the right a destra
  on the right sulla destra
right of way la precedenza
to ring *(bell)* suonare
  (phone) squillare
  it's ringing suona
ring l'anello *(m)*
ring road la circonvallazione
ripe maturo(a)
river il fiume
road la strada
road map la carta stradale
road sign il cartello stradale
roadworks i lavori stradali
roast arrosto(a)
roll *(bread)* il panino
rollerblades i rollerblades
romantic romantico(a)
roof il tetto
roof-rack il portabagagli
room *(hotel)* la camera
  (space) lo spazio
  double room la camera doppia
  family room la camera per famiglia
  single room la camera singola
room number il numero di camera
room service il servizio in camera
root la radice
rope la corda
rose la rosa
rosé wine il vino rosato
rotten *(food)* marcio(a)
rough *(sea)* mosso(a)
round rotondo(a)
roundabout la rotatoria
row *(in theatre, etc)* la fila
to row *(boat)* remare
rowing boat la barca a remi
rubber *(eraser)* la gomma per cancellare
  (material) la gomma
rubber band l'elastico *(m)*
rubber gloves i guanti di gomma
rubbish la spazzatura
rubella la rosolia
rucksack lo zaino
rug *(carpet)* il tappeto
ruins le rovine
ruler *(to measure)* il righello
to run correre

runner beans i fagiolini
rush hour l'ora di punta *(f)*
rusty arrugginito(a)

S
sad triste
saddle la sella
safe *(for valuables)* la cassaforte
safe *(medicine, etc)* senza pericolo ;
  sicuro(a)
  is it safe? è senza pericolo?
safety la sicurezza
safetybelt la cintura di sicurezza
safety pin la spilla di sicurezza
to sail andare in barca
sailboard la tavola da windsurf
sailing la vela
sailing boat la barca a vela
saint il/la santo(a)
salad l'insalata *(f)*
  green salad l'insalata verde
  mixed salad l'insalata mista
  potato salad l'insalata di patate
  tomato salad l'insalata di pomodori
salad dressing il condimento per
  l'insalata
salami il salame
salary lo stipendio
sales *(reductions)* i saldi
salesman/woman il/la commesso(a)
sales rep il/la rappresentante
salt il sale
salt water l'acqua salata *(f)*
salty salato(a)
same stesso(a)
sample il campione
sand la sabbia
sandals i sandali
sandwich il panino ; il tramezzino
  toasted sandwich il toast
sanitary towels gli assorbenti
Sardinia la Sardegna
satellite dish l'antenna parabolica *(f)*
satellite TV la televisione via satellite
satnav *(satellite navigation system, for car)* il
  navigatore satellitare
Saturday il sabato
sauce la salsa
  tomato sauce la salsa di pomodoro
saucepan la pentola
saucer il piattino
sauna la sauna

sausage la salsiccia
to save (life) salvare
  (money) risparmiare
savoury (not sweet) salato(a)
to say dire
scales (weighing) la bilancia
to scan scannerizzare
scan lo scan
scanner lo scanner
scarf la sciarpa
  (headscarf) il foulard
scenery il paesaggio
schedule il programma
  (timetable) l'orario (m)
school la scuola
  primary school la scuola elementare
  secondary school il liceo
scissors le forbici
score il punteggio
to score (goal) segnare
Scot lo/la scozzese
Scotland la Scozia
Scottish scozzese
scouring pad la paglietta
screen lo schermo
screen wash il liquido lavavetri
screw la vite
screwdriver il cacciavite
  phillips screwdriver il cacciavite a
  stella
scuba diving le immersioni subacquee
sculpture la scultura
sea il mare
seacat il catamarano
seafood i frutti di mare
seam (of dress) la cucitura
to search cercare
sea sickness il mal di mare
seaside: at the seaside al mare
season (of year) la stagione
  (holiday) il periodo delle vacanze
  in season di stagione
seasonal stagionale
seasoning il condimento
season ticket l'abbonamento
seat (chair) la sedia
  (theatre, plane, etc) il posto
seatbelt la cintura di sicurezza
seaweed le alghe
second (time) il secondo
second secondo(a)
second class la seconda classe
second-hand di seconda mano
secretary la segretaria

security check il controllo di sicurezza
security guard la guardia giurata
sedative il sedativo
to see vedere
to seize afferrare
self-catering con uso di cucina
self-employed autonomo(a)
self-service il self-service
to sell vendere
  do you sell...? vende...?
sell-by date la data di scadenza
Sellotape® lo Scotch®
to send mandare ; spedire ; inviare
senior citizen l'anziano(a)
sensible pratico(a)
separated separato(a)
separately: to pay separately pagare
  separatamente
September settembre
septic tank la fossa biologica
serious grave
  (not funny) serio(a)
to serve servire
service (in church) la funzione
  (in restaurant) il servizio
  is service included? il servizio è
  incluso?
service charge il servizio
service station la stazione di servizio
set menu il menù turistico/fisso
settee il divano
several alcuni(e)
to sew cucire
sewerage la fognatura
sex (gender) il sesso
  (intercourse) i rapporti sessuali
shade l'ombra (f)
  in the shade all'ombra
to shake (bottle) agitare
shallow basso(a)
shampoo lo shampoo
shampoo and set lo shampoo e messa
  in piega
to share dividere
sharp (razor, blade) affilato(a)
to shave farsi la barba
shaver il rasoio
shaving cream la crema da barba
shawl lo scialle
she ella ; lei
sheep la pecora
sheet (bed) il lenzuolo
shelf la mensola
shell (seashell) la conchiglia

shellfish i frutti di mare
sheltered riparato(a)
to shine brillare
shingles *(illness)* il fuoco di sant'Antonio
ship la nave
shirt la camicia
shock *(mental)* lo shock
  (electric) la scossa
shock absorber l'ammortizzatore *(m)*
shoe la scarpa
shoelaces i lacci delle scarpe
shoe polish il lucido per scarpe
shoe repairer il calzolaio
shoe shop il negozio di calzature
shop il negozio
to shop fare la spesa
  to shop online fare la spesa su internet
shop assistant il/la commesso(a)
shop window la vetrina
shopping: *to go shopping* fare compere ; fare la spesa
shopping centre il centro commerciale
shore la riva
short corto(a)
  (person) basso(a)
short circuit il corto circuito
short cut la scorciatoia
shortage la carenza
shorts i calzoncini corti
short-sighted miope
shoulder la spalla
to shout gridare
show *(theatre)* lo spettacolo
to show mostrare
shower la doccia
  (rain) il rovescio
  to take a shower fare la doccia
shower cap la cuffia da doccia
shower gel il bagnoschiuma
to shrink restringersi
shrub l'arbusto *(m)*
shut *(closed)* chiuso(a)
shutter l'imposta *(f)*
shuttle service la navetta
Sicily la Sicilia
sick *(ill)* malato(a)
  I feel sick mi sento male
  I feel sick (nauseous) ho la nausea
side il lato
side dish il contorno
sidelight la luce di posizione
sidewalk il marciapiede
sieve il setaccio

sightseeing tour il giro turistico
sign il segno
  (on road) il segnale
to sign firmare
signature la firma
signpost il segnale
silk la seta
silver l'argento *(m)*
SIM card la (carta) SIM
similar to simile a
since *(time)* da
to sing cantare
single *(unmarried)* non sposato(a)
  (not double) singolo(a)
  (ticket) di (sola) andata
single bed il letto a una piazza
single room la camera singola
sink il lavandino
sir Signore
sister la sorella
sister-in-law la cognata
to sit sedersi
  please, sit down prego, si accomodi
site *(website)* sito
size *(of clothes)* la taglia
  (of shoes) il numero
to skate *(on ice)* pattinare sul ghiaccio
skateboard lo skateboard
skates *(ice)* i pattini da ghiaccio
  (roller) i pattini a rotelle
to ski sciare
to skid slittare ; sbandare
skis gli sci
ski boots gli scarponi da sci
ski instructor il/la maestro(a) di sci
ski jump il trampolino
ski lift lo ski-lift
ski pass lo skipass
ski pole/stick la racchetta da sci
ski run la pista
ski suit la tuta da sci
skid *(noun)* la slittata ; la sbandata
skin la pelle
skirt la gonna
sky il cielo
sledge la slitta
to sleep dormire
to sleep in dormire fino a tardi
sleeper *(on train)* la cuccetta
sleeping bag il sacco a pelo
sleeping car il vagone letto
sleeping pill il sonnifero
slice *(piece of)* la fetta
sliced bread il pancarrè

slide *(photo)* la diapositiva
to slip scivolare
slippers le pantofole
slow lento(a)
to slow down rallentare
slowly lentamente
small piccolo(a)
 smaller (than) più piccolo (di)
smell l'odore *(m)*
 bad smell la puzza
 nice smell il profumo
to smell *(bad)* puzzare
 to smell of avere odore di
smile il sorriso
to smile sorridere
smoke il fumo
to smoke fumare
 I don't smoke non fumo
 can I smoke? posso fumare?
smoke alarm l'allarme antincendio *(m)*
smoked *(food)* affumicato(a)
smokers *(sign)* fumatori
smooth liscio(a)
SMS message il messaggio SMS
snack lo spuntino
 to have a snack fare uno spuntino
snake il serpente
 (grass) la biscia
snake bite il morso di vipera
to sneeze starnutire
snorkel il boccaglio
snow la neve
to snow: *it's snowing* nevica
snowboard lo snowboard
snowboarding: *to go snowboarding*
 andare a fare lo snowboard
snow chains le catene da neve
snow tyres i pneumatici da neve
snow plough lo spazzaneve
snowed up isolato(a) a causa della neve
soap il sapone
soap powder il detersivo in polvere
sober sobrio(a)
socket *(electric)* la presa
socks i calzini
soda water l'acqua di selz *(f)*
sofa il divano
sofa bed il divano letto
soft soffice ; morbido(a)
soft drink la bibita
software il software
soldier il soldato
sole *(of foot, shoe)* la suola

soluble solubile
some di (del/della)
 (a few) alcuni/alcune
someone qualcuno
something qualcosa
sometimes qualche volta
son il figlio
son-in-law il genero
song la canzone
soon presto
 as soon as possible il più presto
 possibile
sore throat il mal di gola
sorry: *I'm sorry!* mi scusi!
sort il tipo
 what sort? che tipo?
soup la minestra
sour aspro(a) ; agro(a)
soured cream la panna acida
south il sud
souvenir il souvenir
spa la stazione termale
space lo spazio
 (parking) il posteggio
spade il badile
Spain la Spagna
spam *(email)* messaggi indesiderati,
 email spazzatura *(but also spam)*
Spanish spagnolo(a)
spanner la chiave inglese
spare parts i pezzi di ricambio
spare room la stanza degli ospiti
spare tyre la gomma di scorta
spare wheel la ruota di scorta
sparkling frizzante
 sparkling water l'acqua gassata
 sparkling wine il vino frizzante
spark plugs le candele
to speak parlare
 do you speak English? parla inglese?
speaker l'altoparlante *(m)*
special speciale
specialist lo/la specialista
speciality la specialità
special needs:
 people with special needs le persone
 con esigenze particolari *(fpl)*
speech il discorso
speed la velocità
speedboat il motoscafo
speed limit il limite di velocità
 to exceed the speed limit superare il
 limite di velocità

145

speeding l'eccesso di velocità (m)
speeding ticket la multa per eccesso di velocità
speedometer il tachimetro
to spell scrivere
  how's it spelt? come si scrive?
to spend spendere
spice le spezie
spicy piccante
spider il ragno
to spill rovesciare
spinach gli spinaci
spin-dryer la centrifuga
spine la spina dorsale
spirits *(alcohol)* i liquori
splinter la scheggia
spoke *(of wheel)* il raggio
sponge la spugna
spoon il cucchiaio
sport lo sport
sports centre il centro sportivo
sports shop il negozio di articoli sportivi
spot *(stain)* la macchia
  (place) il posto
sprain la slogatura
spring *(season)* la primavera
  (metal) la molla
square *(in town)* la piazza
squash *(game)* lo squash
to squeeze spremere ; stringere
squid il calamaro
stadium lo stadio
staff il personale
stage *(theatre)* il palcoscenico
stain la macchia
stained glass il vetro colorato
stain remover lo smacchiatore
stairs le scale
stale *(bread)* raffermo(a)
stalls *(in theatre)* la platea
stamp il francobollo
to stand stare in piedi
star la stella
starfish la stella marina
start l'inizio (m)
to start cominciare
starter *(food)* l'antipasto (m)
  (in car) il motorino d'avviamento
station la stazione
stationer's la cartoleria
statue la statua
stay il soggiorno
  enjoy your stay! buona permanenza!

to stay *(remain)* rimanere
  I'm staying at the Grand Hotel sono al Grand Hotel
steak la bistecca
to steal rubare
steamed al vapore
to steam cuocere a vapore
steel l'acciaio (m)
steep: *is it steep?* è in salita?
steeple il campanile
steering wheel il volante
step *(stair)* il gradino
stepdaughter la figliastra
stepfather il patrigno
stepmother la matrigna
stepson il figliastro
stereo lo stereo
sterling la sterlina
steward lo steward
stewardess la hostess
to stick *(with glue)* incollare
  (door) incepparsi
sticking plaster il cerotto
still *(motionless)* fermo(a)
  (water) naturale
  (yet) ancora
sting la puntura
to sting pungere
stitches i punti
stock cubes i dadi
stockings le calze
stolen rubato(a)
stomach lo stomaco ; la pancia
stomachache il mal di stomaco
stone la pietra
to stop *(come to a halt)* fermarsi
  (stop doing something) smettere
stop sign lo stop
store *(shop)* il negozio
storey il piano
storm la tempesta ; il temporale
story il racconto
straightaway subito
straight on diritto
strange strano(a)
straw *(drinking)* la cannuccia
strawberries le fragole
stream il ruscello
street la strada
street map la piantina
strength *(of person)* la forza
  (of wine) la gradazione alcolica
stress lo stress
strike *(of workers)* lo sciopero
string lo spago

striped a strisce
stroke *(medical)* l'ictus *(m)*
  to have a stroke avere un ictus
strong forte
  strong coffee il caffè ristretto
  strong tea il tè forte
stuck bloccato(a)
student lo studente/la studentessa
student discount lo sconto per studenti
stuffed farcito(a) ; ripieno(a)
stung punto(a)
stupid stupido(a)
subscription l'abbonamento *(m)*
subtitles i sottotitoli
subway *(train)* la metropolitana
  (passage) il sottopassaggio
suddenly all'improvviso
suede la pelle scamosciata
sugar lo zucchero
sugar-free senza zucchero
to suggest proporre
suit *(man's)* l'abito *(m)*
  (woman's) il tailleur
suitcase la valigia
sum *(of money)* la somma
summer l'estate *(f)*
summer holidays le vacanze estive
summit il vertice
sun il sole
to sunbathe prendere il sole
sunblock la protezione solare totale
sunburn la scottatura solare
suncream la crema solare
Sunday la domenica
sunglasses gli occhiali da sole
sunny: *it's sunny* c'è il sole
sunrise l'alba *(f)*
sunroof *(car)* il tettuccio apribile
sunscreen la crema solare protettiva
sunset il tramonto
sunshade l'ombrellone *(m)*
sunstroke l'insolazione *(f)*
suntan l'abbronzatura *(f)*
suntan lotion la crema abbronzante
supermarket il supermercato
supper *(dinner)* la cena
supplement il supplemento
to supply fornire
sure sicuro(a) ; certo(a)
  I'm sure sono sicuro(a)
to surf fare il surf
  to surf the net navigare in internet
surfboard la tavola da surf
surgery *(surgical treatment)* la chirurgia

surname il cognome
  my surname is... di cognome mi chiamo...
surprise la sorpresa
suspension *(in car)* la sospensione
to survive sopravvivere
to swallow inghiottire
to swear *(bad language)* dire le parolacce
to sweat sudare
sweater il maglione
sweatshirt la felpa
sweet *(not savoury)* dolce
sweetener il dolcificante
sweets le caramelle
to swell gonfiare
to swim nuotare
swimming pool la piscina
swimsuit il costume da bagno
swing l'altalena *(f)*
Swiss svizzero(a)
switch l'interruttore *(m)*
to switch off spegnere
to switch on accendere
Switzerland la Svizzera
swollen gonfio(a)
synagogue la sinagoga
syringe la siringa

T

table la tavola
tablecloth la tovaglia
tablet *(pill)* la pastiglia
table tennis il ping pong
table wine il vino da tavola
tailor il sarto
to take *(carry)* portare
  (to grab, seize) prendere
  how long does it take? quanto tempo ci vuole?
takeaway *(food)* da asporto
to take off decollare
to take out *(of bag)* tirar fuori
talc il borotalco
to talk parlare
tall alto(a)
tampons gli assorbenti interni
tangerine il mandarino
tank la cisterna
  (car) il serbatoio
  (fish) l'acquario *(m)*
tap il rubinetto
tap water l'acqua del rubinetto *(f)*
tape il nastro
tape measure il metro a nastro

tape recorder il registratore
target lo scopo
tart la crostata
taste il sapore
to taste assaggiare ; provare
  can I taste some? ne posso
  assaggiare un po'?
tax la tassa ; l'imposta *(f)*
taxi il taxi
taxi driver il/la tassista
taxi rank il posteggio dei taxi
tea il tè
  herbal tea la tisana
  fruit tea il tè alla frutta
  lemon tea il tè al limone
  tea with milk il tè al latte
tea bag la bustina di tè
tea pot la teiera
to teach insegnare
teacher l'insegnante *(m/f)*
team la squadra
tear *(in material)* lo strappo
teaspoon il cucchiaino
teat *(on bottle)* la tettarella
tea towel lo strofinaccio per i piatti
teenager il/la teenager
teeth i denti
telegram il telegramma
telephone il telefono
to telephone telefonare
telephone box la cabina telefonica
telephone call la telefonata
telephone card la scheda telefonica
telephone directory l'elenco
  telefonico *(m)*
telephone number il numero di
  telefono
television la televisione
to tell dire
temperature la temperatura
  to have a temperature avere la
  febbre
temporary provvisorio(a)
tenant l'inquilino(a)
tendon il tendine
tennis il tennis
tennis ball la pallina da tennis
tennis court il campo da tennis
tennis racket la racchetta da tennis
tent la tenda
tent peg il picchetto
terminal *(airport)* il terminal
terrace la terrazza
terracotta la terracotta
to test *(try out)* provare

testicles i testicoli
tetanus jab l'antitetanica *(f)*
to text mandare un sms
  I'll text you ti manderé un sms
than di
to thank ringraziare
thank you grazie
  thanks very much molte grazie
that quel/quella/quello
  that one quello là
the *(sing)* il/lo/la
  (plural) i/gli/le
theatre il teatro
theft il furto
their il/la loro
them loro ; li ; le
there *(over there)* lì/là
there is/there are c'è/ci sono
thermometer il termometro
these questi/queste
  these ones questi qui
they loro ; essi/esse
thick spesso(a)
thief il/la ladro(a)
thigh la coscia
thin sottile
  (person) magro(a)
thing la cosa
  my things la mia roba
to think pensare
thirsty: to be thirsty avere sete
this questo/questa
  this one questo(a)
those quei/quelle/quegli
  those ones quelli(e)
thread il filo
throat la gola
throat lozenges le pastiglie per la gola
through attraverso
to throw away buttare via
thumb il pollice
thunder il tuono
thunderstorm il temporale
Thursday il giovedì
thyme il timo
ticket *(bus, train, etc)* il biglietto
  (entry fee) il biglietto d'ingresso
  a single ticket un biglietto di (sola)
  andata
  a return ticket un biglietto di andata
  e ritorno
  tourist ticket il biglietto turistico
  book of tickets il blocchetto di
  biglietti
ticket inspector il controllore

148

ticket office la biglietteria
tidy ordinato(a)
to tidy up fare ordine
tie la cravatta
tight stretto(a)
tights i collant ; la calzamaglia
tile *(floor)* la piastrella
till *(cash desk)* la cassa
till *(until)* fino a
  till 2 o'clock fino alle due
time il tempo
  (of day) l'ora *(f)*
  this time questa volta
  what time is it? che ore sono?
  do you have the time? ha l'ora?
timetable l'orario *(m)*
tin *(can)* la scatola di latta ; la lattina
tinfoil la carta stagnola
tin-opener l'apriscatole *(m)*
tip *(to waiter, etc)* la mancia
to tip *(waiter)* dare la mancia
tired stanco(a)
tissues i fazzoletti di carta
to a
  to London a Londra
  to the airport all'aeroporto
toadstool il fungo velenoso
toast *(to eat)* il pane tostato
  (raising glass) il brindisi
tobacco il tabacco
tobacconist's il tabaccaio
today oggi
toe il dito del piede
together insieme
toilet la toilette
  toilet for disabled la toilette per i disabili
toilet brush lo spazzolino del gabinetto
toilet paper la carta igienica
toiletries gli articoli per l'igiene
token *(phone, etc)* il gettone
toll *(motorway)* il pedaggio
tomato il pomodoro
  peeled tomatoes i pelati
  a tin of tomatoes la scatola di pelati
tomato juice il succo di pomodoro
tomato purée il concentrato di pomodoro
tomato sauce la salsa di pomodoro
tomorrow domani
  tomorrow morning domani mattina
  tomorrow afternoon domani pomeriggio
  tomorrow evening domani sera
tongue la lingua

tonic water l'acqua tonica *(f)*
tonight stasera
tonsilitis la tonsillite
too *(also)* anche
  too big troppo grande
  too small troppo piccolo(a)
  too hot troppo caldo(a)
  too noisy troppo rumoroso(a)
tool l'attrezzo *(m)*
toolkit gli attrezzi
tooth il dente
toothache il mal di denti
toothbrush lo spazzolino da denti
toothpaste il dentifricio
toothpick lo stuzzicadenti
top: *the top floor* l'ultimo piano *(m)*
top la cima
  (clothing) il top
  on top of sopra di
topless in topless
torch *(flashlight)* la pila
torn strappato(a)
total il totale
to touch toccare
tough *(meat)* duro(a)
tour il giro
  guided tour la visita guidata
tour guide la guida turistica
tour operator l'operatore turistico *(m)*
tourist il/la turista
tourist information le informazioni turistiche
tourist office l'ufficio turistico *(m)*
tourist route l'itinerario turistico *(m)*
tourist ticket il biglietto turistico
to tow trainare
towbar la barra di traino
tow rope il cavo di traino
towel l'asciugamano *(m)*
tower la torre
town la città
town centre il centro città
town hall il municipio
town plan la piantina
toxic tossico(a)
toy il giocattolo
toy shop il negozio di giocattoli
tracksuit la tuta sportiva
traditional tradizionale
traffic il traffico
traffic jam l'ingorgo *(m)*
traffic lights il semaforo
traffic warden il vigile
trailer il rimorchio

T

train il treno
  the next train il prossimo treno
  the first train il primo treno
  the last train l'ultimo treno
trainers le scarpe da ginnastica
tram il tram
tranquillizer il tranquillante
to transfer trasferire
to translate tradurre
translation la traduzione
to travel viaggiare
travel agent's l'agenzia di viaggi *(f)*
travel documents i documenti di
  viaggio
travel guide la guida
travel insurance l'assicurazione di
  viaggio *(f)*
travel sickness *(sea)* il mal di mare
  (air) il mal d'aria
  (car) il mal d'auto
traveller's cheques i traveller's (cheque)
tray il vassoio
tree l'albero *(m)*
trip la gita ; il viaggio
trolley il carrello
trouble i problemi
trousers i pantaloni
truck il camion
true vero(a)
trunk *(luggage)* il baule
trunks *(swimming)* i calzoncini da bagno
to try provare
to try on *(clothes, etc)* provare
t-shirt la maglietta
Tuesday il martedì
tumble dryer l'asciugatrice *(f)*
tunnel la galleria
Turin Torino
to turn *(handle, wheel)* girare
  to turn around girarsi
to turn off *(light, etc)* spegnere
  (tap) chiudere
to turn on *(light, etc)* accendere
  (tap) aprire
turquoise *(colour)* turchese
tweezers le pinzette
twice due volte ; il doppio
twin beds i letti gemelli
twins i gemelli
to type battere a macchina
typical tipico(a)
tyre la gomma ; il pneumatico
tyre pressure la pressione delle gomme

U

ugly brutto(a)
ulcer *(stomach)* l'ulcera *(f)*
  (mouth) l'afta *(f)*
umbrella l'ombrello *(m)*
  (sunshade) l'ombrellone *(m)*
uncle lo zio
uncomfortable scomodo(a)
unconscious svenuto(a)
under sotto
undercooked poco cotto(a)
underground *(metro)* la metropolitana
underpants le mutande
underpass il sottopassaggio
to understand capire
  I don't understand non capisco
  do you understand? capisce?
underwear la biancheria intima
to undress spogliarsi
unemployed disoccupato(a)
to unfasten slacciare
United Kingdom il Regno Unito
United States gli Stati Uniti
university l'università *(f)*
unleaded petrol la benzina senza
  piombo ; la benzina verde
unlikely improbabile
to unlock aprire
to unpack disfare la valigia
unpleasant sgradevole
to unplug staccare
to unscrew svitare
until fino a
unusual raro(a)
up: to get up alzarsi
upside down sottosopra
upstairs di sopra
urgent urgente
urine l'urina *(f)*
us ci ; noi
to use usare
useful utile
username il nome utente
usual solito(a)
usually di solito
U-turn l'inversione a U *(f)*

V

vacancy *(in hotel)* la camera libera
vacant libero(a)
vacation la vacanza
vaccination la vaccinazione
vacuum cleaner l'aspirapolvere *(m)*

vagina la vagina
valid valido(a)
valley la valle
valuable di valore
valuables gli oggetti di valore
value il valore
valve la valvola
van il furgone
vase il vaso
VAT l'IVA *(f)*
vegan vegetaliano(a)
 I'm vegan sono vegetaliano(a)
vegetables le verdure
vegetarian vegetariano(a)
 I'm vegetarian sono vegetariano(a)
vehicle il veicolo
vein la vena
Velcro® il velcro®
vending machine il distributore
 automatico
venereal disease la malattia venerea
Venice Venezia
ventilator il ventilatore
very molto
vest la canottiera
vet il/la veterinario(a)
via passando per
to video *(from TV)* registrare su
 videocassetta
 to make a video filmare
video il video
video camera la videocamera
video cassette/tape la videocassetta
video game il videogioco
video recorder il videoregistratore
view la vista
villa la villa
village il paese
vinegar l'aceto *(m)*
vineyard la vigna
viper la vipera
virus il virus
visa il visto
visit la visita
to visit visitare
visiting hours l'orario delle visite *(m)*
visitor il visitatore/la visitatrice
vitamin la vitamina
voice la voce
voicemail la casella vocale
volcano il vulcano
volleyball la pallavolo
voltage il voltaggio
to vomit vomitare
voucher il buono

W

wage il salario ; la paga
waist la vita
waistcoat il gilè
to wait (for) aspettare
waiter/waitress il cameriere/la
 cameriera
waiting room la sala d'aspetto
to wake up *(someone)* svegliare
 (oneself) svegliarsi
Wales il Galles
walk la passeggiata
to walk andare a piedi
walking boots gli scarponcini
walking stick il bastone
Walkman® il walkman®
wall il muro ; la parete
wallet il portafoglio
to want volere
 I want... voglio...
 we want... vogliamo...
war la guerra
ward *(hospital)* il reparto
wardrobe l'armadio *(m)*
warm caldo(a)
 it's warm fa caldo
to warm up *(milk, etc)* riscaldare
warning triangle il triangolo
 d'emergenza
to wash lavare
 (to wash oneself) lavarsi
wash and blow dry lo shampoo
 e messa in piega
washbasin il lavandino
washing machine la lavatrice
washing powder il detersivo in polvere
washing-up bowl la bacinella
washing-up liquid il detersivo per i
 piatti
wasp la vespa
wasp sting la puntura di vespa
waste bin il bidone della spazzatura
watch l'orologio *(m)*
to watch guardare
watchstrap il cinturino dell'orologio
water l'acqua *(f)*
 bottled water l'acqua in bottiglia *(f)*
 drinking water l'acqua potabile
 mineral water l'acqua minerale
 sparkling water l'acqua gassata
 still water l'acqua naturale
water heater lo scaldabagno
watermelon l'anguria *(f)*
waterproof impermeabile

to water-ski fare lo sci nautico
watersports gli sport acquatici
waterwings i braccioli salvagente
waves *(on sea)* le onde
waxing *(hair removal)* la ceretta
way in l'entrata *(f)* ; l'ingresso *(m)*
way out l'uscita *(f)*
we noi
weak *(person)* debole
 (tea, coffee, etc) leggero(a)
to wear portare
weather il tempo
weather forecast le previsioni del
 tempo
website il sito web
wedding il matrimonio
wedding anniversary l'anniversario di
 matrimonio *(m)*
wedding present il regalo di
 matrimonio
wedding ring la fede
Wednesday mercoledì
week la settimana
 last week la settimana scorsa
 next week la prossima settimana
 per week alla settimana
 this week questa settimana
 during the week durante la settimana
weekday il giorno feriale
weekend il fine settimana
 next weekend il prossimo fine
 settimana
 this weekend questo fine settimana
weekly settimanale
 weekly pass l'abbonamento
 settimanale *(m)*
to weigh pesare
weight il peso
welcome benvenuto
well bene
well *(for water)* il pozzo
well-done *(steak)* ben cotto(a)
wellington boots gli stivali di gomma
Welsh gallese
west ovest
wet bagnato(a)
wetsuit la muta
what cosa
 what is it? cos'è?
wheat il grano
wheel la ruota
wheelchair la sedia a rotelle
wheel clamp il ceppo bloccaruote
when quando

where dove
which qual/quale
while mentre
 in a while fra poco
whipped cream la panna montata
whisky l'whisky *(m)*
white bianco(a)
who chi
whole tutto
wholemeal bread il pane integrale
whose: *whose is it?* di chi è?
why perché
wide largo(a) ; ampio(a)
widow la vedova
widower il vedovo
width la larghezza
wife la moglie
wig la parrucca
to win vincere
wind il vento
windbreak *(camping)* il frangivento
windmill il mulino a vento
window la finestra
 (shop) la vetrina
 (car) il finestrino
windscreen il parabrezza
windscreen wiper il tergicristallo
to windsurf fare il windsurf
windy: *it's windy* c'è vento
wine il vino
 red wine il vino rosso
 white wine il vino bianco
 dry wine il vino secco
 sweet wine il vino dolce
 rosé wine il vino rosato
 sparkling wine il vino frizzante
 house wine il vino della casa
wine list la lista dei vini
wing *(of bird)* l'ala *(f)*
 (of car) la fiancata
wing mirror lo specchietto laterale
winter l'inverno *(m)*
wire il filo
wireless internet il collegamento a
 internet senza fili
with con
 with ice con ghiaccio
 with milk con latte
 with sugar con zucchero
without senza
 without ice senza ghiaccio
 without milk senza latte
 without sugar senza zucchero
witness il/la testimone

woman la donna
wonderful meraviglioso(a)
wood *(material)* il legno
   (forest) il bosco
wooden di legno
wool la lana
word la parola
work il lavoro
to work *(person)* lavorare
   (machine, car, etc) funzionare
   it doesn't work non funziona
work permit il premesso di lavoro
world il mondo
worried preoccupato(a)
worse peggio
worth *(value)* il valore
   it's worth £5 vale cinque sterline
to wrap up *(parcel)* incartare
wrapping paper la carta da regalo
wrinkles le rughe
wrist il polso
to write scrivere
   please write it down lo scriva per
   favore
writing paper la carta da lettere
wrong sbagliato(a)
   what's wrong? cosa c'è?
wrought iron il ferro battuto

X
x-ray la radiografia
to x-ray radiografare

Y
yacht lo yacht
year l'anno *(m)*
   this year quest'anno
   next year l'anno prossimo
   last year l'anno scorso
yearly *(every year)* annualmente
yellow giallo(a)
Yellow Pages le pagine gialle®
yes sì
yesterday ieri
yet: *not yet* non ancora
yoghurt lo yogurt
   plain yoghurt lo yogurt naturale
yolk il tuorlo
you tu ; voi ; lei
young giovane
your il/la suo(a) ; il/la tuo(a) ; il/la
   vostro(a)

Z
zebra crossing le strisce pedonali
zero lo zero
zip la cerniera
zone la zona
zoo lo zoo

A

a at ; in
abbaglianti *mpl* full-beam headlights
abbiamo... we have...
   non abbiamo... we don't have...
abbigliamento *m* clothes
abbonamento *m* subscription ; season ticket
abbronzatura *f* suntan
abito *m* dress ; man's suit
aborto *m* abortion
   aborto spontaneo miscarriage
abuso *m* misuse
a.C. B.C.
accamparsi to camp
accanto (a) beside ; next (to)
acceleratore *m* accelerator
accendere to turn on ; to light
   accendere i fari switch on your headlights
accendino *m* cigarette lighter
accensione *f* ignition
accento *m* accent *(pronunciation)*
acceso(a) on *(light, engine)*
accesso *m* access
   divieto di accesso no access
accettazione *f* reception
   accettazione bagagli check-in
accomodarsi to make oneself comfortable
   si accomodi do take a seat
accompagnare to accompany
accordo *m* agreement
aceto *m* vinegar
acetone *m* nail polish remover
ACI *m* Automobile Association
acqua *f* water
   acqua calda hot water
   acqua corrente running water
   acqua distillata distilled water
   acqua gassata sparkling water
   acqua minerale mineral water
   acqua naturale still water
   acqua potabile drinking water
acquisto *m* purchase
addetto(a) person in charge
adesso now
adulto(a) adult
aereo *m* plane ; aircraft
aeroplano *m* airplane
aeroporto *m* airport
affari *mpl* business
   per affari on business

affittare to rent ; to let
   affittasi for rent
affitto *m* lease ; rent
affogare to drown
agenda *f* diary
agenzia *f* agency
   agenzia di viaggi travel agent
   agenzia immobiliare estate agent
aggredire to attack
aglio *m* garlic
ago *m* needle
   ago ipodermico hypodermic needle
agosto *m* August
AIDS *m* AIDS
aiutare to help
aiuto! help!
alba *f* dawn
albergo *m* hotel
albero *m* tree ; mast
albicocca *f* apricot
alcolici *mpl* alcoholic drinks
alcolico(a) alcoholic
alcool *m* alcohol
alcuni(e) some ; a few
alcuno(a) any ; some
alimentari *mpl* groceries
allacciare to fasten *(seatbelt, etc)*
allarme *m* alarm
   allarme antincendio fire alarm
allergia *f* allergy
allergico(a) a allergic to
alloggio *m* accommodation
alluvione *f* flood
Alpi *fpl* Alps
alpinismo *m* climbing
alt stop
altezza *f* height
alto(a) high ; tall
   alta stagione high season
   alta marea high tide
altoparlante *m* loudspeaker
altro(a) other
   altri passaporti other passports
alzarsi to get up ; to stand up
amabile sweet *(wine)*
amare to love *(person)*
amarena *f* sour black cherry
amaro(a) bitter *(taste)*
ambasciata *f* embassy
ambiente *m* environment
ambulanza *f* ambulance
ambulatorio *m* surgery ; out-patients
America *f* America

americano(a) American
amico(a) *m/f* friend
ammalato(a) ill
amministratore delegato *m* managing director
ammontare *m* total amount
ammortizzatore *m* shock absorber
amo *m* hook
amore *m* love
analisi del sangue *f* blood test
analcolico *m* soft drink
analcolico(a) non-alcoholic
analgesico *m* painkiller
ananas *m* pineapple
anatra *f* duck
anca *f* hip
anche too ; also ; even
ancora still ; yet ; again
  ancora un po'? a little more?
  non ancora not yet
ancora *f* anchor
andare to go
  andare a cavallo to ride a horse
  andare a piedi to go on foot
  andare bene to fit *(clothes)*
  andare in macchina to go by car
andata: *andata e ritorno* return *(ticket)*
  di (sola) andata single *(ticket)*
andiamo! let's go!
  andiamo a... we're going to...
anestetico *m* anaesthetic
angina pectoris *f* angina
anguria *f* watermelon
anice *m* aniseed
animale *m* animal
  animale domestico pet
annata *f* vintage ; year
  vino d'annata vintage wine
anniversario *m* anniversary
anno *m* year
  buon anno! happy New Year!
annuale annual
annullamento *m* cancellation
annullare to cancel
annuncio *m* announcement ; advert
antibiotico *m* antibiotic
anticipo *m* advance *(loan)*
  in anticipo in advance ; early
anticoncezionale *m* contraceptive
antifurto *m* burglar alarm
antigelo *m* antifreeze ; de-icer
antipasto *m* starter ; hors d'œuvre
antisettico *m* antiseptic

antistaminico *m* antihistamine
anziano(a) *m/f* senior citizen
ape *f* bee
aperitivo *m* apéritif
aperto(a) open
  all'aperto open-air
appartamento *m* flat ; apartment
appendicite *f* appendicitis
appuntamento *m* appointment ; date
apribottiglie *m* bottle opener
aprile *m* April
aprire to open ; to turn on *(tap)*
apriscatole *m* tin-opener
arachide *f* peanut
arancia *f* orange
aranciata *f* orangeade
arancione orange *(colour)*
area *f* area
  area di servizio service area
argento *m* silver
aria condizionata *f* air-conditioning
armadio *m* cupboard ; wardrobe
arrabbiato(a) angry
arredato(a) furnished
arrestare to arrest
arrivare to arrive
arrivederci goodbye
arrivo *m* arrival
  arrivi nazionali domestic arrivals
  arrivi internazionali international arrivals
arrosto *m* roast
arte *f* art ; craft
articolo *m* article
  articoli da dichiarare goods to declare
  articoli da regalo gifts
artigiano(a) *m/f* craftsperson
artista *m/f* artist
artrite *f* arthritis
ascensore *m* lift ; elevator
ascesso *m* abscess
asciugamano *m* towel
asciugare to dry
asciugatrice *f* tumble dryer
ASL local health centre
ascoltare to listen (to)
asma *f* asthma
asparagi *m* asparagus
aspettare to wait (for) ; to expect
aspirapolvere *m* vacuum cleaner
aspirina *f* aspirin
assaggiare to taste

asse m axle (car)
  asse da stiro ironing board
assegno m cheque
assicurato(a) insured
assicurazione f insurance
assistente m/f assistant
assistenza f assistance ; aid
associazione f association
assorbenti mpl sanitary towels
  assorbenti interni tampons
ATM public transport service of Milan
attaccare to attach ; to attack ; to fasten
attacco m fit (seizure)
  attacco cardiaco heart attack
attendere to wait for
attento(a) careful
attenzione f caution
  fare attenzione to be careful
atterraggio m landing (of plane)
atterrare to land (plane)
attestare to declare
attore m actor
attracco m mooring ; berth
attraente attractive
attraversare to cross
attraverso through
attrazione f attraction
attrezzatura f equipment
attrezzo m tool
attrice f actress
auguri! best wishes!
aumentare to increase
Australia f Australia
australiano(a) Australian
austriaco(a) Austrian
autentico(a) genuine
autista m/f driver
auto f car
autobus m bus
autofficina f garage (for repairs)
autoforniture fpl car parts and accessories
autonoleggio m car hire
autore m author
autorimessa f garage
autorizzazione f authorization
autostop m hitchhiking
autostrada f motorway
autunno m autumn
avanti in front ; forward(s)
  avanti! come in!
avere to have

avere bisogno di to need
avere fame to be hungry
avere sete to be thirsty
avvertire to warn
avvisare to inform ; to warn
avviso m notice ; advertisement
azienda f business ; firm
  azienda di soggiorno local tourist board
  Azienda Sanitaria Locale local health centre
azzardo m risk ; hazard
azzurro(a) light blue

B

babbo m daddy
  Babbo Natale Father Christmas
baciare to kiss
bacinella f washing-up bowl
bacio m kiss
baci! love and kisses (in letter)
baffi mpl moustache
bagagli mpl luggage
bagagliaio m boot (of car)
bagaglio m luggage
  bagaglio a mano hand luggage
bagnarsi to bathe ; to get wet
bagnino m lifeguard
bagno m bath ; bathroom
balcone m balcony
ballare to dance
balletto m ballet
ballo m dance
balneazione f bathing
  divieto di balneazione no swimming
balsamo m hair conditioner
bambino(a) m/f child ; baby
bambini mpl children
  per bambini for children
bambola f doll
banana f banana
banca f bank
bancarella f stall ; stand
banchina f platform ; quay
banco m counter ; desk
  banco informazioni enquiry desk
Bancomat® m cash machine ; ATM
banconota f banknote
banda larga f broadband
bandiera f flag
bar m bar ; café
barattolo m tin ; jar

barba *f* beard
barbiere *m* barber
barca *f* boat
barista *m/f* barman/barmaid
basso(a) low ; short
  bassa marea low tide
basta that's enough
battello *m* boat
batteria *f* battery *(car)*
  batteria scarica flat battery
  batteria ricaricabile rechargeable
baule *m* trunk *(luggage)*
bavaglino *m* bib
bello(a) beautiful ; fine ; lovely
benda *f* bandage
bene well ; all right ; OK
benvenuto welcome
benzina *f* petrol
  fare benzina to get petrol
bere to drink
bevanda *f* drink
biancheria *f* linen *(for beds, table)*
  biancheria intima underwear
bianco(a) white ; blank
  lasciate in bianco leave blank
biberon *m* baby's bottle
bibita *f* soft drink
  bibite soft drinks
bicchiere *m* glass *(for drinking)*
bici *f* bike *(pushbike)*
bicicletta *f* bicycle
bidet *m* bidet
bidone *m* bin ; dustbin ; can
biglietteria *f* ticket office
biglietto *m* ticket ; note ; card
  biglietto d'auguri greetings card
  biglietto da visita business card
bin. *(abbreviation of)* **binario**
binario *m* platform
biologico(a) organic
biondo(a) blond *(person)*
biro *f* biro
birra *f* beer
  birra alla spina draught beer
  birra bionda lager
  birra chiara lager
birreria *f* bar ; pub
biscotto *m* biscuit
bisogno *m* need
  avere bisogno di to need
bistecca *f* steak
bloccare to block
  bloccare un assegno to stop a cheque

blocchetto di biglietti *m* book of tickets
blocco *m* block ; notepad
blu blue
blue jeans *mpl* jeans
boa *f* buoy
bocca *f* mouth
boccaglio *m* snorkel
bocce *fpl* bowls *(game)*
bolletta *f* bill
bollire to boil
bollitore *m* kettle
bomba *f* bomb
bombola del gas *f* gas cylinder
bombolone *m* doughnut
borotalco *m* talc
borsa *f* bag ; handbag ; briefcase
  borsa termica cool-box *(for picnic)*
borseggiatore *m* pickpocket
borsellino *m* purse ; wallet
borsetta di plastica *f* plastic bag
bosco *m* wood ; forest
bottega *f* shop
botteghino *m* box office
bottiglia *f* bottle
bottone *m* button
boxer *mpl* boxer shorts
braccialetto *m* bracelet
braccio *m* arm
braccioli *mpl* armbands *(swimming)*
braciola *f* steak ; chop
brindisi *m* toast *(raising glass)*
brioche *f* croissant
britannico(a) *f* British
bronchite *f* bronchitis
bruciare to burn
  masterizzare to burn *(CD)*
bruciore di stomaco *m* heartburn
brutto(a) bad *(weather, news)* ; ugly
buca delle lettere *f* postbox
bucato *m* washing ; laundry
  bucato in lavatrice machine wash
  bucato a mano hand washing
buco *m* hole ; leak
buono(a) good
  buon appetito! enjoy your meal!
  buon compleanno! happy birthday!
  buon giorno good morning/afternoon
  buona notte good night
  buona sera good afternoon/evening
  a buon mercato cheap
buono *m* voucher ; coupon ; token
burattino *m* puppet
burrasca *f* storm

burro m butter
burro di cacao m lip salve
bussare to knock (on door)
busta f envelope
bustina di tè f tea bag
buttare via to throw away

C

cabina f beach hut ; cabin
  cabina telefonica phonebox
cacciavite m screwdriver
cadere to fall
caffè m coffee (espresso)
  caffè corretto espresso with spirit
  such as grappa
  caffè macchiato espresso with a little
  warm milk
  caffè solubile instant coffee
  caffellatte milky coffee
caffettiera f espresso-maker
calamita f magnet
calciatore m football player
calcio m football ; kick
calcolatrice f calculator
caldo(a) hot
calendario m calendar
calle f street (in Venice dialect)
callo m corn (on foot)
calmante m sedative
calmo(a) calm
calpestare to tread on
calvo(a) bald
calza f stocking ; sock
calzamaglia f tights
calzature fpl shoeshop
calze fpl stockings
calzini mpl socks
calzolaio m shoe mender
calzoleria f shoe mender's
calzoncini corti mpl shorts
  calzoncini da bagno swimming trunks
cambiamento m change
cambiare to change
  cambiare autobus/treno to change
  bus/train
  cambiare soldi to change money
  cambiarsi to change one's clothes
cambio m exchange ; gear
camera f room (in house, hotel)
  camera da letto bedroom
  camera doppia double room
  camera libera vacancy (in hotel)

  camera per famiglia family room
  camera singola single room
  camere vacancies
cameriera f chambermaid
cameriere m waiter
camiceria f shirt shop
camicetta f blouse
camicia f shirt
  camicia da notte nightdress
camion m lorry
camminare to walk
camoscio m chamois
campagna f countryside ; campaign
campanello m bell
campeggiare to camp
campeggio m camping ; campsite
  campeggio libero free campsite
camping gas m gas da campeggio
campione m sample ; champion
campo m field ; court
  campo da tennis tennis court
  campo di calcio football pitch
  campo di golf golf course
  campo sportivo sports ground
camposanto m cemetery
Canada m Canada
canadese Canadian
canale m canal ; channel
cancellare to erase ; to cancel
cancellazione f cancellation
cancro m cancer
candeggina f bleach
candela f candle ; spark plug
candida f thrush (candida)
cane m dog
canile m kennel
canna da pesca f fishing rod
cannuccia f straw (for drinking)
canoa f canoe
canottaggio m rowing
canottiera f vest
canotto m dinghy (rubber)
cantante m/f singer
cantare to sing
cantiere m building site
cantina f cellar ; wine cellar
canzone f song
capelli mpl hair
capire to understand
  capisce? do you understand?
  non capisco I don't understand
capitale f capital (city)
capitolo m chapter

capo m head ; leader ; boss
Capodanno m New Year's day
capogruppo m group leader
capolavoro m masterpiece
capolinea m terminus
capoluogo m county town
capotreno m guard (on train)
cappella f chapel
cappello m hat
cappotto m overcoat
cappuccino m cappuccino
capra f goat
carabiniere m policeman
caraffa f carafe
caramelle fpl sweets
carbone m coal ; charcoal
carburante m fuel
carburatore m carburettor
carcere m prison
caricare to charge (battery)
  devo ricaricare il telefonino I need to charge my phone
carico m load ; shipment ; cargo
carino(a) pretty ; lovely ; nice
carne f meat
carnevale m carnival
caro(a) dear ; expensive
carote fpl carrots
carrello m trolley
carriera f career
carro m cart
  carro attrezzi breakdown van
carrozza f carriage
  carrozze cuccette couchettes
  carrozza letto sleeper
carrozzeria f bodywork
carrozzina f pram
carta f paper ; card ; map
  carta assegni cheque card
  alla carta à la carte
  carta d'argento senior citizen's rail card
  carta di credito credit card
  carta di circolazione log book
  carta famiglia family rail card
  carta d'identità identity card
  carta igienica toilet paper
  carta d'imbarco boarding card
  carta stradale road map
  carta verde green card
carte da gioco fpl playing cards
cartella f briefcase ; folder
cartello m sign ; signpost

cartine fpl cigarette papers
cartoccio m paper bag
cartoleria f stationer's
cartolina f postcard
casa f house ; home
  a casa at home
casalinga f housewife
casalinghi mpl household articles
cascata f waterfall
casco m helmet
casella postale f post-office box
casella vocale f voicemail
casinò m casino
caso: in caso di in case of
cassa f till ; cash desk
  cassa chiusa position closed
cassaforte f safe (for valuables)
cassetta f cassette
  cassetta delle lettere letterbox
cassetto m drawer
cassiere(a) m/f cashier ; teller
castello m castle
catena f chain ; mountain range
  catene (da neve) snow chains
cattedrale f cathedral
cattivo(a) bad ; nasty ; naughty
cattolico(a) Catholic
causa f cause ; case (lawsuit)
  a causa di because of
cavalcare to ride (horse)
cavallo m horse
cavatappi m corkscrew
cavo m cable
  cavo da rimorchio tow rope
  cavo del cambio gear cable
  cavo del freno brake cable
cavolfiore m cauliflower
CD m CD
  CD vuoto blank CD
c'è there is
cedro m cedar ; lime (fruit)
CE f EC
celibe m single man (not married)
cellulare m mobile phone
cena f dinner (evening meal)
cenare to have dinner
cenone m New Year's Eve dinner
centesimo m cent (euro)
centimetro m centimetre
cento hundred
centrale central
centralino m switchboard

centro m centre
  centro affari business centre
  centro città city centre
  centro commerciale shopping centre
  centro storico old town
ceppo bloccaruote m wheel clamp
cera f wax (for furniture)
ceramica f ceramics ; pottery
cercare to look for
ceretta f waxing (hair removal)
cerini mpl matches
cerniera f zip
cerotto m sticking plaster
certificato m certificate
  certificato di nascita birth certificate
cervello m brain
cestino m basket ; waste paper bin
cetriolo m cucumber
chatroom m chatroom (internet)
che what ; who ; which
  che gusto? what flavour?
  che ore sono? what time is it?
cherosene m paraffin
chi? who?
  di chi è? whose is it?
chiamare to call
  chiamare per telefono to phone
chiamarsi to be called (name)
  come si chiama? what's your name?
chiamata f call (telephone)
chiave f key
  chiave elettronica keycard
  chiave inglese spanner
chiavetta di memoria f memory stick
  (for camera, etc)
chiedere to ask ; to ask for
chiesa f church
chilo m kilo
chilogrammo m kilogram
chilometraggio m mileage (in km)
chilometro m kilometre
chiodo m nail (metal)
chirurgia f surgery (operations)
chitarra f guitar
chiudere to close ; to turn off (tap)
  chiudere a chiave to lock
chiuso(a) closed
  chiuso per turno closed for weekly
  day off
  chiuso per ferie closed for holidays
chiusura centralizzata f central
  locking (car)
ciabatta f slipper ; type of bread

ciao! hi! ; bye!
cibo m food
cielo m sky
ciliegia f cherry
cinghia della ventola f fan belt
cintura f belt
  cintura di sicurezza seatbelt
cinturino dell'orologio m watchstrap
cioccolato m chocolate
cipolla f onion
circo m circus
circolare to move (traffic)
circolazione f traffic
circonvallazione f ring road
cisterna f cistern ; tank
cisti f cyst
cistite f cystitis
citofono m intercom
città f city ; town
cittadinanza f citizenship
cittadino(a) citizen
classe f class
clavicola f collar bone
cliente m/f customer
climatizzato(a) air-conditioned
clinica f clinic
cocco m coconut
cocomero m watermelon
coda f tail ; queue
codice m code
  codice a barra barcode
  codice postale postcode
  codice stradale highway code
cofano m bonnet (car)
cognata f sister-in-law
cognato m brother-in-law
cognome m surname
  di cognome mi chiamo...
  my surname is...
coincidenza f connection (train, etc) ;
  coincidence
colazione f breakfast ; lunch
collana f necklace
collant mpl tights
collega m/f colleague
collegamento a internet senza fili m
  wireless internet
colletto m collar
collina f hill
collo m neck ; package
colluttorio m mouthwash
colomba f dove ; Easter cake
colore m colour

Colosseo m Coliseum
colpa f fault
  non è colpa mia it's not my fault
coltello m knife
combustibile m fuel
come like ; as ; how
  come? how? *(in what way)*
  come si chiama? what's your name?
  come si pronuncia? how is it pronounced?
  come si scrive? how is it spelt?
  come sta? how are you?
  come va? how's it going?
cominciare to begin
commesso(a) m/f assistant ; clerk
commissariato m police station
commozione cerebrale f concussion
comodo(a) comfortable
compagnia f company
  compagnia aerea airline
compilare to fill in *(form)*
compleanno m birthday
completo(a) no vacancies ; full
completo m outfit
comporre to dial *(number)*
comprare to buy
compreso(a) included
compressa f tablet
computer m computer
  computer palmare palmtop
  computer portatile laptop
comune m town hall ; commune
con with
  con bagno with bathroom
  con filtro filter-tipped
  con ghiaccio with ice
concerto m concert
conchiglia f seashell
condimento m seasoning ; dressing *(for food)*
conducente m/f driver *(taxi, bus)*
confermare to confirm
confine m boundary ; border
congelatore m freezer
congratulazioni! congratulations!
congresso m conference
cono m cone
  cono gelato ice-cream cone
conoscere to know *(to be acquainted with)*
consegna f consignment ; delivery
conservante m preservative
consigliare to advise
consiglio m advice
consumare to use up
  da consumarsi entro best before

consumazione f drink
contanti mpl cash
  pagare in contanti to pay cash
contatore m electricity meter
contento(a) happy
continuare to continue
conto m account ; bill
  conto corrente current account
  conto dettagliato itemised bill
  conto in banca bank account
contorno m vegetable side dish
contrabbando m smuggling
contratto m contract
contravvenzione f fine
contro against ; versus
controllare to check
controllo m check ; control
  controllo passaporti passport control
controllore m ticket collector
convalida f date stamp
convalidare to validate *(ticket)*
convincere to persuade
coperta f blanket
coperto m place setting ; cover charge
copertura f cover *(insurance)*
coppa gelato f ice cream served in goblet/tub
coppia f couple *(two people)*
copriletto m bedspread
coraggioso(a) brave
corda f rope
cordless m cordless phone
cornetto m ice cream cone
corpo m body
corrente f current *(electric, water)*
  corrente d'aria draught
correre to run
corridoio m corridor
corriere m courier
corsa f race ; journey
  corsa semplice single fare
corsia f lane ; hospital ward ; route
  corsia di emergenza hard shoulder
  corsia di sorpasso outside lane
corso m course ; avenue
  corso dei cambi exchange rates
  corso intensivo crash course
cortile m courtyard
corto(a) short
cos'è? what is it?
  cos'è successo? what happened?
cosa f thing
  cosa? what?
coscia f thigh

così so ; thus *(in this way)*
cosmetici *mpl* cosmetics
costa *f* coast
  Costa Azzurra French Riviera
costare to cost
costoletta *f* chop
costoso(a) expensive
costruire to build
costume *m* custom ; costume
  costume da bagno swimsuit
cotone *m* cotton
  cotone idrofilo cotton wool
cotto(a) cooked
  poco cotto(a) medium rare *(steak)*
cotton fioc® *m* cotton bud
crampi *mpl* cramps
cravatta *f* tie
credere to believe
credito *m* credit
  carta di credito credit card
  non si fa credito no credit given
crema *f* cream ; custard
  crema da barba shaving cream
  crema solare suncream
crescere to grow
crespella *f* fried pastry twist
cric *m* jack *(for car)*
crisi epilettica *f* epileptic fit
cristallo *m* crystal
  di cristallo made of crystal
croccante *f* crisp
croce *f* cross
crocevia *m* crossroads
crociera *f* cruise
crollo *m* collapse
cronaca *f* news
cruciverba *m* crossword puzzle
crudo(a) raw
cuccetta *f* couchette ; sleeper
cucchiaino *m* teaspoon
cucchiaio *m* spoon ; tablespoon
cucina *f* cooker ; kitchen ; cooking
  cucina a gas gas cooker
cucinare to cook
cucire to sew
cuffia *f* bathing cap
cuffie *fpl* earphones
cugino(a) *m/f* cousin
culla *f* cradle
cuocere to cook
  cuocere a vapore to steam
  cuocere alla griglia to grill
cuoco *m* chef

cuoio *m* leather
cuore *m* heart
cupola *f* dome
curva *f* bend ; corner
cuscino *m* cushion
custode *m* caretaker
custodia *f* case ; holder
cyber-café *m* internet cafe

D

da from ; by ; worth
  da asporto take-away
  dall'Inghilterra from England
  dalla Scozia from Scotland
  da vedere worth seeing
  da 100 euro worth 100 euros
dadi *m* stock cubes
danneggiare to spoil ; to damage
danno *m* damage
dappertutto everywhere
dare to give
  dare su to overlook ; to give onto
  dare la precedenza give way
  dare da mangiare to feed
  dare la mancia to tip *(waiter, etc)*
data *f* date
  data di nascita date of birth
  data di scadenza sell-by date
dati *mpl* data
dattero *m* date *(fruit)*
davanti a in front of ; opposite
dazio *m* customs duty
d.C. A.D.
debito *m* debt
decaffeinato(a) decaffeinated
decollare to take-off
decollo *m* takeoff
delizioso(a) delicious
dente *m* tooth
dentiera *f* dentures
dentifricio *m* toothpaste
dentro in ; indoors ; inside
deodorante *m* deodorant
  deodorante per ambienti air
  freshener
deposito bagagli *m* left-luggage
descrivere to describe
descrizione *f* description
desiderare to want ; to desire
destinazione *f* destination
destra *f* right
detergente *m* cleanser

detersivo m detergent
  detersivo in polvere soap powder
  detersivo per i piatti washing-up liquid
detrazione f deduction
dettagli mpl details
deviazione f detour ; diversion
di of ; some
  di cristallo/plastica made of crystal/plastic
  di Giovanni Giovanni's
  di lusso luxury (hotel, etc)
  di mattina in the morning
  di pomeriggio in the afternoon
  di moda fashionable
  di notte at night
  di stagione in season
  di valore of value ; valuable
diabete m diabetes
diabetico(a) diabetic
diaframma m cap (diaphragm)
dialetto m dialect
diamante m diamond
diapositiva f slide (photo)
diarrea f diarrhoea
dicembre m December
dichiarare to declare
dichiarazione f declaration
dieta f diet
  essere a dieta to be on a diet
dietro behind ; after
  dietro di behind
difetto m fault
difficile difficult
diga f dam ; dyke
digerire to digest
digestivo m after-dinner liqueur
dimenticare to forget
Dio m God
dipinto(a) painted
diramazione f fork (in road)
dire to say ; to tell
diretto(a) direct
  treno diretto through train
  in diretta live (TV programme, etc)
direttore m manager ; director
direzione f management ; direction
dirigere to manage (be in charge of)
diritto(a) straight
  sempre diritto straight on
disabile disabled (person)
disastro m disaster
dischetto m floppy disk ; diskette

disco m disk ; record
  disco orario parking disk
discoteca f disco
disdire to cancel
disegno m drawing
disfare la valigia to unpack
disinfettante m disinfectant
disoccupato(a) unemployed
dispiacere: mi dispiace I'm sorry
disponibile available
distaccare to detach ; to unplug
distante far ; distant
distanza f distance
distorsione f sprain
distributore m dispenser
  distributore di benzina petrol station
disturbare to disturb
disturbo m trouble
dito m finger
  dito del piede toe
ditta f firm ; company
diurno(a) day(time)
divano m sofa ; divan
  divano letto sofa bed
diversi(e) several ; various
diverso(a) different
divertente funny (amusing)
divertimento m entertainment ; fun
divertirsi to enjoy oneself
dividere to share
divieto forbidden ; not allowed
  divieto di sorpasso no overtaking
  divieto di sosta no parking
divisa f uniform
divorziato(a) divorced
dizionario m dictionary
DOC (abbreviation of) **denominazione di origine controllata** (guarantee of wine quality)
doccia f shower
docente m/f lecturer
DOCG (abbreviation of) **denominazione di origine controllata e garantita** (guarantee of wine quality)
documenti mpl papers (passport)
dogana f customs
dolce sweet (not savoury) ; mild
dolce m sweet ; dessert ; cake
dolcelatte m creamy blue cheese
dolcificante m sweetener
dolciumi mpl sweets
dollari mpl dollars
dolore m pain ; grief

doloroso(a) painful
domanda f question
domandare to ask (a question)
domani tomorrow
  domani mattina tomorrow morning
  domani pomeriggio tomorrow
    afternoon
  domani sera tomorrow evening/night
domattina tomorrow morning
domenica Sunday
donna f woman
  donne ladies ; women
dopo after ; afterward(s)
dopobarba m aftershave
dopodomani the day after tomorrow
doppio(a) double
dormire to sleep
dove? where?
dovere to have to
droga f drugs (narcotics)
drogheria f grocery shop
duepezzi m two-piece suit ; bikini
duomo m cathedral
durante during
durare to last
duro(a) hard ; tough ; harsh
DVD m DVD
  lettore DVD DVD player

E

e and
E east (abbreviation)
è is (to be)
ebreo(a) Jewish
ecc. etc.
eccedenza f excess ; surplus
eccesso m excess
  eccesso di velocità speeding
eccezionale exceptional
eccezione f exception
ecco here is/are
ecologico(a) ecological
economico(a) cheap
ecoturismo m eco-tourism
edicola f newsstand ; kiosk
edificio m building
effetto m effect
  effetti personali belongings
egregio(a) dear (in formal letter)
elastico m rubber band
elenco m list
  elenco telefonico phone directory

elettricista m/f electrician
elettricità f electricity
elettrico(a) electric(al)
elettrodomestici mpl electrical goods
elettronico(a) electronic
  agenda elettronica electronic
    organizer
elisoccorso m air ambulance
emergenza f emergency
emicrania f migraine
emorroidi fpl haemorrhoids
enoteca f wine shop ; wine bar
ente m corporation ; body
entrambi(e) both
entrare to come/go in ; to enter
entrata f entrance
  entrata abbonati season ticket
    holders' entrance
  entrata libera free admission
epatite f hepatitis
epilessia f epilepsy
epilettico(a) epileptic
equitazione f horse-riding
erba f grass
ernia f hernia
errore m mistake
esame m examination
esatto(a) exact ; accurate
esaurimento nervoso m nervous
    breakdown
esaurito(a) exhausted ; out of print
  tutto esaurito sold out
esca m fishing bait
escluso(a) excluding
escursione f excursion
esente exempt
  esente da dogana duty-free
esempio example
  per esempio for example
esercizio m exercise ; business
esigenza f requirement
esperto(a) expert ; experienced
esplosione f explosion
esportare to export
esposto(a) exposed
  esposto(a) a nord north-facing
espresso m express train ; coffee
espresso(a) express (parcel, etc)
essere to be
  essere assicurato(a) to be insured
  essere capace (di) to be able (to)
  essere d'accordo to agree
  essere nato(a) to be born

est *m* east
estate *f* summer
esterno(a) outside ; external
estero(a) foreign
  all'estero abroad
estintore *m* fire extinguisher
estivo(a) summer
età *f* age
etichetta *f* luggage tag ; label
euro euro
euro cent *m* centesimo
Europa *f* Europe
eventuale possible
evitare to avoid

F

fa ago
  un anno fa a year ago
fabbrica *f* factory
fabbricare to manufacture
faccia *f* face
facile easy
fagiano *m* pheasant
fagiolini *m* runner beans
fallire to fail
fallito(a) bankrupt
fallo *m* foul *(football)*
falso(a) fake
fame *f* hunger
  avere fame to be hungry
famiglia *f* family
familiare family ; familiar
famoso(a) famous
fanale *m* light
fanalino dello stop *m* brake light
fango *m* mud
farcito(a) stuffed ; filled
fare to do ; to make
  fare attenzione to be careful
  fare la spesa to go shopping
  fare la spesa su internet to shop
  online
farfalla *f* butterfly
fari *mpl* headlights
farina *f* flour
farmacia *f* chemist's ; pharmacy
  farmacie di turno duty chemists
  farmacista pharmacist
farmaco *m* drug *(medicine)*
faro *m* headlight ; lighthouse
fascia *f* band ; bandage
fastidio: non mi dà fastidio I don't mind

fatelo da voi *m* DIY
fatto a mano hand-made
fatto di ... made of ...
fattoria *f* farm ; farmhouse
fattura *f* invoice
favore *m* favour
  per favore please
fax *m* fax
fazzoletto *m* handkerchief
  fazzoletto di carta tissue
febbraio February
febbre *f* fever
  avere la febbre to have a temperature
  febbre da fieno hay fever
fede *f* wedding ring ; faith
federa *f* pillowcase
fegato *m* liver
felice happy
felpa *f* sweatshirt
femmina *f* female
feriale workday *(Monday-Saturday)*
ferie *fpl* holiday(s)
  essere in ferie to be on holiday
ferire to injure
ferita *f* wound ; injury ; cut
ferito(a) injured
fermare to stop
fermata *f* stop
  fermata dell'autobus bus stop
fermo(a) still ; off *(machine)*
  stare fermo to stay still
ferro da stiro *m* iron *(for clothes)*
ferrovia *f* railway
festa *f* festival ; holiday ; party
  festa nazionale public holiday
festivo(a) sundays/public holiday
fetta *f* slice
fiamma *f* flame
fiammifero *m* match
fico *m* fig
fidanzato(a) engaged *(to marry)*
fieno *m* hay
fiera *f* fair *(trade)*
  fiera dell'artigianato craft fair
figlia *f* daughter
figlio *m* son
fila *f* line *(row, queue)*
  fare la fila to queue
filiale *f* branch ; subsidiary
film *m* film *(at cinema)*
filo *m* thread ; wire
  filo interdentale dental floss

filtro m filter
  filtro dell'olio oil filter
finanza f finance
  Guardia di finanza Customs and Excise
fine f end
  fine settimana weekend
  fine stagione end of season
fine elegant ; fine
finestra f window
finestrino m window *(car, train)*
finire to finish
finito(a) finished
fino a until ; as far as
  fino alle due till 2 o'clock
fior di latte m cream *(ice cream flavour)*
fiori mpl flowers
fiorista m/f florist
Firenze Florence
firma f signature
firmare to sign
  firmare il registro to sign the register
fiume m river
floppy disk m floppy disk
focaccia f flat salted bread
foglia f leaf *(of tree, etc)*
fogna f sewer ; drain
folla f crowd
folle mad
  in folle in neutral *(car)*
fon m hairdryer
fondo m back *(of room)* ; bottom
fontana f fountain
fonte f source
foratura f puncture
forbici fpl scissors
  forbicine nail scissors
forchetta f fork *(for eating)*
foresta f forest
forfora f dandruff
formaggio m cheese
fornaio m baker
fornello m stove ; hotplate
fornitore m supplier
forno m oven
  forno a microonde microwave
forse perhaps
forte strong ; loud ; high *(speed)*
fortunato(a) lucky
forza f strength ; force
foto f photo
fotocamera digitale f digital camera
fotocopia f photocopy
fotocopiare to photocopy
fotocopiatrice f photocopier

fototessera f passport-type photo
foulard m headscarf
fra between ; among(st)
  fra 2 giorni in 2 days
  fra poco in a while
fragile breakable
fragola f strawberry
frana f landslide
francese French
francese m French *(language)*
Francia f France
francobollo m stamp
frappé m milk shake
fratello m brother
frattura f fracture
frazione f village
freccia f indicator *(car)* ; arrow
freddo(a) cold
frenare to brake
freno m brake
  freno a mano handbrake
frequente frequent
fretta f hurry
  avere fretta to be in a hurry
friggere to fry
frigorifero m refrigerator
frittata f omelette
fritto(a) fried
frizione f clutch *(car)*
frizzante fizzy ; sparkling
fronte f forehead ; front
  di fronte a facing ; opposite
frontiera f frontier ; border
frullato m milkshake
frutta f fruit
  frutta secca dried fruit
frutti di mare mpl seafood
fruttivendolo m greengrocer
FS Italian State Railways
fuga f escape ; leak *(gas)*
fuggire to escape
fulmine m lightning
fumare to smoke
  non fumo I don't smoke
fumatori smokers
fumo m smoke
funerale m funeral
funghi mpl mushrooms
  funghi porcini boletus mushrooms
  funghi secchi dried mushrooms
funicolare f funicular railway
funzionare to work *(mechanism)*
  non funziona it doesn't work
fuoco m fire ; focus
  fuochi d'artificio fireworks

fuori outside ; out
  fuori servizio out of order
furgone *m* van
furto *m* theft
fuseaux *mpl* leggings
fusibile *m* fuse
futuro *m* future

G

gabinetto *m* lavatory
  gabinetto biologico chemical toilet
  gabinetto medico doctor's surgery
galleria *f* tunnel ; gallery ; arcade ; circle *(theatre)*
  galleria d'arte art gallery
Galles *m* Wales
gallese Welsh
gamba *f* leg
gara *f* race *(sport)*
garanzia *f* guarantee ; warranty
gas *m* gas
gasolio *m* diesel
gassato(a) fizzy
gassosa *f* lemonade
gastrite *f* gastritis
gatto *m* cat
gay gay *(person)*
gel per capelli *m* hair gel
gelateria *f* ice-cream shop
gelatina *f* jelly
gelato *m* ice cream
gelo *m* frost
geloso(a) jealous
gemelli *mpl* twins ; cufflinks
genere *m* kind *(type)* ; gender
genero *m* son-in-law
genitori *mpl* parents
Genova *f* Genoa
gentile kind *(person)*
Germania *f* Germany
gesso *m* chalk ; plaster *(for limb)*
gettare to throw
  non gettare rifiuti no dumping
gettone *m* token
  gettone di presenza attendance fee
ghiaccio *m* ice
ghiacciolo *m* ice lolly
giacca *f* jacket
giallo *m* thriller *(book or film)*
giallo(a) yellow ; amber *(light)*
giardiniere *m* gardener
giardino *m* garden

gilè *m* waistcoat
gin *m* gin
  gin tonic gin and tonic
ginecologo/a *m/f* gynaecologist
ginocchio *m* knee
giocare to play ; to gamble
giocattolo *m* toy
gioco *m* game
  gioco a quiz quiz show
gioielleria *f* jeweller's
gioielli *mpl* jewellery
gioielliere *m* jeweller
giornalaio *m* newsagent
giornale *m* newspaper
giornalista *m/f* journalist
giornata *f* day
giorno *m* day
  giorni feriali Monday-Saturday
  giorni festivi Sundays/holidays
giovane young
giovedì *m* Thursday
girare to turn ; to spin
  girarsi to turn around
girasole *m* sunflower
giro *m* tour ; turn
  fare un giro a piedi to go for a stroll
  giro turistico sightseeing tour
gita *f* trip ; excursion
  gita in barca boat trip
  gita in pullman coach trip
giù down ; downstairs
giubbotto salvagente *m* life jacket
giudice *m* judge
giugno *m* June
giusto(a) fair ; right *(correct)*
gli the ; to him/it
globale inclusive *(costs)*
glutine glutin
goccia *f* drop *(of liquid)* ; drip
gola *f* throat ; gorge
golfo *m* gulf
gomito *m* elbow
gomma *f* rubber ; tyre
  gomma a terra flat tyre
  gomma da cancellare eraser
gommone *m* dinghy *(inflatable)*
gonfiare to inflate
gonfio(a) swollen
gonfiore *m* lump *(swelling)*
gonna *f* skirt
Gps *m* GPS (global positioning system)
gradazione *f* content *(of alcohol)*
gradevole pleasant

gradino m step ; stair
Gran Bretagna f Great Britain
grana f parmesan cheese
granaio m barn
granchio m crab
grande large ; great ; big
grande magazzino m department store
grandine f hail
granita f water ice *(flavoured)*
grappa f strong spirit *(often drunk with coffee)*
grasso(a) fat ; greasy
gratis free of charge
grattacielo m skyscraper
grattugia f grater
grattugiato(a) grated
gratuito(a) free of charge
  il servizio è gratuito service included
grave serious
grazie thank you
gridare to shout
grigio(a) grey
griglia f grill
  alla griglia grilled
grissini mpl breadsticks
grosso(a) big ; thick
grucce fpl crutches
gruccia f coat hanger
gruppo m group
  gruppo sanguigno blood group
guadagnare to earn
guanciale m pillow
guanto m glove
  guanto da forno oven glove
  guanto di spugna facecloth
  guanti di gomma rubber gloves
guardacoste m coastguard
guardare to look (at) ; to watch
guardaroba m cloakroom
guardia f guard
  Guardia di finanza Customs and Excise
guasto out of order
guerra f war
guida f guide *(person or book)* ; directory
  guida a sinistra left-hand drive
  guida telefonica telephone directory
  guida turistica tour guide
guidare to drive ; to steer
guidatore m driver
guinzaglio m lead *(for dog)*
gustare to taste ; to enjoy
gusto m flavour

H

ha...? do you have...?
  ha l'ora? do you have the time?
hamburger m burger
herpes m cold sore ; herpes
ho... I have...
  ho ... anni I'm ... years old
  ho bisogno di... I need...
  ho fame I'm hungry
  ho fretta I'm in a hurry
  ho sete I'm thirsty
hostess f stewardess

I

i the *(plural)*
identificare to identify
idratante m moisturizer
idraulico m plumber
ieri yesterday
il the *(singular)*
imbarcarsi to embark
imbarcazione f boat
imbarco m boarding
  carta d'imbarco boarding card
imbottigliato(a) bottled
imbucare to post *(letter, etc)*
immediatamente at once
immergere to dip *(into liquid)*
immersioni subacquee fpl scuba diving
immobilizzatore m immobilizer *(on car)*
immondizie fpl rubbish
immunizzazione f immunisation
impanato coated in breadcrumbs
imparare to learn
impasto m mixture
imperatore m emperor
impermeabile m raincoat
impero m empire
impiego m use ; employment
impiegato(a) m/f employee ; white-collar worker
importante important
importare to import ; to matter
  non importa it doesn't matter
importo m (total) amount
impossibile impossible
imposta f tax *(on income)* ; shutter
  imposta sul valore aggiunto (IVA) value-added tax (VAT)
improbabile unlikely
in in ; to
  in Spagna to Spain
  in vacanza on holiday

inalatore m inhaler
inadempienza f negligence
incantevole charming
incaricarsi di to take charge of
incartare to wrap up (parcel)
incassare to cash (a cheque)
incendio m fire
inchiostro m ink
incidente m accident
incinta pregnant
incluso(a) included ; enclosed
incontrare to meet
incontro m meeting (by chance)
incrocio m crossroads ; junction
indicatore m indicator ; gauge
  indicatore del livello dell'olio oil gauge
indicazioni fpl directions
indice m index ; contents
indietro backwards ; behind
indirizzo m address
infarto m heart attack
infatti in fact ; actually
infermeria f infirmary
infermiera f nurse
infezione infection
infiammabile inflammable
infiammazione f inflammation
influenza f flu
informare to inform
  informarsi (di) to inquire (about)
informazioni fpl information
infuso di erbe f herbal tea
ingessatura f plaster cast
Inghilterra f England
inghiottire to swallow
inglese English
ingorgato(a) blocked (pipe, sink)
ingorgo m blockage ; hold-up
  ingorgo stradale traffic jam
ingresso m entry/entrance
  ingresso gratuito free entry
iniezione f injection
inizio m start
innocuo(a) harmless
inondazione m flood
inoltre besides
inquinato(a) polluted
insalata f salad
  insalata di patate potato salad
  insalata di pomodori tomato salad
  insalata mista mixed salad
  insalata verde green salad

insegnante m/f teacher
insegnare to teach
inserire to insert
  inserire le banconote una per volta insert banknotes one at a time
insettifugo m insect repellent
insetto m insect
insieme together
insolazione f sunstroke
insulina f insulin
interessante interesting
internazionale international
internet m internet
  collegamento a internet senza fili wireless internet
  sei collegato a internet? do you have internet access?
interno m inside ; extension (phone)
intero(a) whole
interpretazione f interpretation
interprete m/f interpreter
interruttore m switch
intervallo m half-time ; interval
intervento m operation
inversione f U-turn
intervista f interview
intestato(a) a registered in the name of
intimi donna mpl ladies' underwear
intorno around
intossicazione alimentare f food-poisoning
introdurre to introduce
inutile unnecessary ; useless
invalido(a) disabled ; invalid
invece di instead of
invernale winter
inverno m winter
investire to knock down (car)
inviare to send
invitare to invite
invito m invitation
io I
ipermercato m hypermarket
ipermetrope long-sighted
iPod m iPod
Irlanda f Ireland
  Irlanda del Nord Northern Ireland
irlandese Irish
iscritto m member
  per iscritto in writing
iscriversi a to join (club)
iscrizione f inscription ; enrolment
isola f island

istituto m institute
istruttore(trice) m/f instructor
istruzioni fpl instructions
Italia f Italy
italiano(a) Italian
itinerario m route
  itinerario turistico scenic route
itterizia f jaundice
IVA f VAT

J
jolly m joker (cards)

L
la the ; her ; it ; you
là there
  per di là that way
labbra fpl lips
lacca f lacquer ; hair spray
ladro m thief
lago m lake
lamette fpl razor blades
lampada f lamp
lampadina f lightbulb
lampone m raspberry
lana f wool
largo(a) wide ; broad
lasciare to leave ; to let (allow)
lassativo m laxative
lassù up there
latte m milk
  latte a lunga conservazione long-life milk
  latte di soia soya milk
  latte fresco fresh milk
  latte in polvere powdered milk
  latte intero whole milk
  latte scremato skimmed milk
  latte parzialmente scremato semi-skimmed milk
lattuga f lettuce
lavabile washable
lavaggio m washing
  lavaggio auto car wash
  per lavaggi frequenti for frequent use
lavanderia f laundry (place)
  lavanderia automatica launderette
lavandino m sink
lavare to wash
  lavare a secco to dry-clean
lavarsi to wash (oneself)
lavasecco m dry-cleaner's

lavastoviglie f dishwasher
lavatrice f washing machine
lavorare to work (person)
lavoro m job ; occupation ; work
  lavori stradali road works
  lavori in corso road works
le the ; them ; to her ; to you
legge f law
leggere to read
leggero(a) light (not heavy) ; weak
legno m wood (material)
lei she ; her ; you
lentamente slowly
lente f lens (of glasses)
  lente d'ingrandimento magnifying glass
  lenti a contatto contact lenses
lento slow
lenzuolo m sheet (bed)
lesbica lesbian
lesione f injury
lettera f letter
  lettera raccomandata registered letter
lettino m cot
letto m bed
  letto a una piazza single bed
  letto matrimoniale double bed
  letti gemelli twin beds
  letti a castello bunk beds
lettore CD m CD player
  lettore di MP3 MP3 player
lì there (over there)
libero(a) free/vacant
libreria f bookshop
libretto m booklet ; log book (for car)
  libretto degli assegni cheque book
libro m book
licenza f licence ; permit
  licenza di caccia hunting permit
  licenza di pesca fishing permit
limetta per le unghie f nail file
limite m limit ; boundary
  limite di velocità speed limit
limone m lemon
linea f line ; route
  linea aerea airline
lingua f language ; tongue
lino m linen
liquido m liquid
  liquido dei freni brake fluid
  liquido lavavetri screen wash
  liquido per lenti a contatto contact lens solution
liquore m liqueur

liquori *mpl* spirits *(alcohol)*
liscio(a) smooth ; straight ; plain
lista *f* list
  lista dei vini wine list
listino prezzi *m* price list
litro *m* litre
livello *m* level
lo him ; it
locale local
locale *m* room ; place ; local train
  locale notturno nightclub
località di vacanza *f* resort
locanda *f* inn
Londra *f* London
lontano(a) far
lozione *f* lotion
  lozione solare suntan lotion
lucchetto *m* padlock
  lucchetto della bici bike lock
luce *f* light
lucertola *f* lizard
luglio *m* July
lui him
lumaca *f* snail
luna *f* moon
  luna di miele honeymoon
luna park *m* funfair
lunedì *m* Monday
lunghezza *f* length
lungo(a) long
  lungo la strada along the street
  a lungo for a long time
lungomare *m* promenade ; seafront
luogo *m* place
  luogo di nascita place of birth
lupo *m* wolf
lusso *m* luxury
  di lusso luxury *(hotel, etc)*

M

ma but
macchia *f* stain ; mark
macchina *f* car ; machine
  macchina a noleggio hire car
  macchina fotografica camera
  fotocamera digitale digital camera
  macchina sportiva sports car
macedonia *f* fruit salad
macellaio *m* butcher's
macinato(a) ground *(coffee, meat)*
madre *f* mother
magazzino *m* warehouse

maggio *m* May
maggiore larger ; greater ; older ;
  largest ; greatest ; oldest
maglietta *f* t-shirt
maglione *m* jumper ; sweater
magro(a) thin *(person)* ; low-fat ;
  lean *(meat)*
mai never ; ever
maiale *m* pig ; pork
maionese *f* mayonnaise
mal *see* **male**
malato(a) ill ; sick
malattia *f* disease
  malattia venerea venereal disease
male badly *(not well)*
male *m* pain ; ache
  mal d'aria air sickness
  mal d'auto car sickness
  mal d'orecchi earache
  mal di denti toothache
  mal di gola sore throat
  mal di mare sea sickness
  mal di pancia stomachache
  mal di testa headache
maltempo *m* bad weather
mamma *f* mum(my)
mancia *f* tip *(to waiter, etc)*
mandare to send
  mandare per fax to fax
  mandare un sms to text
mango *m* mango
mangiare to eat
  mangiare fuori to eat out
manica *f* sleeve
  la Manica the English Channel
manicure *m* manicure
mano *f* hand
  fatto(a) a mano handmade
Mantova *f* Mantua
manuale di conversazione *m* phrase
  book
manzo *m* beef
marca *f* brand *(make)*
marcia *f* gear *(car)* ; march
marciapiede *m* pavement
mare *m* sea ; seaside
  Mare del Nord North Sea
margarina *f* margarine
margherita *f* daisy
marina *f* navy
marito *m* husband
marmellata *f* jam
  marmellata d'arance marmalade

marrone m brown ; chestnut
marsupio m bumbag ; money belt
martedì m Tuesday
  martedì grasso Shrove Tuesday
martello m hammer
marzo m March
maschera f mask ; fancy dress
maschile masculine ; male
massaggio m massage
massimo(a) maximum
masticare to chew
materassino m airbed ; lilo
materasso m mattress
materiale m material
matrigna f stepmother
matrimonio m wedding
mattina f morning
  di mattina in the morning
matto(a) mad
mazza f mallet
  mazze da golf golf clubs
meccanico m mechanic ; repair shop
medicina f medicine
medico m doctor
Mediterraneo m Mediterranean
medusa f jellyfish
megabyte m megabyte (Mb)
meglio better ; best
  meglio di better than
mela f apple
melanzana f aubergine ; eggplant
melone m melon
membro m member
meningite f meningitis
meno less ; minus
mensa f canteen
mensile monthly
mensilmente monthly
mensola f shelf
menta f mint
mento m chin
mentre while ; whereas
menù m menu
  menù alla carta à la carte menu
  menù a prezzo fisso set-price menu
  menù turistico set menu
meraviglioso(a) wonderful
mercatino dell'usato m flea market
mercato m market
merce f goods
merci fpl freight ; goods
mercoledì m Wednesday
merenda f snack

meridionale southern
mese m month
messa f mass (in church)
messaggio m message
  messaggio SMS SMS message
mestruazioni fpl period (menstrual)
metà f half
  metà prezzo half-price
metro m metre
  metro a nastro tape measure
metropolitana f underground ; metro
mettere to put ; to put on (clothes)
  mettersi in contatto con to contact
mezzanotte f midnight
mezzi mpl means ; transport
mezzo m middle
mezzo(a) half
  mezza pensione half board
mezzogiorno m midday ; noon
  il Mezzogiorno the south of Italy
mezz'ora f half an hour
mi me ; to me ; myself
mia my
microfono m microphone
miele m honey
migliorare to improve
migliore better ; best
Milano Milan
miliardo m billion
milione m million
mille thousand
millimetro m millimetre
minestra f soup
minidisk m minidisk
minimo m minimum
ministro m minister (political)
minorenne underage
minori mpl minors
minuto m minute
mio my
miscela f blend
misto(a) mixed
mittente m/f sender
MM metro ; underground (in Milan)
mobili mpl furniture
moda f fashion
moderno(a) modern
modo m way ; manner
modulo m form (document)
  modulo d'iscrizione registration form
moglie f wife
molletta f clothes peg
  molletta per capelli hairgrip

molo m jetty ; quay ; pier
molti(e) many
  molte grazie thanks very much
molto much ; a lot ; very
  molto tempo for a long time
  molta gente lots of people
monastero m monastery
moneta f coin ; currency
montagna f mountain
monumento m monument
mordere to bite
morire to die
morsicare to bite
morsicato(a) bitten
morso m bite
morso(a) bitten
morto(a) dead
mosca f fly
moscerino m midge ; gnat
moschea f mosque
mosso(a) rough (sea) ; ruffled
mostra f exhibition
mostrare to show
moto f motorbike
motore m engine ; motor
motorino m moped
motorino d'avviamento m starter motor
multa f fine (to be paid)
municipio m town hall
muro m wall
museo m museum
musica f music
muta f wetsuit
mutande fpl underpants
mutandine fpl knickers ; panties

N

N north (abbreviation)
nafta f diesel
Napoli Naples
nascita f birth
naso m nose
nastro m tape ; ribbon
nato(a) born
nauseato(a) nauseous
nave f ship
navigatore satellitare m satellite navigation system (for car)
nave-traghetto f ferry
nazionale national ; domestic (flight)
nazionalità f nationality
nazione f nation

né ... né neither ... nor
nebbia f fog
necessario(a) necessary
negativo m negative (photo)
negozio m shop
nero(a) black
nessuno(a) no ; nobody ; none
netto m net
  al netto di IVA net of VAT
neve f snow
nevicare to snow
niente nothing
  niente da dichiarare nothing to declare
nipote m/f nephew/niece
nipotina f granddaughter
nipotino m grandson
noce f walnut
nocivo(a) harmful
nodo m knot ; bow
  nodo ferroviario junction (railway)
noi we
noleggiare to hire
noleggio m hire
  noleggio auto car hire
  noleggio barche boat hire
  noleggio bici bike hire
  noleggio sci ski hire
nolo m hire
nome m name ; first name
  nome da ragazza maiden name
  nome utente username
non not
  non ancora not yet
  non c'è there isn't
  non funziona it doesn't work
  non capisco I don't understand
  non pericoloso(a) safe
non-fumatore m/f non-smoker
nonna f grandmother
nonno m grandfather
nord m north
nostro(a) our
notare to notice
notizie fpl news
notte f night
  notte di San Silvestro New Year's Eve
  di notte at night
novembre m November
nubile single (woman)
nulla nothing ; anything
nullo(a) void (contract)

numero m number ; size (of shoe)
  numero di camera room number
  numero di cellulare mobile number
  numero del conto account number
  numero di telefono phone number
nuora f daughter-in-law
nuotare to swim
Nuova Zelanda f New Zealand
nuovo(a) new
  di nuovo again
nuvoloso(a) cloudy

O

o or
O west (abbreviation for Ovest)
obbligatorio(a) compulsory
oceano m ocean
occasione f opportunity ; bargain
occhiali mpl glasses
  occhiali da sci skiing goggles
  occhiali da sole sunglasses
occhio m eye
occupato(a) busy/engaged
odore m smell
offerta f offer
officina f workshop ; repair shop
oggetto m object
oggi today
OGM (privo(a) di organismi
  geneticamente modificati) GM-free
ogni each ; every
  ogni giorno every day ; daily
  ogni quanto? how often?
  ogni tanto occasionally
olio m oil
  olio solare suntan oil
  olio di girasole sunflower oil
  olio d'oliva olive oil
olive fpl olives
oltre beyond ; besides
ombra f shade
  all'ombra in the shade
ombrello m umbrella
ombrellone m sun umbrella
ombretto m eye shadow
omeopatico(a) m/f homeopathic
  (remedy etc)
  omeopatia homeopathy
omogeneizzati mpl baby food
omosessuale homosexual
onde fpl waves
onestà f honesty
onesto(a) honest

opera f opera
operatore turistico m tour operator
operazione f operation (surgical)
opuscolo m brochure
ora now
ora f hour
  ora di punta rush hour
  che ore sono? what's the time?
orario m timetable
  in orario on time
  orario di apertura opening hours
  orario di cassa banking hours
  orario visite visiting hours
ordinare to order ; to prescribe
ordine f order (in restaurant)
ordinato(a) tidy
orecchini mpl earrings
orecchio m ear
orecchioni mpl mumps
oreficeria f jeweller's
orina f urine
ormeggiare to moor
ormeggio m mooring
oro m gold
  placcato oro gold-plated
orologeria m watchmaker's
orologio m clock ; watch
orticaria f rash (skin)
ortografia f spelling
ospedale m hospital
ospite m/f guest ; host/hostess
osso m bone
ostello m hostel
  ostello della gioventù youth hostel
osteria f inn
ottenere to get ; obtain
  ottenere la linea to get through
  (on phone)
ottimo(a) excellent
ottobre m October
otturazione f filling (in tooth)
ovest m west

P

pacchetto m packet
pacco m package ; parcel
padella f frying-pan
Padova Padua
padre m father
padrone(a) m/f owner
paesaggio m scenery ; countryside
paese m country (nation) ; village
pagare to pay ; to pay for

pagato(a) paid
pagina f page
paio m pair
palazzo m building ; block of flats ; palace
palestra f gym
palla f ball
pallina f ball (small)
  pallina da golf golf ball
  pallina da tennis tennis ball
pallone m football
pandoro m Italian Christmas cake
pane m bread ; loaf
  pane integrale wholemeal bread
  pane carré sandwich bread
  pane e coperto cover charge
  pane di segale rye bread
panettone m Italian Christmas cake
panetteria f baker's
pangrattato m breadcrumbs
panificio m bakery
panino m bread roll
  panino imbottito sandwich
paninoteca f sandwich bar
panna f cream
panno m cloth ; fabric
pannolini mpl nappies
pantaloni mpl trousers
  pantaloni corti shorts
pantofole fpl slippers
papa m pope
papà m daddy
parabrezza m windscreen
paramedico m paramedic
paraurti m bumper (on car)
parcheggiare to park
parcheggio m car park
  parcheggio custodito supervised car park
  parcheggio libero free parking
  parcheggio sotterraneo underground car park
parchimetro m parking meter
parco m park
  parco nazionale national park
parente m/f relation ; relative
Parigi f Paris
parlare to speak ; to talk
parmigiano m parmesan
  parmigiano grattugiato grated parmesan
parola f word
  parola d'ordine password

parolaccia f swear word
parrucchiere(a) m/f hairdresser
parte f share ; part ; side
partenza f departures
  partenze internazionali international departures
  partenze nazionali domestic departures
partire to depart ; to leave
partita f match ; game
  partita di calcio football match
passaggio m passage ; lift (in car)
  dare un passaggio to give a lift
passaporto m passport
passeggiata f walk ; stroll
passeggino m pushchair
passo m pace ; pass (mountain)
  passo carrabile keep clear
  passo chiuso pass closed.
  fare quattro passi to go for a stroll
pasticcino m cake (small, fancy)
pastiglia f tablet (pill)
pasto m meal
pastorizzato pasteurised
patata f potato
patatine fpl crisps
  patatine fritte chips
patente f permit ; driving licence
patrigno m stepfather
pavimento m floor
paziente m/f patient
pecora f sheep
pedaggio m toll (motorway)
pedale m pedal
pedalò m pedalboat
pedicure m chiropodist
pedoni mpl pedestrians
peggio worse
pelati mpl tinned tomatoes
pelle f skin ; hide ; leather
pellegrino m pilgrim
pelletterie fpl leather goods
pellicola f film (for camera)
  pellicola a colori colour film
  pellicola in bianco e nero black and white film
pelo m fur
pene m penis
penicillina f penicillin
penisola f peninsula
penna f pen
pensare to think

pensione f guesthouse
  pensione completa full board
  mezza pensione half board
  pensione familiare bed and breakfast
pentola f saucepan
pepe m pepper (spice)
peperoncino m chilli
peperone m pepper (vegetable)
per for ; per ; in order to
  per esempio for example
  per favore please
  per via aerea air mail
pera f pear
perché why ; because ; so that
percorso m walk ; journey ; route
  percorso panoramico scenic route
perdere to lose ; to miss (train, etc)
perdita f leak (of gas, liquid)
pericolante unsafe
pericolo m danger
pericoloso(a) dangerous
  non pericoloso(a) safe
periferia f outskirts ; suburbs
permanente continua parking
  restrictions still apply
permanenza f stay ; residency
permesso m licence ; permit
  permesso! excuse me! (to get by)
  permesso di soggiorno residence
  permit
permettere to allow
perso(a) lost (object) ; missed (train, plane,
  etc)
persona f person
  le persone con esigenze particolari
  people with special needs
personale m staff
pesante heavy
pesare to weigh
pesca f angling ; fishing ; peach
  divieto di pesca no fishing
pescare to fish
pesce m fish
pesche m peaches
pescivendolo m fishmonger's
peso m weight
pettine m comb
petto m chest ; breast
  petto di pollo chicken breast
pezzo m piece ; bit ; cut (of meat)
piacere to please
  le piace? do you like it?
  piacere! pleased to meet you!

piangere to cry (weep)
piano slowly ; quietly
piano m floor (of building) ; plan
pianta f map ; plan ; plant
pianterreno m ground floor
piantina f street map
piatto m dish ; course ; plate
  primo piatto first course
piazza f square (in town)
piazzale m large square
piazzola (di sosta) f lay-by
piccante spicy ; hot
picchetto m tent peg
piccolo(a) little ; small
piede m foot
  a piedi on foot
pieno(a) full
pietra f stone
pigiama m pyjamas
pigro(a) lazy
pila f battery ; torch
pillola f pill
pinne fpl flippers
pino m pine
pinze fpl pliers
pinzette fpl tweezers
pioggia f rain
piombo m lead (metal)
piovere to rain
piscina f swimming pool
  piscina per bambini paddling pool
piselli m peas
pista f track ; race track
  pista da ballo dance floor
  pista da sci ski run
più more ; most ; plus
  più di more than
  più economico(a) cheaper
  più tardi later
piumino m duvet
pizzeria m pizza restaurant
pizzico m pinch ; sting
pizzo m lace
plastica f plastic
  di plastica made of plastic
pneumatico m tyre
po' a little (shortened form of **poco**)
pochi(e) few
poco(a) little ; not much
  un po' a little
podologo m chiropodist
poi then
polizia f police
  polizia stradale traffic police

poliziotto m policeman
polizza f policy
pollo m chicken
polmone m lung
poltrona f armchair ; seat in stalls
pomata f ointment
pomeriggio m afternoon
  di pomeriggio in the afternoon
pomodoro m tomato
pompa f pump
  pompa da bicicleta bicycle pump
pompelmo m grapefruit
ponte m bridge ; deck
  ponte macchine car deck
pontile m jetty ; pier
porcellana f china
porri m leeks
porta f door ; gate ; goal
  porta di sicurezza emergency exit
portabagagli m luggage rack ; porter (at airport, station, etc)
portacenere m ashtray
portafoglio m wallet
portare to carry/bring ; to wear
portiere m porter (doorkeeper) ; goalkeeper
portineria f caretaker's lodge
porto m port ; harbour
  porto di scalo port of call
Portogallo m Portugal
porzione f portion ; helping
posate fpl cutlery
posologia f dosage
possiamo we can
  non possiamo we cannot
posso I can
  non posso I cannot
posta f post office ; mail
  posta elettronica e-mail
  posta raccomandata registered mail
posteggio m car park
  posteggio taxi taxi rank
posto m place ; job ; seat
  posti in piedi standing room
  posti a sedere seating capacity
  posti prenotati reserved seats
potabile ok to drink
potere to be able
pranzo m lunch
pré-maman m maternity dress
preavviso m advance notice
precotto(a) ready-cooked
predeterminare l'importo desiderato select required amount

preferire to prefer
preferito(a) favourite
prefisso m prefix ; area code
  prefisso telefonico dialling code
pregare to pray
  si prega... please...
prego don't mention it!
prelievo m collection ; sample
premere to push ; to press
premio m prize
prendere to take ; to catch (bus, etc)
  prendere il sole to sunbathe
  prendere in prestito to borrow
prenotare to book ; to reserve
prenotato(a) reserved
prenotazione f reservation
preoccupato(a) worried
preparare to prepare ; to get ready
presa f socket (electric)
preservativo m condom
pressione del sangue f blood pressure
prestare to lend
presto early ; soon
prete m priest
previsione f forecast
  previsioni del tempo weather forecast
previsto(a) scheduled ; expected
  come previsto as expected
prezzo m price
  prezzo al dettaglio retail price
  prezzo fisso set price
  prezzo di catalogo list price
  prezzo al minuto retail price
  prezzo d'ingresso entrance fee
prima di before
primavera f spring (season)
primo(a) first ; top ; early
  primo piano first floor
  primo piatto first course
principale main
principiante m/f beginner
privato(a) private
problema m problem
professione f profession
professore m/f teacher ; professor
profondità f depth
profondo(a) deep
profumeria f perfume shop
progettare to plan
programma m programme ; syllabus ; schedule
proibire to ban ; to prohibit
proibito(a) forbidden ; prohibited

prolunga f extension (electrical)
promettere to promise
pronto(a) ready
  pronto! hello! (on telephone)
  pronto soccorso casualty
proprietario(a) m/f owner
proprio(a) own
prosciutto cotto m ham (cooked)
prosciutto crudo m ham (cured)
prossimamente coming soon
prossimo(a) next
proteggislip m panty liner
protesi dell'anca f hip replacement
protestante Protestant
provare to try ; to test (try out) ; to try on (clothes)
provvisorio(a) temporary
prugna f plum
PTP abbreviation of **Posto Telefonico Pubblico**
pubblicità f advertisement
pubblico m audience ; public
pulce f flea
pulito(a) clean
pulizia f cleaning
  pulizia del viso facial
pullman m coach
pulmino m minibus
punteggio m score
puntine fpl points
punto m point ; stitch ; full stop
  punto d'incontro meeting place
puntura f bite ; sting ; injection
puzzle m jigsaw
puzza f bad smell

Q

qua here
quaderno m exercise book
quadro m picture ; painting
qual(e) what ; which ; which one
qualche some
  qualche volta sometimes
qualcosa something ; anything
qualcuno someone ; somebody
qualificato(a) qualified
qualità f quality
qualsiasi any
qualunque any
quando? when?
quanto(a)? how much?
  quanti(e)? how many?
quartiere m district

quarto m quarter
  quarto d'ora quarter of an hour
quattro four
quei those ; those ones
quel(la) that ; that one
quelli(e) those ; those ones
quello(a) that ; that one
questi(e) these ; these ones
questo(a) this ; this one
questura f police station
qui here
quindi then ; therefore
quindici giorni fortnight
quotidiano m daily (paper)
quotidiano(a) daily

R

rabarbaro m rhubarb
rabbia f anger ; rabies
racchetta f racket ; bat
  racchetta da neve snowshoe
  racchetta da sci ski pole
raccomandare to recommend
racconto m story
radiatore m radiator
radio f radio
radiografia f x-ray
raffreddore m cold (illness)
  raffreddore da fieno hay fever
ragazza f young woman ; girlfriend
  ragazza alla pari au pair
ragazzo m young man ; boyfriend
RAI f Italian State Broadcasting
rallentare to slow down
rapido m express train
rapido(a) high-speed ; quick
rasoio m razor
  rasoio elettrico electric razor
reato m crime
recarsi alla cassa pay at cash desk
recentemente recently
reclamo m complaint
recupero monete returned coins
regalo m present ; gift
reggiseno m bra
regione f region ; district ; area
registrare to record
registratore m cassette player
registro m register
Regno Unito m United Kingdom
regolamento m regulation
regolare regular ; steady
remare to row (boat)

rendersi conto di to realize
rene m kidney
reparto m department ; ward
restare to stay ; to remain
restituire to return ; to give back
restituzione f return ; repayment
resto m remainder ; change (money)
restringersi to shrink
rete f net ; goal
   rete portabagagli rack (luggage)
retro m back
   vedi retro please turn over
retromarcia f reverse gear
reumatismo m rheumatism
ricambio m spare part ; refill
ricaricare to recharge (battery)
   caricatelefono m recharger (mobile) ;
   caricabatterie (battery)
ricetta f prescription ; recipe
ricevere to receive ; to welcome
ricevitore m receiver (phone)
ricevuta f receipt
richiedere to require
richiesta f request
riciclare to recycle
riconoscere to recognize
riconoscimento m identification
ricordare to remember
   non mi ricordo I don't remember
ricordo m souvenir ; memory
ricorrere a to resort to
ricoverare to admit (to hospital)
recovero per auto m car port
ridere to laugh
ridurre to reduce
riduttore m adaptor
riduzione f reduction
riempire to fill
rientro m return ; return home
rifare to do again ; to repair
rifiutare to refuse
rifiuti mpl rubbish ; waste
rifugio m mountain inn ; shelter
righello m ruler (for measuring)
rigore m penalty (football)
riguardo m care ; respect
   riguardo a... regarding...
rilasciato(a) a issued at
rimandare to postpone
rimanere to stay ; to remain
rimborsare to reimburse
rimborso m refund
rimessa f remittance ; garage

rimettere to put back
rimettersi to recover (from illness)
rimorchiare to tow
rimorchio m trailer
   a rimorchio on tow
rimozione f removal ; towing away
Rinascimento m Renaissance
rinfreschi mpl refreshments
ringraziare to thank
rinnovare to renew
rinunciare to give up
riparare to repair
riparato(a) sheltered ; repaired
riparazione f repair
ripetere to repeat
ripido(a) steep
ripiegare to fold
ripieno m stuffing
riposarsi to rest
riposo m rest (repose)
risalita f reascent
risarcimento m compensation
riscaldamento m heating
riscaldare to heat up (food)
rischio m risk
risciacquare to rinse
riscuotere to collect ; to cash
riserva f reserve ; reservation
   riserva di caccia private hunting
   riserva naturale nature reserve
riservare to reserve
riservato(a) reserved
riso m rice ; laugh
risotto m rice cooked in stock
risparmiare to save (money)
rispondere to answer ; to reply
risposta f answer
ristorante m restaurant
ritardo m delay
ritirare to withdraw
ritiro m retirement ; withdrawal
   ritiro bagagli baggage reclaim
ritornare to return (go back)
ritorno m return
riunione f meeting
riuscita f result ; outcome
riva f bank ; shore
riviera f riviera
rivista f magazine ; revue
rivolgersi a to refer to (for info)
roba f stuff ; belongings
roccia f rock
rognoni mpl kidneys

romanico(a) Romanesque
romanzo m novel
  romanzo rosa romantic novel
rompere to break
rondine f swallow (bird)
rosa pink
rosa f rose
rosmarino m rosemary
rosolia f German measles ; rubella
rossetto m lipstick
rosso(a) red
rosticceria f shop selling cooked food
rotonda f roundabout
rotondo(a) round
rotto(a) broken
roulotte f caravan
rovesciare to spill ; to knock over
rovine fpl ruins
rtd delay (abbreviation for **ritardo**)
rubare to steal
rubinetto m tap
rubrica f address book
ruggine f rust
rughe fpl wrinkles
rullino m roll of film
rum m rum
rumore m noise
rumoroso(a) noisy
ruota f wheel
  ruota di scorta spare wheel
rupe f mountain cliff
ruscello m stream
russare to snore

S

S south (abbreviation)
sabato Saturday
sabbia f sand
saccarina f saccharin
sacchetto m small bag
  sacchetto di carta paper bag
  sacchetto di plastica plastic bag
sacco m large bag
  sacco a pelo sleeping bag
  sacco della spazzatura bin bag
sacerdote m priest
sagra f local food festival
sala f hall ; auditorium
  sala da pranzo dining room
  sala d'aspetto waiting room
  sala partenze departure lounge
salame m salami
salario m wage

salato(a) salted ; savoury
saldare to settle (bill) ; to weld
saldi sale
saldo m payment ; balance
sale m salt
salire to rise ; to go up
  salire in to get in (vehicle)
salita f climb ; slope
  in salita uphill
salmone m salmon
  salmone affumicato smoked salmon
salone m lounge ; salon
salotto m living room ; lounge
salsa f sauce
salsiccia f sausage
saltare to jump
saltato(a) sautéed
salumeria f delicatessen
salumi mpl cured pork meats
salute f health
  salute! cheers!
saluto m greeting
salvagente m life belt
salvare to rescue ; to save (life)
salvavita m circuit breaker
salve! hello!
salvia f sage (herb)
salvietta f serviette
salviettine per bambini fpl baby wipes
salvo except ; unless
sandali mpl sandals
sangue m blood
  al sangue rare (steak)
sanguinare to bleed
sapere to know
sapone m soap
sapore m flavour ; taste
saporito(a) tasty
Sardegna f Sardinia
sarto m tailor
sartoria f tailor's ; dressmaker's
sasso m stone
sauna f sauna
sbagliato(a) wrong
sbaglio m mistake
sbandare to skid
sbandata f skid
sbarco m landing (boat)
sbrigare to hurry
scadente low (standard, quality)
scadenza f expiry
scadere to expire (ticket, etc)
scaduto(a) out-of-date ; expired

scala f scale ; ladder ; staircase
  scala antincendio fire escape
  scala mobile escalator
scalare to climb
scaldabagno m water heater
scaldare to heat up
scale fpl stairs
scalino m step
scalo m stopover
scaloppina f veal escalope
scannerizzare to scan
  lo scan scan
  lo scanner scanner
scarico(a) flat *(battery)*
scarpa f shoe
  scarpe da ginnastica trainers
scarponcini mpl walking boots
scarponi da sci mpl ski boots
scatola f box ; tin
  scatola di pelati tinned tomatoes
scegliere to choose
scelta f range ; selection ; choice
scendere to go down
  scendere da to get off *(bus, etc)*
scheda f slip *(of paper)* ; card
  scheda telefonica phonecard
schiena f back *(of body)*
sci m ski ; skiing
  sci di fondo cross-country skiing
  sci nautico water-skiing
scialuppa di salvataggio f lifeboat
sciare to ski
sciarpa f scarf
sciogliere to melt
sciopero m strike
sciovia f ski-lift
scivolare to slip
scomodo(a) inconvenient ; uncomfortable
scomparire to disappear
scompartimento m compartment
scongelare to defrost
sconto m discount
  sconti reductions
scontrino m ticket ; receipt ; chit
scopa f broom *(brush)*
scopio (di pneumatico) m blowout *(of tyre)*
scorso(a) last
scossa f shock *(electric)*
scottatura f burn
  scottatura solare sunburn
Scozia f Scotland

scozzese Scottish
scrivania f desk
scrivere to write ; to spell
scultura f sculpture
scuola f school
  scuola di sci ski school
  scuola materna nursery school
scuro(a) dark *(colour)*
scusare to excuse ; to forgive
scusarsi to apologise
scusi? pardon?
se if ; whether
sé oneself
seconda f second gear
secondo m second *(time)* ; main course *(meal)*
secondo(a) second ; according to
  seconda classe second class
  di seconda mano secondhand
sedano m celery
sede f head office
sedersi to sit down
sedia f chair
  sedia a rotelle wheelchair
  sedia a sdraio deckchair
sedile per bambini m babyseat *(car)*
seggiolone m highchair
seggiovia f chair-lift
segnale m signal ; road sign
segnare to score *(goal)*
segreteria telefonica f answering machine
seguente following
seguire to follow ; to continue
sella f saddle
selvatico(a) wild
semaforo m traffic lights
semifreddo m dessert made with ice cream
seminterrato basement
semplice plain ; simple
sempre always ; ever
  per sempre for ever
senape f mustard
senso unico one-way street
  senso vietato no entry
sentiero m path ; footpath
sentire to hear
sentirsi to feel
senza without
separato(a) separated
sera f evening
serbatoio m tank *(car)*
  serbatoio dell'acqua cistern

serio serious (not funny)
serpente m snake
serratura f lock
servire to serve
servizio m service ; report (in press)
  servizio al tavolo waiter service
  servizio compreso service included
servizi mpl facilities ; bathroom
sesso m sex
seta f silk
sete f thirst
  avere sete to be thirsty
settembre m September
settentrionale northern
settimana f week
  settimana bianca week's skiing holiday
settimanale weekly
sfida f challenge
sfuso(a) loose ; on tap (wine)
sganciare to lift receiver
sì yes
Sicilia f Sicily
sicurezza f safety ; security
  controllo di sicurezza security check
sicuro(a) sure
sidro m cider
Sig. Mr abbreviation of **Signor**
Sig.ra Mrs/Ms abbreviation of **Signora**
sigaretta f cigarette
sigaro m cigar
Sig.na Miss abbreviation of **Signorina**
Signor: *il Signor Grandi* Mr Grandi
signora f lady ; madam ; Mrs ; Ms
  signore ladies
signore m gentleman ; sir
  signori gents
signorina f young woman ; Miss
silenzio m silence
SIM f SIM card
simile a similar to
simpatico(a) pleasant ; nice
sindacato m trade union
sindaco m mayor
singolo(a) single
sinistra f left
sistemare to arrange
sito m site
  sito web website
skipass m skipass
slacciare to unfasten ; to undo
slavina f snowslide ; landslide
slegato(a) loose (not fastened)
slittata f skid

slogatura f sprain
smarrito(a) missing (thing)
smettere to stop doing something
soccorso m assistance ; help
  soccorso alpino mountain rescue
socio m associate ; member
soggiorno m stay ; sitting room
soldi mpl money
sole m sun ; sunshine
solito: *di solito* usually
sollevare to raise ; to relieve
sollievo m relief
solo(a) alone ; only
solubile soluble
  caffè solubile instant coffee
sonnifero m sleeping pill
sono I am (to be)
sopra on ; above ; over
  di sopra upstairs
sopracciglia fpl eyebrows
sopravvivere to survive
sorella f sister
sorpassare to overtake (in car)
sorpresa f surprise
sorridere to smile
sorriso m smile
sospeso(a) suspended ; postponed
sosta f stop
  divieto di sosta no parking
sott'acqua underwater
sotterraneo(a) underground
sotto underneath ; under ; below
Spagna f Spain
spagnolo(a) Spanish
spalla f shoulder
sparire to disappear
spazzatura f rubbish
spazzola f brush
  spazzola per capelli hairbrush
  spazzolino da denti toothbrush
speciale special
specialità f speciality
specialmente especially
spedire to send ; to dispatch
spegnere to turn off ; to put out
spendere to spend (money)
spento(a) turned off ; out (light, etc)
sperare to hope
spese fpl shopping ; expenses
spesso often
spettacolo m show ; performance
spezzatino m stew
spiaggia f beach ; shore
  spiaggia privata private beach

spiccioli *mpl* small coins ; change
 non ho spiccioli I've no change
spiegare to explain
spina *f* bone *(of fish)* ; plug *(electric)*
spinaci *m* spinach
spingere to push
spirale *f* coil *(IUD)*
spogliatoio *m* dressing room
sporco(a) dirty
sportello *m* counter ; door *(train, car)*
sportivo(a) informal *(clothes)*
sposarsi to get married
sposato(a) married
 non sposato(a) single
spremuta *f* freshly squeezed juice
spugna *f* sponge
spuma *f* hair mousse
spumante *m* sparkling wine
spuntino *m* snack
squadra *f* team
squillare to ring *(phone)*
Srl Ltd
stabilimento *m* factory
stadio *m* stadium
stagione *f* season
 di stagione in season
stalla *f* stable
stampata *f* printout
stampatello *m* block letters
stanco(a) tired
stanza *f* room
 stanza da bagno bathroom
 stanza dei giochi playroom
stare to be ; to keep
 stare attento(a) a... beware of..
 stare bene to be well
 stare in piedi to stand
 come sta? how are you?
 stai zitto! keep quiet!
stasera tonight ; this evening
Stati Uniti *mpl* United States
stazione *f* station ; resort
 stazione balneare seaside resort
 stazione dell'autobus bus station
 stazione di servizio petrol station
 stazione ferroviaria train station
stella *f* star
sterlina *f* sterling ; pound
stesso(a) same
stirare to iron
stitichezza *f* constipation
stitico(a) constipated
stivali *mpl* boots

storia *f* history
storico(a) historic(al)
 centro storico old town
strada *f* road ; street
 strada chiusa road closed
 strada panoramica scenic route
 strada sbarrata road closed
 strada statale main road
 strada senza uscita no through road
stradina *f* lane
straniero(a) foreign ; foreigner
strano(a) strange
stupido(a) stupid
su on ; onto ; over ; about ; up
sua his ; her(s) ; its ; your(s)
 (with fsing)
subito at once ; immediately
succedere to happen
succo *m* juice
 succo d'arancia orange juice
 succo di frutta fruit juice
 succo di mela apple juice
 succo di pomodoro tomato juice
succursale *m* branch *(of bank, etc)*
sud *m* south
sue his ; her(s) ; its ; your(s) *(with fpl)*
suo(i) his ; her(s) ; its ; your(s) *(with mpl)*
suocera *f* mother-in-law
suocero *m* father-in-law
suola *f* sole *(of foot, shoe)*
suonare to ring ; to play
suono *m* sound
superare to exceed ; to overtake
supermercato *m* supermarket
supplemento *m* supplement
supposta *f* suppository
surf *m* surf
surgelato(a) frozen
sveglia *f* alarm clock/call
svegliare to wake up
svenire to faint
sviluppare to develop *(photos)*
Svizzera *f* Switzerland
svizzero(a) Swiss
svolta *f* turn

T

tabaccaio *m* tobacconist's
tacco *m* heel
tachimetro *m* speedometer
taglia *f* size *(of clothes)*
tagliare to cut

tailleur *m* women's suit
tallone *m* heel
tangenziale *f* ring road
tanti(e) so many
tanto(a) so much ; so
tappo *m* cork ; plug ; cap
  tappo del serbatoio petrol cap
tardi late
targa *f* numberplate *(car)*
tariffa *f* tariff ; rate
  tariffa economica cheap rate
  tariffa festiva rate on holidays
  tariffa ore di punta peak rate
tartufo *m* truffle
tasca *f* pocket
tassa *f* tax
tasso *m* rate
  tasso di cambio exchange rate
tavola *f* table ; plank ; board
  tavola calda hot snacks
  tavola da surf surfboard
  tavola a vela windsurfing board
taxi *m* taxi
tazza *f* cup
tè *m* tea
  tè al latte tea with milk
  tè al limone lemon tea
  tè freddo iced tea
teatro *m* theatre ; drama
tedesco(a) German
telecomando *m* remote control
telefonare to (tele)phone
telefonata *f* phone call
telefonino *m* mobile phone
telefono *m* telephone
  telefono pubblico payphone
televisione *f* television
telone impermeabile *m* groundsheet
temperatura *f* temperature
temperino *m* penknife
tempesta *f* storm
tempio *m* temple
tempo *m* weather ; time
temporale *m* thunderstorm
tenda *f* curtain ; tent
tendalino *m* awning *(for caravan etc.)*
tendine *m* tendon
tenere to keep ; to hold
tenore *m* tenor *(singer)*
tenore alcolico *m* alcohol content
tergicristallo *m* windscreen wiper
terminal *m* terminal *(airport)*
termometro *m* thermometer

termosifone *m* heater
terra *f* earth ; ground
terrazza *f* terrace
terremoto *m* earthquake
terza *f* third gear
terzi *mpl* third party
terzo(a) third
tessera *f* pass ; season ticket ; card
tessuto *m* fabric
testa *f* head
testicoli *mpl* testicles
tettarella *f* dummy *(for baby)*
tetto *m* roof
tettuccio apribile *m* sunroof *(car)*
Tevere *m* Tiber
thermos *m* thermos flask
thriller *m* thriller
timone *m* rudder
tirare to pull
toccare to touch ; to feel
  non toccare do not touch
togliere to remove ; to take away
toilette *f* toilet
tonno *m* tuna
topo *m* mouse
Torino *f* Turin
tornare to return ; to come/go back
torneo *m* tournament
toro *m* bull
torre *f* tower
torrone *m* nougat
torta *f* cake ; tart ; pie
Toscana *f* Tuscany
tosse *f* cough
tossico(a) toxic
tossire to cough
totale *m* total *(amount)*
tovaglia *f* tablecloth
tovagliolo *m* napkin
tra between ; among(st) ; in
tradizionale traditional
tradurre to translate
traduzione *f* translation
traffico *m* traffic
traghetto *m* ferry
tramezzino *m* sandwich
trampolino *m* diving board ; ski jump
tranquillante *m* tranquillizer
tranquillo(a) quiet *(place)*
trasferire to transfer
trasporto *m* transport
trattoria *f* restaurant
traveller's cheque *mpl* traveller's cheque

traversata f crossing
treno m train
  treno merci goods train
triangolo d'emergenza m warning triangle
tribuna f stand (stadium)
tribunale m law court
trimestre m term (school)
triste sad
tritare to mince ; to chop
troppi(e) too many
troppo too much ; too
trovare to find
trucco m make-up
tu you (familiar)
tubo m pipe ; tube
  tubo di scappamento exhaust
tuffarsi to dive
turno m turn ; shift
  di turno on duty
tuta sportiva f tracksuit
tutti (e) all ; everybody
  tutte le direzioni all routes
tutto everything ; all

U

ubriaco(a) drunk
uccello m bird
uccidere to kill
UE European Union
ufficio m office ; church service
  ufficio informazioni information bureau
  ufficio oggetti smarriti lost property office
  ufficio postale post office
ufficio turistico tourist office
uguale equal ; even
ulcera f ulcer
ultimo(a) last
un a ; an ; one
unghia f nail (finger, toe)
unione f union
  Unione Europea European Union
università f university
uno(a) a ; an ; one
uomo m man
  uomini gents
uova mpl eggs
uovo m egg
  uovo di Pasqua Easter egg
  uova di polli ruspanti free range eggs
  uovo sodo hard-boiled egg

uragano m hurricane
urgente urgent
usare to use
uscire to go/come out
uscita f exit/gate
  uscita di sicurezza emergency exit
uso m use
utile useful
uva f grapes

V

va bene all right (agreed)
vacanza f holiday(s)
  vacanze estive summer holidays
vaccinazione f vaccination
vagina f vagina
vaglia m money order
vagone m carriage ; wagon
  vagone letto sleeper
  vagone ristorante restaurant car
valanga f avalanche
valico m pass (mountain)
valido(a) valid
  valido fino a... valid until...
valigia f suitcase
valore m value; worth
  di valore valuable
valuta f currency
valvola f valve
varicella f chickenpox
vasetto m jar
vaso m vase
vassoio m tray
vecchio(a) old
vedere to see
vedova f widow
vedovo m widower
vegetaliano(a) vegan
vegetariano(a) vegetarian
veicolo m vehicle
vela f sail ; sailing
veleno m poison
velenoso(a) poisonous
veloce quick
velocemente quickly
velocità f speed
vena f vein
vendere to sell
  vendesi for sale
vendita f sale
  vendita al minuto retail
  vendita a rate hire purchase
venerdì m Friday

venerdì santo *m* Good Friday
Venezia *f* Venice
venire to come
ventaglio *m* fan *(hand-held)*
ventilatore *m* electric fan
vento *m* wind
verde green
verdura *f* vegetables
verde green
vergine blank *(disk, tape)*
vermut *m* vermouth
vernice *f* paint
verniciare to paint
vero(a) true ; real ; genuine
versamento *m* payment ; deposit
versare to pour
vertice *m* summit
vescica *f* blister
vespa *f* wasp
vestaglia *f* dressing gown
vestirsi to get dressed
vestiti *mpl* clothes
vestito *m* dress
vetrina *f* shop window
vetro *m* glass *(substance)*
via *f* street ; by *(via)*
  per via aerea by air mail
viaggiare to travel
viaggiatore *m* traveller
viaggio *m* journey ; trip ; drive
  viaggio d'affari business trip
  viaggio organizzato package tour
viale *m* avenue
vicino (a) near ; close by
vicolo *m* alley ; lane
  vicolo cieco cul-de-sac
videocamera *f* videocamera
videocassetta *f* videocassette
videofonino *m* camera phone
videogioco *m* computer game
videoregistratore *m* video recorder
vietato forbidden
  vietato accendere fuochi do not light fires
  vietato fumare no smoking
  vietato l'ingresso no entry
  vietato ingresso veicoli no entry for vehicles
  vietato scendere no exit
vigili del fuoco fire brigade
vigilia *f* eve
  Vigilia di Natale Christmas Eve
vigna *f* vineyard

vincere to win
vino *m* wine
  vino bianco white wine
  vini da pasto table wines
  vino da tavola table wine
  vini pregiati quality wines
  vino rosso red wine
violentare to rape
virus *m* virus
visita *f* visit
  visite guidate guided tours
visitare to visit
vista *f* view
visto *m* visa
vita *f* life ; waist
  vita notturna night life
vitamina *f* vitamin
vite *f* vine ; screw
vivavoce *m* hands-free kit *(for phone)*
vivere to live
vivo(a) live ; alive
voce *f* voice
volante *m* steering wheel
volare to fly
voler dire to mean *(signify)*
volere to want
volo *m* flight
  volo di linea scheduled flight
  volo charter charter flight
volta *f* time
  una volta once
  due volte twice
voltaggio *m* voltage
vomitare to vomit
vongola *f* clam
vostro(a) your ; yours
vulcano *m* volcano
vuoto(a) empty ; blank *(disk, tape)*

Z

zanzara *f* mosquito
zanzariera *f* mosquito net
zia *f* aunt
zio *m* uncle
zona *f* zone
  zona blu restricted parking zone
  zona pedonale pedestrian
zucchero *m* sugar
zucchini *mpl* courgettes
zuppa *f* soup
  zuppa inglese type of trifle

How Italian Works

Nouns

> A **noun** is a word such as **car**, **horse** or **Mary** which is used to refer to a person or thing.

In Italian all nouns are either masculine or feminine. Where in English we say *the apple* and *the book*, in Italian it is **la mela** and **il libro** because **mela** is feminine and **libro** is masculine. The gender of nouns is shown in the article (**il**, **la**, **un**, **una**, etc.).

the: *masc. sing.* **il**
                    l' *(+vowel)*
                    lo *(+z, gn, pn, ps, x, s +consonant)*
                                   fem. sing. **la**
                                   l' *(+vowel)*

    masc. plur. **i**
                    gli *(+vowel, +z, gn, pn, s +consonant)*   *fem. plur.* **le**

a, an: *masc.* **un**
                    uno *(+z, gn, pn, s +consonant)*   *fem.* **una**
                                                un' *(+vowel)*

NOTE: Definite articles (**il**, **la**, **i**, **le**, etc.) used after the prepositions **a** (*to, at*), **da** (*by, from*), **su** (*on*), **di** (*of, some*) and **in** (*in, into*) contract as follows:

a + il = **al**	**da + il** = **dal**	**su + il** = **sul**
a + lo = **allo**	**da + lo** = **dallo**	**su + lo** = **sullo**
a + l' = **all'**	**da + l'** = **dall'**	**su + l'** = **sull'**
a + la = **alla**	**da + la** = **dalla**	**su + la** = **sulla**
a + i = **ai**	**da + i** = **dai**	**su + i** = **sui**
a + gli = **agli**	**da + gli** = **dagli**	**su + gli** = **sugli**
a + le = **alle**	**da + le** = **dalle**	**su + le** = **sulle**
di + il = **del**	**in + il** = **nel**	
di + lo = **dello**	**in + lo** = **nello**	
di + l' = **dell'**	**in + l'** = **nell'**	
di + la = **della**	**in + la** = **nella**	
di + i = **dei**	**in + i** = **nei**	
di + gli = **degli**	**in + gli** = **negli**	
di + le = **delle**	**in + le** = **nelle**	

e.g. **alla casa** (*to the house*)   **sul tavolo** (*on the table*)

Formation of Plurals

For most nouns, the singular ending changes as follows:

masc. sing.	*masc. plur.*	*example*
o	i	libro ➜ libri
e	i	padre ➜ padri
a	i	artista ➜ artisti

NOTE: Nouns ending in **e** can be either masculine or feminine. In the plural they all end in **i**, e.g.:

la televisione	le televisioni
il mare	i mari

NOTE: Most nouns ending in **co** and **go** become **chi** and **ghi** in the plural to keep the **c** and **g** hard sounding. Some exceptions occur in the masculine, e.g. **amico – amici**.

fem. sing.	fem. plur.	example
a	e	mela → mele
e	i	madre → madri

NOTE: Nouns ending in **ca** and **ga** become **che** and **ghe** in the plural to keep the **c** and **g** hard sounding. Nouns ending in **cia** and **gia** often become **ce** and **ge** to keep the **c** and **g** soft sounding, e.g.:

la barca	le barche
la boccia	le bocce

Adjectives

> An **adjective** is a word such as **small**, **pretty** or **practical** that describes a person or thing, or gives extra information about them.

Adjectives normally follow the noun they describe in Italian, e.g. **la mela <u>rossa</u>** (*the <u>red</u> apple*).

Some common exceptions which go before the noun are:

bello beautiful, **breve** short, **brutto** ugly, **buono** good, **cattivo** bad, **giovane** young, **grande** big, **lungo** long, **nuovo** new, **piccolo** small, **vecchio** old
e.g. una **bella** giornata (a beautiful day).

Italian adjectives have to reflect the gender of the noun they describe. To make an adjective feminine, an **a** replaces the **o** of the masculine, e.g. **ross<u>o</u> – ross<u>a</u>**. Adjectives ending in **e**, e.g. **giovane**, can be either masculine or feminine. The plural forms of the adjective change in the way described for nouns (above).

My, Your, His, Her, Our, Their

These words also depend on the gender and number of the noun they accompany, and not on the sex of the 'owner'.

	with masc. sing. noun	with fem. sing. noun	with masc. plur. noun	with fem. plur. noun
my	il mio	la mia	i miei	le mie
your (polite)	il suo	la sua	i suoi	le sue
your (familiar)	il tuo	la tua	i tuoi	le tue
your (plural)	il vostro	la vostra	i vostri	le vostre
his/her	il suo	la sua	i suoi	le sue
our	il nostro	la nostra	i nostri	le nostre
their	il loro	la loro	i loro	le loro

Pronouns

> A **pronoun** is a word that you use to refer to someone or something when you do not need to use a noun, often because the person or thing has been mentioned earlier. Examples are **it**, **she**, **something** and **myself**.

SUBJECT		OBJECT	
I	**io**	me	**mi**
you	**lei**	you	**la**
he	**lui/egli**	him	**lo/l'** (+vowel)
she	**lei/ella**	her	**la/l'** (+vowel)
it (masc.)	**esso**	it (masc.)	**lo/l'** (+vowel)
it (fem.)	**essa**	it (fem.)	**la/l'** (+vowel)
we	**noi**	us	**ci**
you	**voi**	you	**vi**
they	**loro**	them (masc.)	**li**
(things:masc.)	**essi**	them (fem.)	**le**
(things:fem.)	**esse**		

The object pronouns shown above are also used to mean *to me*, *to us*, etc., except:

to him/to it	= **gli**
to her/to it/to you	= **le**
to them	= **loro**

Object pronouns (other than **loro**) usually go before the verb:

lo vedo	but	**scriverò loro**
I see him		I will write to them

When used with an infinitive (the verb form given in the dictionary), the pronoun follows and is attached to the infinitive less its final **e**:

voglio comprarlo   I want to buy it

Subject pronouns (**io**, **tu**, **egli**, etc.) are often omitted in Italian, since the verb ending generally distinguishes the person:

parlo	I speak
parliamo	we speak
parlano	they speak

In Italian there are two forms for *you* – **Lei** (singular) and **voi** (plural).
Tu, the familiar form for **you**, should only be used with people you know well, or children.

Verbs

> A **verb** is a word such as **sing**, **walk** or **cry** which is used with a subject to say what someone or something does or what happens to them. **Regular verbs** follow the same pattern of endings. **Irregular verbs** do not follow a regular pattern so you need to learn the different endings.

There are three main patterns of endings for verbs in Italian – those ending -**are**, -**ere** and -**ire** in the dictionary. Two examples of the -**ire** verbs are shown, since two distinct groups of endings exist. Subject pronouns are shown in brackets because these are often not used:

	PARL<u>ARE</u>	TO SPEAK
(io)	**parlo**	I speak
(tu)	**parli**	you speak
(lui/lei)	**parla**	(s)he speaks
(noi)	**parliamo**	we speak
(voi)	**parlate**	you speak
(loro)	**parlano**	they speak

past participle: **parlato** (with **avere**)

	VEND<u>ERE</u>	TO SELL
(io)	**vendo**	I sell
(tu)	**vendi**	you sell
(lui/lei)	**vende**	(s)he sells
(noi)	**vendiamo**	we sell
(voi)	**vendete**	you sell
(loro)	**vendono**	they sell

past participle: **venduto** (with **avere**)

	DORM<u>IRE</u>	TO SLEEP
(io)	**dormo**	I sleep
(tu)	**dormi**	you sleep
(lui/lei)	**dorme**	(s)he sleeps
(noi)	**dormiamo**	we sleep
(voi)	**dormite**	you sleep
(loro)	**dormono**	they sleep

past participle: **dormito** (with **avere**)

	FIN<u>IRE</u>	TO FINISH
(io)	**finisco**	I finish
(tu)	**finisci**	you finish
(lui/lei)	**finisce**	(s)he finishes
(noi)	**finiamo**	we finish
(voi)	**finite**	you finish
(loro)	**finiscono**	they finish

past participle: **finito** (with **avere**)

Irregular Verbs

Among the most important irregular verbs are the following:

	ESSERE	TO BE
(io)	**sono**	I am
(tu)	**sei**	you are
(lui/lei)	**è**	(s)he is
(noi)	**siamo**	we are
(voi)	**siete**	you are
(loro)	**sono**	they are

past participle: **stato** (with **essere**)

AVERE	TO HAVE
ho	I have
hai	you have
ha	(s)he has
abbiamo	we have
avete	you have
hanno	they have

past participle: **avuto** (with **avere**)

	ANDARE	TO GO
(io)	**vado**	I go
(tu)	**vai**	you go
(lui/lei)	**va**	(s)he goes
(noi)	**andiamo**	we go
(voi)	**andate**	you go
(loro)	**vanno**	they go

past participle: **andato** (with **essere**)

FARE	TO DO
faccio	I do
fai	you do
fa	(s)he does
facciamo	we do
fate	you do
fanno	they do

past participle: **fatto** (with **avere**)

	POTERE	TO BE ABLE
(io)	**posso**	I can
(tu)	**puoi**	you can
(lui/lei)	**può**	(s)he can
(noi)	**possiamo**	we can
(voi)	**potete**	you can
(loro)	**possono**	they can

past participle: **potuto** (with **avere**)

VOLERE	TO WANT
voglio	I want
vuoi	you want
vuole	(s)he wants
vogliamo	we want
volete	you want
vogliono	they want

past participle: **voluto** (with **avere**)

	DOVERE	TO HAVE TO (MUST)
(io)	**devo**	I must
(tu)	**devi**	you must
(lui/lei)	**deve**	he/she must
(noi)	**dobbiamo**	we must
(voi)	**dovete**	you must
(loro)	**devono**	they must

past participle: **dovuto** (with **avere**)

Past Tense

> To make a simple past tense you need an **auxiliary verb** with the past participle of the main verb, e.g. **I have** (auxiliary) **been** (past participle), **I have** (auxiliary) **eaten** (past participle). In Italian the basic auxiliary verbs are **avere** (to have) and **essere** (to be).

To form the simple past tense, I spoke/I have spoken, I sold/I have sold, etc. combine the present tense of the verb **avere** – *to have* with the past participle of the verb, e.g.

ho parlato	I spoke/I have spoken
ho venduto	I sold/I have sold

PARL*ARE* (past)

ho parlato	I spoke
hai parlato	you spoke
ha parlato	(s)he spoke
abbiamo parlato	we spoke
avete parlato	you spoke
hanno parlato	they spoke

VEND*ERE* (past)

ho venduto	I sold
hai venduto	you sold
ha venduto	(s)he sold
abbiamo venduto	we sold
avete venduto	you sold
hanno venduto	they sold

DORM*IRE* (past)

ho dormito	I slept
hai dormito	you slept
ha dormito	(s)he slept
abbiamo dormito	we slept
avete dormito	you slept
hanno dormito	they slept

FIN*IRE* (past)

ho finito	I finished
hai finito	you finished
ha finito	(s)he finished
abbiamo finito	we finished
avete finito	you finished
hanno finito	they finished

NOTE: Not all verbs take **avere** (**ho**, **hai**, etc.) as their auxiliary verb, some take **essere** (**sono**, **sei**, etc.). These are mainly verbs of motion or staying, e.g. **andare** – *to go*, **stare** – *to be* (located at):

sono andato	I went
sono stato a Roma	I was in Rome

When the auxiliary verb **essere** is used, the past particple (**andato**, **stato**) becomes an adjective and should agree with the subject of the verb, e.g.:

sono anda**ta**	I went *(fem. sing.)*
siamo stat**i**	we went *(masc. plural)*

...ke a sentence negative e.g. I am not eating, you use **non** before the

...on mangio	I am not eating
...n sono andato	I did not go